Winning Lebanon

By the mid-twentieth century, youth movements around the globe ruled the streets. In Lebanon, young people in these groups attended lectures, sang songs, and participated in sporting events; their music tastes, clothing choices, and routine activities shaped their identities. Yet scholars of modern Lebanon often focus exclusively on the sectarian makeup and violent behaviors of these sociopolitical groupings, obscuring the youth cultures that they forged. Using unique sources to highlight the daily lives of the young men and women of Lebanon's youth politics, Dylan Baun traces the political and cultural history of a diverse set of youth-centric organizations, from the 1920s to 1950s, to reveal how these youth movements played significant roles in the making of the modern Middle East.

Outlining how youth movements established a distinct type of politics and populism, *Winning Lebanon* reveals that these groups both encouraged the political socialization of different types of youth, and, through their attempts to "win" Lebanon – physically and metaphorically – around the 1958 War, helped produce sectarian violence.

Dylan Baun is Assistant Professor of Modern Middle East and Islamic World History at the University of Alabama in Huntsville. He is the author of numerous articles on the history of youth and young people in the modern Middle East in journals including the *Arab Studies Journal* and *International Journal for the History of Sport*.

T0364202

Cambridge Middle East Studies

Cambridge Middle East Studies has been established to publish books on the nineteenth- to twenty-first-century Middle East and North Africa. The series offers new and original interpretations of aspects of Middle Eastern societies and their histories. To achieve disciplinary diversity, books are solicited from authors writing in a wide range of fields including history, sociology, anthropology, political science, and political economy. The emphasis is on producing books affording an original approach along theoretical and empirical lines. The series is intended for students and academics, but the more accessible and wide-ranging studies will also appeal to the interested general reader.

A list of books in the series can be found after the index.

Winning Lebanon

Youth Politics, Populism, and the Production of Sectarian Violence, 1920–1958

Dylan Baun

University of Alabama in Huntsville

CAMBRIDGE
UNIVERSITY PRESS

CAMBRIDGE
UNIVERSITY PRESS

University Printing House, Cambridge CB2 8BS, United Kingdom

One Liberty Plaza, 20th Floor, New York, NY 10006, USA

477 Williamstown Road, Port Melbourne, VIC 3207, Australia

314-321, 3rd Floor, Plot 3, Splendor Forum, Jasola District Centre, New Delhi - 110025, India

103 Penang Road, #05-06/07, Visioncrest Commercial, Singapore 238467

Cambridge University Press is part of the University of Cambridge.

It furthers the University's mission by disseminating knowledge in the pursuit of
education, learning and research at the highest international levels of excellence.

www.cambridge.org
Information on this title: www.cambridge.org/9781108798396
DOI: 10.1017/9781108863230

First published 2021
First paperback edition 2022

A catalogue record for this publication is available from the British Library

Library of Congress Cataloging in Publication data
Names: Baun, Dylan, 1986– author.
Title: Winning Lebanon : youth politics, populism, and the production of
sectarian violence, 1920–1958 / Dylan Baun, University of Alabama in Huntsville.
Description: Cambridge, United Kingdom ; New York, NY : Cambridge
University Press, 2020. | Series: Cambridge Middle East studies | Includes
bibliographical references and index.
Identifiers: LCCN 2020015214 | ISBN 9781108491525 (hardback) | ISBN
9781108863230 (epub)
Subjects: LCSH: Youth – Political activity – Lebanon – History – 20th century. |
Political violence – Lebanon – History – 20th century.
Classification: LCC HQ799.9.P6 B38 2020 | DDC 303.60835–dc23
LC record available at https://lccn.loc.gov/2020015214

ISBN 978-1-108-49152-5 Hardback
ISBN 978-1-108-79839-6 Paperback

To my love, Nicole

And the Youth of a Nation are the trustees of Posterity.
—Benjamin Disraeli, *Sybil* (1845)

He alone, who owns the youth, gains the Future!
—Adolf Hitler, speech (1935)

You young people, full of vigor and vitality, are in the bloom of life, like the sun at eight or nine in the morning. Our hope is placed on you. The world belongs to you. China's future belongs to you.
—Mao Zedong, meeting with students (1957)

Oh youth, blossom in life and search for vigor. I did not lax in your radiant coat as a coward!
—The Arab Nationalist Youth, poem titled "Youth" (1952)

Contents

Figures, Maps, and Tables

Figures

Maps

Tables

Acknowledgments

This book has been many years in the making. It is the culmination of countless conversations, brainstorming sessions, presentations, drafts, writing retreats, rewrites, and grant applications. To start, I find it very difficult to imagine *Winning Lebanon* without the logistical and financial support I have received over the years to conduct archival research in Lebanon, the UK, and US. I thank the organizations and institutions that have made this research possible: the Confluencenter for Creative Inquiry at the University of Arizona, the School of Middle Eastern and North African Studies at the University of Arizona, the Social and Behavioral Sciences Research Institute at the University of Arizona, the Committee on Grants at Franklin & Marshall College, the Office of Research and Economic Development at the University of Alabama in Huntsville, and the Humanities Center at the University of Alabama in Huntsville.

Like any historian, I am bound by my sources. Thankfully, I had amazing support finding archival material in Lebanon (Map 0.1). Before conducting dissertation fieldwork in 2013 in Lebanon, I had no idea how familiar I would become with the microfilm reading room at Jafet Library at the American University of Beirut! Their newspaper collection on microfilm is essential to this book. I am indebted to the staff at Jafet for helping me find what I needed. In particular, I thank library staff Rania Kanj and Claude Matar (now retired, *alif mabrouk!*) for your assistance accessing microfilm, and those employees of the Archives and Special Collections Department who guided me through the Linda Sadaqah Collection, including Kaokab Chebaro, Samar Mikati, Yasmine Younes, and Rana Kassas. Also, I acknowledge those other libraries, institutes, and foundations in Lebanon, the UK, and US that facilitated my research: the Lebanese National Archives, the Institute for Palestine Studies, the Orient Institute, the Kamel Mroueh Foundation, the Center for Arab and Middle East Studies at the American University of Beirut, Bibliothèque Orientale at the University of Saint Joseph, the Salah Barakat Gallery, the Friends of Kamal Jumblatt Association, Dar al-Taqaddumiyya in Moukhtara, the Kata'ib Museum in Haret Sakher, the ʿAmiliyya Islamic Benevolent Society in Beirut, the British National Archives in London, the UN Archives and Records Management in New York, the US National Archives at College Park, the Widener Collection of Newspapers on Microfilm at Harvard University, and the main libraries at the University of Arizona, Franklin & Marshall College, and the University of Alabama in Huntsville.

Like any ethnographer, I am at the mercy, benevolence, and hospitality of my interlocutors, many of whom are still associated with the youth organizations-cum-political parties at the center of *Winning Lebanon*. I appreciate the time, energy, and resources afforded to me by these people, especially when it came to fulfilling my long-winded requests or answering my equally winded questions. In particular, I appreciate the assistance of Ghassan Ahmed ʿIssa, Wassim Jabre, Joy Homsi, ʿAbboudi Bou and Marwan Jaoudeh, ʿAbbas Khalaf, Khalil Ahmad Khalil, and one of my closest friends, Walid Nuwayhid. Although associated with very different groups, ideologies, and backgrounds, you collectively aided my understanding of youth politics and activism in the history of modern Lebanon. Without the conversations and sources you provided, understanding the popular culture of these organizations, daily life within them, and the local scene in which they emerged, would still be far beyond my grasp. No one book can please everyone, and my book is of course no exception. It is my hope that even if you do not agree with my conclusions, you appreciate the attention and nuance I have brought to this subject.

As I spent seven years at the School of Middle Eastern and North African Studies at the University of Arizona, one year at Franklin & Marshall College in the Department of History, and four years at the University of Alabama in Huntsville in the Department of History, I must emphasis the assistance of these institutions as well. Broadly, I thank my colleagues (especially the Department of History at UAH!), staff, and my students for their assistance, whether it was talking through an idea, printing out a source, providing feedback, or just listening to me go on and on about my upcoming deadlines. Specifically, I would like to thank my dissertation committee at the University of Arizona, including Leila Hudson, my committee chair, Maha Nassar, Aomar Boum, and Faten Ghosn. Collectively, you are a diverse group of accomplished scholars that make this work, in my humble opinion, a testament to the merits of interdisciplinary research. I also need to thank those individuals across these three institutions and others who have read drafts of this book, provided feedback, or general writing, research, and/or publishing advice. They include, but are not limited to, Ziad Abu Rish, Kristine Alexander, Catherine Batruni, Adel Beshara, Elizabeth Bishop, Tylor Brand, Juan Cole, Andrei Gandila, Jim Gelvin, Wilson Jacob, Rick Jobs, Rashid

Khalidi, Akram Khater, Zeina Maasri, Kevin Martin, Heidi Morrison, Wassim Mroueh, Nicole Pacino, Graham Auman Pitts, Linda Sayid, Nadya Sbaiti, Hoda Yousef, Joey Taylor, Libby Thompson, Farzin Vejdani, Peter Wien, and Murat Yıldız.

I would also like to thank my family: my mother, Barbara, father, William, brother, Clinton, sister-in-law, Marie, spouse, Nicole Zaleski, and father-in-law, Joseph. Thanks for always taking the time to ask me how the book was going, and then actually listening to my detailed responses. A lot of the intangibles in this book have come out of our conversations and our diversions. And Nicole, more so than anyone, you have seen me grow throughout the course of this book and been my partner through it all. Thank you, most of all, for your patience and confidence in me and my work. You are my all and everything, and I dedicate this book to you.

Of course, I am missing many more with whom I had conversations about this work and others that helped along the way. I thank you all, for this book simply would not be without your guidance.

A Note on Conventions

This book largely uses the transliteration guide of the *International Journal of Middle East Studies*. "Al-," the Arabic definite article, is used at first mention of an individual's full name that includes the definite article (Muhyi al-Din al-Nasuli) or a proper noun (*al-futuwwa*, al-Tala'i'). The article is omitted thereafter (*futuwwa* or Tala'i') or when only noting the last name of an individual (Nasuli, not al-Nasuli, Shamali, not al-Shamali). In cases where an Arabic noun has a common English spelling, the latter is used (Sidon, not Saida, Saadeh not Sa'adeh). With Arab newspaper titles, the article is always included for uniformity when mentioned, as some newspaper titles necessitate it for correct translation (*al-Bashir*, "the Omen," not *Bashir*, "Omen"). Arabic terms are glossed where they first appear (*al-shabab*, "the youth"), whether in text or notes.

This book chooses not to use acronyms for organizational names for the sake of clarity and to mirror, as best possible, the way these groups are discussed in Arabic (not PSP, but in Arabic, Progressive Socialist Party). When discussing organizational actions, I use the singular form (the Kata'ib was), unless discussing the actions of members (Kata'ib youth were). At first mention of major leaders of these organizations, I include their range of life and activity as such: Kamal Jumblatt (1917–1977).

In terms of notes, at first mention of a source I include the full citation followed by a short citation thereafter. At first mention in a new chapter, I include the publication year – Baun, *Winning Lebanon* (2021) – followed by a shorter citation at subsequent mentions in that chapter (Baun, *Winning Lebanon*). Only the first mention of an archival source will include where the source is located (*Records at the Lebanese National Archives*). For newspaper citations, I only note the newspaper name and date (*al-Nahda*, November 13, 1937), not the issue number or location of the cited material in that issue. The very few websites that are included were last accessed in late 2019; these sources are only mentioned in the notes, not the bibliography.

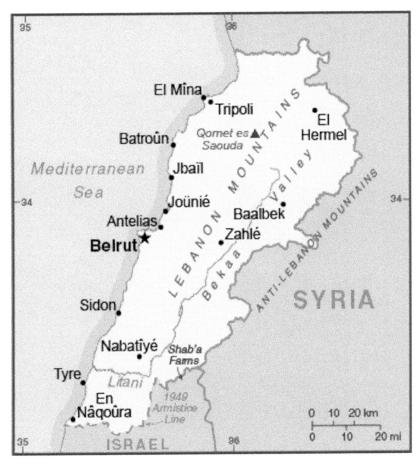

Map 0.1 Map of Lebanon. Courtesy of *The World Factbook.*

Introduction

Ma dama al-shabab m'ana fainana la shaka najihun

With the youth at our side, there is no doubt we will succeed.[1]

This slogan from the Kata'ib, a Lebanese youth organization, reflects a sentiment shared across the globe in the twentieth century: "youth," however defined – by age, class, gender, race – mattered. Kata'ib leadership knew this, and surely had the youth with them, whether measured by the tens of thousands of young members, their investment in the group's ideology, or their participation in party rituals. In July 1958, for example, the group held a ceremony for new members at its headquarters in Beirut, Bayt al-Kata'ib, or the "Kata'ib home." In the space that hosted many gatherings, ranging from lectures to sports tournaments, young men and women congregated alongside party officials and supporters to "perform the oath" (*ta'diyya al-yamin*). This included the routine dedication to party and nation, "in service of Lebanon," another party slogan since the 1930s. Thereafter, recruits received membership cards from their president, Pierre Gemayel, who congratulated each individual on his or her "engagement in the new party life."[2] The event then ended with the singing of the Kata'ib anthem, played by its very own band.

In a nearby neighborhood of Beirut, another youth organization paired music and pageantry in late 1958. Najjadeh members marched through the streets of Basta close to its home, Bayt al-Najjadeh. An observer describes the festival as follows:

During a visit to Basta area on 20 August, Major Boldt, Major Pendergast and I were present during a parade. The parade took place at 1715 and included approximately 120 men mostly in khaki uniforms, the majority armed with French-British rifles with a band in front, 5 drums and scouts … [.] The parade

---

[1] This slogan was taken from the famous Egyptian nationalist Saad Zaghloul. Lebanese Kata'ib Party, *Ila al-Shabab* [To the Youth] (1940). Lebanese Kata'ib Party Files, Linda Sadaqah Collection, American University of Beirut.

[2] *Al-'Amal*, July 13, 1958.

was welcomed by nearly the whole population in the area it passed by and many people fired their guns because of happiness; it is a miracle that nobody was hurt.[3]

These types of events, showcasing the size, order, rituals, and culture of youth-centric organizations, were commonplace in twentieth-century Lebanon. What was unique about these two particular gatherings is their timing – the summer of 1958, in the midst of a war that witnessed 4,000 deaths. Perhaps this is one reason the individual above, United Nations observer Captain Friis of the Royal Danish Army, was shocked that no was injured. Friis also wrote that these young Najjadeh members were "the soldiers who fought" in the war for the fate of Lebanon, and that when "all the trouble had settled down, then they would make a march through the town."[4]

The particular context of 1958 is even more palpable in the Kata'ib oathing festival, as described in a report included in the group's newspaper, al-'Amal ("the Action"). After the young recruits were lined up, George 'Amireh, a member of the Kata'ib leadership council, told them that in the face of the "enmity of our enemies," which included the Najjadeh, "we will not surrender (lan nastaslim)." As long as they were still fighting, working, and sweating, 'Amireh stressed that the Kata'ib, and its vision for Lebanon, "will not die."[5] Indeed, with the youth by their side, the Kata'ib and Najjadeh believed there was no doubt they could succeed in their goals, wartime or otherwise.

Winning Lebanon takes up this history of youth politics in mid-twentieth-century Lebanon. In this period, well before the devastating Lebanese Civil War (1975–1990), the majority of young people were politically engaged and active. This context allows for a multilayered exploration of young men and women as more than victims of a broken political system or a war-torn country. Instead, they were participants in community belonging, the site of power politics, agents of popular culture, and the producers of radical social change. To investigate these various roles, this book focuses on a particular subset of young socio-political actors, what I refer to collectively as "popular organizations," with special attention to their rituals and cultures. These types of groups are diverse, including scout and sports organizations – like the Kata'ib and Najjadeh – social justice movements, transnational student clubs, and workers' associations, all with populist, anti-colonial, and

---

[3] AG-020, United Nations Office for Special Affairs (1955–1991), S-0166, United Nations Observation Group in Lebanon (UNOGIL), Situation in Basta Area, Friis to Chief of Staff, August 19, 1958. *Records at the United Nations Archives and Record Management*, New York. While Friis does not mention the Najjadeh by name, they were the only youth group to have its headquarters in Basta and wear khaki uniforms.
[4] Ibid.   [5] *Al-'Amal*, July 13, 1958.

anti-elite agendas. With popular organizations at the center, I ask what are they, how did they become popular, in what ways did they expand their base, and why and how did they participate in the 1958 War?

From New York to Calcutta, these types of youth-centric organizations ruled the street during the mid-twentieth century. They waved flags and banners in public and gathered in houses and group headquarters to practice politics. With their shared platforms, styles, and rituals, they constitute a global phenomenon that this book explores in the Lebanese milieu; an area of study that currently lacks a focus on the history and culture of youth politics. I frame this study in terms of how these organizations attempted to "win" Lebanon: *demographically*, by adding more members and new types of members; *symbolically*, by pushing their own, distinct image of Lebanon; and *politically*, by gaining access to official and unofficial power structures. I find that these intermediaries, and their rich primary source material, provide a window into the world inhabited by young people, between adult mobilization strategies and their own youthful experiences.

The central argument of *Winning Lebanon* is that these predominantly middle-class, professional, and non-elite actors were critical to the making of modern Lebanon and the broader Middle East in three particular ways. First, they established a distinct type of popular politics, populism, which was centered around young people, and against elites, colonialism, and the status quo. Second, they encouraged the political socialization of new groups and categories of people outside educated, middle-class, male youth, such as young women, rural and working-class populations, and diasporic youth that lived outside Lebanon. Third, in the midst of the 1958 War, popular organizations helped produce sectarian violence. Discursively, the way that popular organizations and others explained and justified the conflict fused categories that had once defied sectarianism, specifically youth and youthfulness, to the unfolding violence. Whether that linkage was explicit – the enemy's youth as sectarian – or coded – the enemy's youth as "punks" – or whether it was detailed by combatants at the time or observers thereafter, conceiving of youth as prone to violence was a new feature in the historical construction of sectarianism. Furthermore, and in terms of group participation and practices during the war, the environment of 1958 that they shaped was unique in that the violence was performed by young people, it was fought across the country, and it was typified by populist rhetoric. In words and actions, this is not unlike subsequent moments of so-called sectarian violence in the Middle East or beyond in the twentieth and twenty-first centuries.

To demonstrate this significance, *Winning Lebanon* takes a bottom-up approach, examining the cultural production (i.e., textual, oral, aural, and visual sources, ranging from organizational newspapers to group songs), rituals (learning, marching, and playing), and youth cultures (belonging, sociability, and discipline) of these types of groups. The book starts in the 1920s, when the first popular organizations were founded during the French mandate era (1920–1943), and ends in 1958, in the midst of Lebanon's first war of the early independence period (1943–1958). The remainder of this introduction sketches the history of these types of groups, and the fields of study that they are linked to, including popular politics, populism, young people, and sectarianism.

The History of Popular Politics, Populism, and Popular Organizations in Modern Lebanon

At the turn of the twentieth century, inhabitants of the Ottoman Empire witnessed a set of major transformations. They ranged from the seizing of Ottoman lands in North Africa by the French and British to the increase of government-run schools throughout the remaining provinces. Perhaps most important for the history of mass or popular politics in modern Lebanon was the creation of a public sphere.[6] Across the empire, and particularly in its city centers (Istanbul, Cairo, Beirut, Damascus), individuals experienced the impacts of urban planning, the growth of the printing press, and the saturation of coffeehouses, where these developments and more were discussed. In this new meeting ground, those concerned about a changing world, whether under Ottoman centralization or European colonialism, began to form "associations," or *jam 'iyyat* in Arabic. Associations provided an opportunity for the often male students and middle-class professionals, who were also a product of these transformations, to mobilize beyond and against the state. The most famous were the Young Ottomans and Young Turk movement in Istanbul, active since the 1860s, the National Party in Alexandria, led by Mustafa Kamil and founded in the 1890s, and the Young Tunisians of Tunis, which was inspired by the Young Turk Revolution of 1908. Although their ideologies diverged, they were united in their use of the public sphere, principally in the form of public meetings and demonstrations, the use of newspapers and journals, and their forward thinking, typified by the use of "young" (*fata* in Arabic or *jön* in Turkish), the "youth" (*al-shabab* in Arabic or

---

[6] For more information on the centrality of the public sphere in Arab popular politics, see James L. Gelvin, *Divided Loyalties: Nationalism and Mass Politics in Syria at the Close of Empire* (Berkeley, CA: University of California Press, 1998).

gençler in Turkish), or "new" (*jadid* in Arabic *or yeni* in Turkish) in their names.[7]

This was also the context in which extra-governmental associations took shape in Bilad al-Sham, or "Greater Syria," and its largest, most cosmopolitan port: Beirut. They included Butrus al-Bustani's Syrian Association, linked to the Arabic Nahda (or "renaissance") movement, and the transregional leftist networks that ran through Beirut.[8] Like their counterparts in Istanbul or Cairo, these groups were common in their anti-colonial platforms, nationalist – or localist – pride, and forward-looking visions. These traits were only solidified in the tumultuous context of the second decade of twentieth-century Bilad al-Sham. The Ottoman Empire's entrance into the Great War in late 1914, the Entente's naval blockade of the Eastern Mediterranean in 1915, the imposition of Ottoman martial law in Bilad al-Sham starting in 1915, and a few crippling winters throughout the war led to the death of hundreds of thousands and the forced migration – within and well beyond the Eastern Mediterranean – of many more. Also destroyed was the Ottoman Empire and its control over its Arab provinces, including Beirut and Damascus. Following the Treaty of Sevrès in 1920, the two provinces and others nearby were fully separated, and granted to France as the "mandates" of Syria and Lebanon. While the League of Nations member state promised "progressive development" in its mandates, Lebanon was little more than a colonial holding.[9] This was the particular milieu in which the first youth-centric organizations emerged. Like earlier generations of associations, these groups used the public sphere as their launching point. Unlike others, however, they not only embodied the concept of young, but targeted young people as the panacea to the unprecedented trauma caused by the Great War and drivers of a brighter future.

From the 1920s to 1940s in mandate Lebanon, these youth-centric organizations used the weapons of the public sphere to challenge French colonialism and the elites that supported it. These elites, or *zu'ama'*, were the traditional holders of political, social, and economic power in the Arab provinces of the Ottoman world since the sixteenth century. The *zu'ama'* also represented the community they came from – Sunni

---

[7] For more information on these earliest associations and their intellectual milieu, see Albert Hourani, *Arabic Thought in the Liberal Age, 1798–1939* (Cambridge: Cambridge University Press, 1983); and Jens Hanssen and Max Weiss, eds., *Arabic Thought beyond the Liberal Age: Towards an Intellectual History of the Nahda* (Cambridge: Cambridge University Press, 2016).

[8] For more information on these networks and their use of the public sphere, see Ilham Khuri-Makdisi, *The Eastern Mediterranean and the Making of Global Radicalism, 1860–1914* (Berkeley, CA: University of California Press, 2013).

[9] "French Mandate for Syria and the Lebanon," *The American Journal of International Law* 17, no. 3, Supplemental Official Documents (July 1923): 177.

Muslims in coastal Lebanon, Shi'i Muslims in the south, and Druze, Maronite Christian, or Greek Orthodox in Mount Lebanon. Their claim to kinship, coupled with their roles as patrons, providers, and protectors, made the zu'ama' a fixture in Lebanese politics. Yet, their privileged, intermediary positions were complicated by both the transformations in the public sphere and the emerging relationship between these leaders and colonial powers. These shifts in the early twentieth century gave youth-centric movements, whether they were organized according to sect or not, or even when their leaders were from the landed elite, a platform to draw recruits away from traditional sources of power. In petitions, speeches, and slogans, these groups distinguished the complicity, corruption, and outdatedness of the zu'ama' to the virtue of al-sha'b, or "the people." Such stances led to the repression of these groups, ranging from the jailing of members to the forced exile of leaders. At the same time, their stand against the status quo, as well as their novelty in distinction to it, cemented their populist and radical credentials.

After the Lebanese gained their independence in 1943, and the French fully terminated the mandates of Lebanon and Syria in 1946 following World War II, youth-centric organizations had the chance to transform to political parties and make up the parliamentary and governmental system. While these groups ranged in their willingness to join in state building, they all grew during the postindependence period. They held large festivals to commemorate their achievements, established branch offices throughout and outside the country, and even participated in national elections. Even though they often did not win any seats (at least until the 1960s), they were influencers through their styles, newspapers, sizable memberships, and ideologies. They may have shared the vision that youth would build the future, but all mobilized different ideologies to get there. They hinged on their understanding of Lebanon's relationship to the region and globe. Some groups were Lebanese nationalist, in support of the government's conception of Lebanon as independent, diverse, and nonaligned. Others thought of Lebanon as part of a broader, fully integrated Arab world. Others were socialist or communist, and went even further, conceiving of Lebanon as part of an international, anti-colonial front.

Accordingly, rivalries between groups were as common as clashes with the police. Yet, there were no major disputes between different varieties of movements in the first thirty years of their respective histories.[10] This

---

[10] An exception to this coordination is the 1949 Gemmayzeh incident. For more information, see Dylan Baun, "The Gemmayzeh Incident of 1949: Conflict over Physical and Symbolic Space in Beirut," *Arab Studies Journal* 25, no. 1 (2017): 92–122; and Adel Beshara, *Outright Assassination: The Trial and Execution of Antun Sa'adeh, 1949* (Reading, UK: Ithaca Press, 2010).

peace was shattered in the 1950s. The pressures associated with the Arab-Israeli conflicts of the late 1940s to early 1950s, the international Cold War and subsequent pro-West and anti-colonial defensive pacts, the authoritarianism of Lebanese President Camille Chamoun, and the Union of Egypt and Syria under Egyptian President Gamal Abdel Nasser in February 1958, culminated with the 1958 War in Lebanon. Most of the youth-centric organizations at the middle of *Winning Lebanon* participated in this war, some on the side of the government, others against it.

***

Scholars of modern Lebanon have taken up this history before, referring to these groups operating in the fields of popular and youth politics in the twentieth century as "political parties," "ideological parties," or "para-military youth organizations."[11] Michael W. Suleiman's *Political Parties in Lebanon: The Challenge of a Fragmented Political Culture* (1967) was the first, and only, English-language study to take these groups in Lebanon as a whole and follow them from their founding to the contemporary. Those after often focused on only one group in relation to others.[12] Simply stated, I believe there is a critical need for an updated historical evaluation of these types of groups. First, I find the terminology of "parties," which is still utilized to study these groupings, limits the scope of analysis. This is because the logic that undergirds this term is based on modernization theory, which views democracy and its political actors, political parties, as the most evolved. On one level, groups that were not political parties, including scout and social clubs, are then left out of the fold. On another level, even for the groups that used the term "party" (or in Arabic, *hizb*), the English translation appears rigid and teleological – that is, a certain group *always* wanted to be a parliamentary actor, even before they could legally organize as one. Moreover, the emphasis on party politics favors descriptions of ideology and sect makeup over equally important traits that *Winning Lebanon* takes up, including the everyday life, practices, and

---

[11] Michael W. Suleiman, *Political Parties in Lebanon: The Challenge of a Fragmented Political Culture* (Ithaca, NY: Cornell University Press, 1967); Shifaq Juha, *Ma'rakat Masir Lubnan fi 'Ahd al-Intidab al-Faransi, 1918–1946* [Battle for the Fate of Lebanon in the French Mandate Period], vol. 2 (Beirut: Maktabat Ra's Bayrut, 1995), 239; and Fawwaz Traboulsi, *A History of Modern Lebanon* (London: Pluto Press, 2007), 102.

[12] For three important examples, see Labib Zuwiyya Yamak, *The Syrian Social Nationalist Party: An Ideological Analysis* (Cambridge, MA: Center for Middle Eastern Studies, 1966); John Entelis, *Pluralism and Party Transformation in Lebanon: Al-Kata'ib, 1936–1970* (Leiden: E. J. Brill, 1974); and Nazih Richani, *Dilemmas of Democracy and Political Parties in Sectarian Societies: The Case of the Progressive Socialist Party 1949–1996* (New York: St. Martin's Press, 1998).

rituals of these groups. Indeed, these groups do not only provide a survey into the ideologies of the time, but the cultural milieu of youth politics.[13]

The second need for this study is historiographical in thrust. In the last sixty years, scholarship on these organizations has shifted from overall optimistic to pessimistic, with little revaluation of this shift in knowledge. Before the Lebanese Civil War of 1975–1990, many political scientists argued that these grassroots organizations fostered political openness, cross-sect dialogue, and modernization to the benefit of Lebanon.[14] These hypotheses were, of course, complicated by the war. As these groups were the center of the fighting throughout the 1970s to 1990s, they have, in turn, been positioned at the center of scholarly explanations for the war.[15] This violent reality, however, is often projected onto the earliest history of these groups in the 1920s to 1950s.[16] While I acknowledge and unpack the cultural and social roots of violence within these groups in the following chapters, I find that overemphasizing their trajectory from good party to bad militia works to obscure the popularity and mundanity of these groups well before the 1970s. For these reasons, I study these groups ethnographically, in all their subjectivity and transformations, from their own sources, for the sake of understanding the youth cultures that are shaped by them. In short, then, *Winning Lebanon* is a cultural history of youth politics and youth organization in the mid-twentieth century.

Additionally, I use the more flexible term "popular organizations" when discussing these actors of Lebanon's youth politics as a whole. I define popular organizations as a class of groups emerging in Lebanon during the first half of the twentieth century. They ranged from athletic clubs to labor unions. Some represented certain sects while others did not. Some can be

---

[13] My methodology of using rituals to "read" culture is inspired by the work of historians and anthropologists alike. They include Natalie Zemon Davis, "The Rites of Violence: Religious Riot in Sixteenth-Century France," *Past & Present* 59 (1973): 51–91; Clifford Geertz, "Deep Play: Notes on the Balinese Cockfight," *Daedalus* 134, no. 4 (2005): 56–86; and Bertram Wyatt-Brown, *Southern Honor: Ethics and Behavior in the Old South* (New York: Oxford University Press, 2007).

[14] For studies that paint these groups favorably, see Yamak, *The Syrian Social Nationalist Party*; Suleiman, *Political Parties in Lebanon*; and Entelis, *Pluralism and Party Transformation in Lebanon*.

[15] For three examples, see Kamal Salibi, *Crossroads to Civil War: Lebanon 1958–1976* (Ann Arbor, MI: Caravan Books, 1976); Farid el-Khazen, *The Breakdown of the State in Lebanon 1967–1976* (New York: I.B. Tauris, 2000); and Samir Khalaf, *Civil and Uncivil Violence in Lebanon: A History of the Internationalization of Communal Conflict* (New York: Columbia University Press, 2002).

[16] For two prime examples of this trend, see Itamar Rabinovich, *The War for Lebanon, 1970–1985*, revised ed. (Ithaca, NY: Cornell University Press, 1985); and William Harris, *Faces of Lebanon: Sects, Wars, and Global Extensions* (Princeton, NJ: Markus Wiener Publishers, 1997).

characterized as youth movements based on the average age of their members, while others embodied youthful energies and ideas. Regardless of these differences, the groups were collectively grassroots, urban-based, and dominated by middle-class young men, although the class, gender, and geographic components of these groups would change by the 1940s to 1950s. Their leaders, often middle-class male professionals, mobilized populist discourses, claiming to support and defend the people and popular demands. While these demands varied from group to group and depend on context, all popular organizations claimed to be anti-colonial and protested against establishment politics.

Accordingly, these groups were pivotal to, but not an exclusive part of, contentious and popular politics in mid-twentieth-century Lebanon. A number of scholars have focused on mass-based movements, popular politics, and the public sphere in twentieth-century Lebanon.[17] Even more have done such in the field of modern Middle East history.[18] Yet, there are very few that engage directly with the term "populism," or *sha'biyya*.[19] My understanding and deployment of the term is informed by particular studies that define populism as a discursive frame within popular politics, centered on notions of the people (in-group, *al-sha'b*)

---

[17] For works on popular politics in Lebanon, see Elizabeth Thompson, *Colonial Citizens: Republican Rights, Paternal Privilege and Gender in French Syria and Lebanon* (New York: Columbia University Press, 2000); Betty Anderson, *The American University of Beirut: Arab Nationalism and Liberal Education* (Austin, TX: University of Texas Press, 2011); Khuri-Makdisi, *The Eastern Mediterranean and the Making of Global Radicalism*; and Ziad Munif Abu-Rish, "Conflict and Institution Building in Lebanon, 1946–1955" (PhD diss., University of California, Los Angeles, 2014).

[18] For studies on popular politics in the modern Middle East, see Juan R. I. Cole, *Colonialism and Revolution in the Middle East: Social and Cultural Origins of Egypt's 'Urabi Movement* (Princeton, NJ: Princeton University Press, 1993); Gelvin, *Divided Loyalties*; Joel Beinin, *Workers and Peasants in the Modern Middle East* (Cambridge: Cambridge University Press, 2001); Orit Bashkin, *The Other Iraq: Pluralism and Culture in Hashemite Iraq* (Stanford, CA: Stanford University Press, 2009); Ziad Fahmy, *Ordinary Egyptians: Creating the Modern Nation through Popular Culture* (Stanford, CA: Stanford University Press, 2011); Asef Bayat, *Life as Politics: How Ordinary People Change the Middle East* (Stanford, CA: Stanford University Press, 2010); and John Chalcraft, *Popular Politics in the Making of the Modern Middle East* (Cambridge: Cambridge University Press, 2016).

[19] Gelvin and Bashkin are rare exceptions. Gelvin incorporates literature on populism into his analysis of the Syrian Arab Kingdom of 1918–1920, discussing the role that the populist "discursive field" (our true nation vs. elite exploitation) played in the creation of Syrian popular committees. Gelvin, *Divided Loyalties*, 207–220. And while Bashkin does not draw on populism studies in her work on Iraq in the interwar period, she does explore a social movement in mid-1930s Iraq called *sha'biyya*, or what she refers to as "people-ism," which was socially conscious, democratic, and leftist. Bashkin, *The Other Iraq*, 67–68. Similarly, all popular organizations in Lebanon distinguished their just cause from "the other," all supported pluralism (even those that adapted fascist aesthetics), all eventually promoted cross-class solidarity, and all served as a venue to discuss plans meant to alleviate poverty.

and the elite (out-group, *al-zu'ama'*).[20] With their critical distinction between the leaders/system and the people/youth, populism was elemental to the ethos and culture of the organizations at the crux of *Winning Lebanon*. Moreover, both in the context of the 1958 War, and the later civil war in Lebanon, a particular populist discourse (in short, our just, popular cause vs. their abomination) was central to group justifications for war.[21] For these reasons, I considered populism a key mode by which to enrich our understanding of popular politics and popular organizations, both when comparing group to group, and as a collective field.

The popular organizations that constitute the subsequent analysis include:

- **Lebanese People's Party** (al-Hizb al-Sha'b al-Lubnani) – a workers' association founded in 1924 by journalist Yusuf Yazbak and labor activist Fuad al-Shamali; later became known as the Lebanese Communist Party (al-Hizb al-Shiyu'i al-Lubnani)
- **Syrian Social Nationalist Party** (al-Hizb al-Suri al-Qawmi al-Ijtima'i) – a social club founded in 1932 by journalist and teacher Antoun Saadeh
- **Lebanese Kata'ib** ("Phalanx") **Organization** (Munazzamat al-Kata'ib al-Lubnaniyya or in French, Phalanges Libanaises) – a youth club founded in 1936 by pharmacist and football enthusiast Pierre Gemayel
- **Najjadeh** ("Helpers") **Organization** (Munazzamat al-Najjadeh) – a scout movement founded in 1937 by newspaper owner and parliamentarian Muhyi al-Din al-Nasuli
- **Tala'i'** ("Vanguard") **Organization** (Munazzamat al-Tala'i') – a youth club founded in 1944 by philanthropist and parliamentarian Rashid Baydun
- **Progressive Socialist Party** (al-Hizb al-Ishtiraki al-Taqaddumi) – a social justice movement founded in 1949 by intellectual and parliamentarian Kamal Jumblatt

---

[20] For more information on those that explore populism as a discourse, see Francisco Panizza, "What Do We Mean When We Talk about Populism?" in *Latin American Populism in the Twenty-First Century*, ed. Carlos de la Torre and Cynthia J. Arnson (Baltimore, MD: Johns Hopkins University Press, 2013), 85–115; Paris Aslanidis, "Populism and Social Movements," in *The Oxford Handbook of Populism*, ed. Cristóbal Rovira Kaltwasser et al. (Oxford: Oxford University Press, 2017), 10–26; and Gelvin, *Divided Loyalties*.

[21] For more information on this line of reasoning, see Dylan Baun, "Populism and War-Making: Constructing the People and the Enemy during the Early Lebanese Civil War Era," in *Mapping Populism: Approaches and Methods*, ed. Amit Ron and Majia Nadesan (Abingdon, Oxon: Routledge, 2020), 146–157.

- **Arab Nationalist Youth** (al-Shabab al-Qawmi al-'Arabi) –
a transnational student organization founded in 1951 by medical doctor
George Habash; later became known as the Arab Nationalist
Movement (Harakat al-Qawmiyyin al-'Arab)

These groups were not the only non-state, sociopolitical, youth-centric
groups during this period. Rather, they are some of the largest, most
popular, comprehensive (in terms of four out of the seven groups representing the major religio-communal groups in Lebanon – Sunni,
Maronite, Shia, and Druze), and consequential to understanding the
political and cultural history of modern Lebanon.

Moreover, these groups left behind multitudes of material evidence,
ranging from organization newspapers to group songs and uniforms.
Their sources, especially read as artifacts of group culture, are under-
represented in the literature on Lebanon and the broader Middle East.
To fill this gap, this book most embraces the richness of Lebanon's
print history. A vestige of European missionary work, the nineteenth-
century Nahda movement, and the broader growth of the public
sphere, printing was common among multiple types of associations in
twentieth-century Lebanon. In the 1930s to 1950s, popular organizations ran multipage, high-end productions, ranging from pamphlets to
licensed newspapers.[22] I am not only interested in their reporting of
events, but the place of clearly subjective articles, ads, essays, and
pictures in the process of cultural formation. Through this framing
and source focus, *Winning Lebanon* seeks to add new perspectives on
popular culture and youth social formation in the history of the modern
Middle East.

Being Young in the Modern Middle East and Global South

If populism constitutes one angle by which to reposition these groups and
emphasize their cultures, youth is another. Even though the history of
youth is not as famous as its nearby counterpart, the history of children
and childhood, it is a well-established field in areas across the world.
Studies include the historical construction of youth summer camps in
nineteenth-century North America, youth delinquency in early Soviet

---

[22] For more information on the history of print culture in modern Lebanon, see Nabil
A. Dajani, *Disoriented Media in a Fragmented Society: The Lebanese Experience* (Beirut:
American University of Beirut, 1992); Ami Ayalon, *The Press in the Arab Middle East:
A History* (Oxford: Oxford University Press, 1995); and William A. Rugh, *Arab Mass
Media: Newspapers, Radio, and Television in Arab Politics* (Westport, CT: Praeger
Publishers, 2004).

Russia, and youth backpacking in post-war Europe.[23] To study the history of being young in the modern Middle East, however, is fairly uncharted territory. Several scholars have taken up the topic of scouting in the modern Middle East, including Jennifer Dueck's *The Claims of Culture at Empire's End: Syria and Lebanon under French Rule* (2010).[24] Nevertheless, there is only one historical survey on youth: Haggai Erlich's *Youth and Revolution in the Changing Middle East, 1908–2014* (2014).[25] *Winning Lebanon* builds on these studies and other works on youth and children in the modern Middle East to explore the concepts of "youth" and "being young" in several ways.[26]

The first is to approach youth as a lived historical phenomenon. In the late nineteenth century in the colonized Global South, notions of modernity and modern living were in the air. As it pertains to youth, mostly young men in their teens and twenties began to live in cities by themselves, away from their parents, to explore new ideas and experiences. In the context of the late Ottoman Empire, in part due to centralizing reforms, mass migration to cities, a burgeoning public sphere, the introduction of liberal and emancipatory education, and the creation of the middle class, young people became "free" to do just that – be young. Their days became split between non-leisure (often schooling) and leisure (all different types of play and activity) time. Thus, they were old enough to begin thinking about their role in society and what careers they would take on in the future. While this future was jeopardized in the midst of the Great War and the colonial period, being hip, mobile, and innovative became a way of life to escape that instability and participate in what I call the "global grammar of

[23] For a sampling of works on the world history of youth, see Anne E. Gorsuch, *Youth in Revolutionary Russia: Enthusiasts, Bohemians, Delinquents* (Bloomington, IN: Indiana University Press, 2000); Abigail A. Van Slyck, *A Manufactured Wilderness: Summer Camps and the Shaping of American Youth, 1890–1960* (Minneapolis, MN: University of Minnesota Press, 2006); and Richard Ivan Jobs, *Backpack Ambassadors: How Youth Travel Integrated Europe* (Chicago, IL: University of Chicago Press, 2017).
[24] For more information on a particular type of popular organization, the scout movement, see Jennifer Dueck, *The Claims of Culture at Empire's End: Syria and Lebanon under French Rule* (Oxford: Oxford University Press, 2010); Keith David Watenpaugh, *Being Modern in the Middle East: Revolution, Nationalism, Colonialism, and the Arab Middle Class* (Princeton, NJ: Princeton University Press, 2006); and Wilson Chacko Jacob, *Working Out Egypt: Effendi Masculinity and Subject Formation in Colonial Modernity, 1870–1940* (Durham, NC: Duke University Press, 2011).
[25] Haggai Erlich, *Youth and Revolution in the Changing Middle East, 1908–2014* (Boulder, CO: Lynne Reinner Publishers, Inc., 2014).
[26] The history of childhood in the modern Middle East is equally new. Beyond the richness of childhood memoirs, two very recent academic examples are Nazan Maksudyan, *Orphans and Destitute Children in the Late Ottoman Empire* (Syracuse, NJ: Syracuse University Press, 2014); and Heidi Morrison, *Childhood and Colonial Modernity in Egypt* (New York: Palgrave Macmillan, 2015).

youth."[27] Regardless of ideology or demographic background, all popular organizations in Lebanon engaged in this art of being young and looking the part.

Given that this historical phenomenon is observable through the material evidence that young people, and their overseers, leave behind, this book also considers youth as a category of analysis. I argue that shifting the focus toward young people, and their political engagement through the associations and groups they were affiliated with, can highlight new things about the history of the modern Middle East. While age, class, race, and gender are common ways to approach youth and consider who actually has access to youth (often accepted as age fifteen to twenty-four and middle- to upper-class, in-group men), I analyze the broader positionality of young people in the twentieth century. That is, once the historical category is constructed and experienced – by age, class, gender, or race – the youth are potential drivers of social change, experiencing intense biological change, all under the specter of adults and the state. These challenges for young people are most clear around times of transformation, whether it is the colonial period examined in *Winning Lebanon* or the contemporary one. In fact, the competing trends of youth empowerment and control on display in events like the 2011 Arab Spring, and the violent state response against mostly youth protesters, hark back to twentieth-century youth politics in the Middle East.

Lastly, I conceptualize youth as both a rite of passage and a state of mind. This means that rituals matter when discussing the making of youth culture and youth politics in Lebanon and beyond. Whether it is joining an organization, swearing an oath, or attending study groups, investigating the meanings of these practices works to highlight both the creation of a collective identity prefaced on being young, and how one officially enters and exits that stage. Moreover, just because individuals go beyond this stage of life, it does not mean they fall out of youth. "Youthfulness" is not bound by age or biological development alone, but can also be defined by ideas and practices. Hence, as young members of youth-centric organizations grow older, get married, and have a family, they can still be connected to their youth through a certain performativity that is classified as "youthful."

---

[27] For more on these broader trends as they pertain to youth, see Thompson, *Colonial Citizens*; Akram Fouad Khater, *Inventing Home: Emigration, Gender, and the Middle Class in Lebanon, 1870–1920* (Berkeley, CA: University of California Press, 2001); Watenpaugh, *Being Modern in the Middle East*; and Erlich, *Youth and Revolution in the Changing Middle East*.

While youthfulness is certainly a global concept, it is my hope that *Winning Lebanon* adds nuance to it in the context of the Middle East, and in particular, for understanding the trajectories of popular organizations in modern Lebanon. The most fitting translation of youthfulness in Arabic is *al-futuwwa*. This concept has been in use since at least the eighth century and holds positive or negative connotation depending on context. Its entry in a standard Arabic–English dictionary points to its elasticity; senses include "youth, adolescence," "chivalrous qualities of a man," and "bully, brawler [and] rowdy."[28] More specifically, in early Islamic genealogy, this term referred to the practices by which one become a morally sound and pious individual, especially in Sufism. In the twentieth century and beyond, however, *futuwwa* became a wildness associated with youth masculinity, one that should be avoided or at least contained.[29]

To be clear, *futuwwa* is not a term that popular organizations often use. However, I find its queerness beneficial to understanding how these groups, and young people within them, were perceived, both by other groups, state officials, the *zu'ama'*, and the population at large. In their early histories, it was their youthfulness that made them the potential building blocks of a future, utopian society, and if anything, *futuwwa* was to be cultivated. In another context, specifically 1958, it was their youthfulness that made them uncontrollable, and hence, *futuwwa* must be stopped at all costs. By understanding youthfulness as an experience, identifier, and feeling, this book helps reconstruct the critical, yet complex, part young men and women of Lebanon played in both extra-parliamentarian politics in Lebanon and global, disruptive politics. Indeed, since the early twentieth-century Middle East, similarly to other parts of the Global South, when categories of modernity, citizenship, nationalism, and education were articulated and practiced, young people have been agents for and a site of radical change.

Sectarianism, Sectarian Violence, and the 1958 War

When discussing popular organizations in Lebanon, and their mostly young members, many scholars either assume that they are, or describe them as, "sectarian." More specifically, three out of the seven groups are often characterized as sectarian, because they are made up almost

---

[28] *The Hans Wehr Dictionary of Modern Written Arabic*, 4th ed., ed. J. M. Cowan (Urbana, IL: Spoken Language Services, Inc., 1994), 815.

[29] For my understanding and use of *al-futuwwa*, I benefited from the work of and conversations with Wilson Chacko Jacob. For more information on *futuwwa*, in all its complexities, see Jacob, *Working Out Egypt*, 225–262.

exclusively of one sect, whether it be Maronite Christians (the Kata'ib), Sunni Muslims (the Najjadeh), or Shi'i Muslims (the Tala'i'). The need to preface a description of a group with a sectarian signifier (the Maronite Christian Kata'ib, for example) is the product of the long-standing analytical frame of "sectarianism," or *ta'ifiyya*. Whether those who use it are historians or journalists, outside observers or active participants, the frame accepts that national, secular identity is progress, and any group identity is sectarian, often in a pejorative sense.[30]

For instance, historian Stephen Hemsley Longrigg wrote in 1958 that popular organizations of mandate-era Syria and Lebanon, especially of the scout and paramilitary variety, with "its leaders and salutes and narrow devotions," were a "damaging obstacle to the sound national development which the world would gladly have acclaimed."[31] However, as will be shown in *Winning Lebanon*, these groups were at the center of national, "secular" development, particularly in regards to the construction of populist youth politics. They all believed that socializing young people, under the group, of course, was a cure to all types of backwardness. They also all acted upon this belief by implementing non- and anti-sectarian membership requirements and principles. To complicate Longrigg's words even more, when these groups do engage in sectarianism, or what I define as the politics and culture of socioreligious identity, sectarianism should not be assumed as static or value negative. Instead, sect is one of many, overlapping aspects of collective identity for young people in modern Lebanon, tied to family, nation, class, gender, and group affiliation.

Pertaining to the field of identity politics and sectarianism, my approach is the result of groundbreaking works of the last twenty years on Lebanon and the broader Middle East. They have shown that sectarianism is not just "out there" or primordial, but historically produced in the modern period. In his 2000 study, *The Culture of Sectarianism: Community, History, and Violence in Nineteenth-Century Ottoman*

---

[30] Three examples include Stephen Hemsley Longrigg, *Syria and Lebanon under French Mandate* (Oxford: Oxford University Press, 1958); Kamal Salibi, *The Modern History of Lebanon* (New York: Frederick A. Praeger, Inc., 1965); and Phillip K. Hitti, *Lebanon in History: From the Earliest Times to the Present*, 3rd ed. (London: Macmillan and Company Limited, 1967). While these scholars set a precedence for the analytical tradition, especially in the English-language literature on Lebanon, the foundations for sectarianism as an analytical frame date back to nineteenth-century Lebanon. For more information on the analytical trend, see Axel Havemann, "Historiography in 20th-Century Lebanon: Between Confessional Identity and National Coalescence," *Bulletin of the Royal Institute for Inter-Faith Studies* 4, no. 2 (2002): 49–69.

[31] Longrigg, *Syria and Lebanon under French Mandate*, 229–230.

Lebanon, Ussama Makdisi explores the moment at which European deci-sion-making changed the rules of the game in Mount Lebanon. He writes:

This encounter [between Ottoman and European imperial policy and local interpre-tations of that policy] profoundly altered the meaning of religion in the multiconfes-sional society of Mount Lebanon because it emphasized sectarian identity as the only viable marker of political reform and the only authentic basis for political claims.[32]

Through a discursive analysis of the 1860 War in Lebanon, Makdisi shows how even if sects predate sectarianism, the colonial encounter and interpretations of reform created a "culture of sectarianism" (i.e., investment in one's confessional identity as their main political marker) that had not existed prior and has existed in Lebanon and the broader Middle East ever since.

In his 2010 book, *In the Shadow of Sectarianism: Law, Shiʻism, and the Making of Modern Lebanon,* Max Weiss examines the subtle institutional changes under which Shi'i Muslims "became sectarian" during the later mandate period.[33] While one could read Makdisi as favoring the imperial contributions to sectarianism, Weiss focuses on "sectarianism from below"; for example, how Shia began, in the 1920s to 1930s, calling for personal status laws that matched their socially and politically more powerful Christian and Sunni Muslim compatriots.[34]

Chronologically speaking, *Winning Lebanon* fills a lacuna, starting where Makdisi and Weiss left off in early twentieth-century Lebanon. Moreover, it is grounded in a period, the mid-twentieth century, that is not often characterized by sectarianism. Thematically, this book builds from these two works, alongside others both from and beyond the Middle East, to synthesize a bottom-up approach to sectarianism.[35] This approach is grounded in the beliefs, rituals, practices, and cultures of particular groups, and in relation to the broader structures they exist in. In other words, while I agree with those scholars that have highlighted the role that nationalism, colonialism, and universalist discourses play in creating the context for sectarian politics and identities, someone or

---

[32] Ussama Makdisi, *The Culture of Sectarianism: Community, History, and Violence in Nineteenth-Century Ottoman Lebanon* (Berkeley, CA: University of California Press, 2000), 2.

[33] Max Weiss, *In the Shadow of Sectarianism: Law, Shiʻism, and the Making of Modern Lebanon* (Cambridge, MA: Harvard University Press, 2010), 3.

[34] Ibid., 11.

[35] For more examples, see Sean Farrell, *Rituals and Riots: Sectarian Violence and Political Culture in Ulster, 1784–1886* (Lexington, KY: University Press of Kentucky, 2009); Justin Jones, *Shi'a Islam in Colonial India: Religion, Community and Sectarianism* (Cambridge: Cambridge University Press, 2012); and Toby Matthiesen, *The Other Saudis: Shiism, Dissent and Sectarianism* (Cambridge: Cambridge University Press, 2015).

something has to breathe it to life for it then to be a distinguishable phenomenon.[36] In the course of the 1958 War, key agents in the production of a particular type of sectarian discourse and practice, what I refer to as sectarian violence, were popular organizations.

To be clear, *Winning Lebanon* is not a book on sectarian violence and difference, as the majority of it focuses on the coexistence and connectivity between youth-centric groups. Yet, it does culminate with an examination of discourses and practices of violence, often carried out by young people, that became known as sectarian. To explain the relationship between populism and violence, youth and violence, and sectarianism and violence, I find Pierre Bourdieu's theories most useful, particularly his concept of distinction.[37] Bourdieu advocates for structured or bounded agency; that is, even as groups have the ability to shape the terms of social life as agents of history through their practices, they are still bound by broader structures.[38] Given these dynamics that shape the local, sociopolitical field, in this study, youth and popular politics in mid-twentieth-century Lebanon, popular organizations try to stay relevant, boast, and survive by creating difference – both within and between groups – through their discourses and practices. Stated differently, through their ideologies, their ideals, their tastes, their styles, and their rituals, they distinguish themselves.[39]

Bourdieu focuses on class structures, predominantly in Europe, as the basis for the distinctions that high intellectuals make "between the beautiful and the ugly, the distinguished and the vulgar."[40] While class plays an integral role in the social structure, something *Winning Lebanon* takes up in subsequent chapters, the historical context of modern Lebanon necessities a shift beyond Bourdieu's specific framing. In summation, the politics of reform around the 1860s, the creation of sect-based politics under the French during the 1920s to 1940s, and its continuation by way of sect-based quotas following the National Pact of 1943 – six to five in

---

[36] For excellent structural approaches to sectarianism, see Saba Mahmood, *Religious Difference in a Secular Age: A Minority Report* (Princeton, NJ: Princeton University Press, 2016); and Maya Mikdashi, "Sextarianism: Notes on Studying the Lebanese State," in *The Oxford Handbook of Contemporary Middle-Eastern and North African History*, ed. Amal Ghazal and Jens Hanssen (Oxford Handbooks Online, 2018).

[37] Pierre Bourdieu, *Distinction: A Social Critique of the Judgment of Taste*, trans. Richard Nice (Cambridge, MA: Harvard University Press, 1984).

[38] Pierre Bourdieu, *Outline of a Theory of Practice*, trans. Richard Nice (Cambridge: Cambridge University Press, 1977), 73.

[39] Pierre Bourdieu, *Language and Symbolic Power*, ed. John B. Thompson, trans. Gino Raymond and Matthew Adamson (Malden, MA: Polity Press, 1992); and Pierre Bourdieu, *The Field of Cultural Production: Essays on Art and Literature*, ed. Randal Johnson (New York: Columbia University Press, 1993).

[40] Bourdieu, *Distinction*, 6.

favor of Christians over Muslims in parliament and civil service – place socioreligious difference as a necessary, but not sufficient, feature of the social structure in mid-twentieth-century Lebanon.[41]

Consequently, I focus on the ways that popular organizations distinguish between what they perceive as sectarian and its converse: popular, defensible, and anti-sectarian. Their usage of this discourse, however, depends on their position within the system. For example, as Maronite Christians historically benefited more from this system than Shi'i Muslims, a group made up mostly of Maronites is going to imbue the term sectarian with a different meaning or avoid it altogether. Regardless of particular position though, distinction creates the context for group differentiation in its most routine forms, and in its extreme form, the normalization of violent practices.

The latter, including the act of killing someone of another sect, even when the name of that sect is not mentioned, are explored in the context of the 1958 War. What some call the "war," others the "crisis," "events," or "revolution," 1958 in Lebanon has garnered considerable attention.[42] Most scholarship either focuses on domestic elites, and their reaction to the war, or the broader geopolitics of this event, including UN and US–UK intervention.[43] *Winning Lebanon* addresses a gap by focusing on the local scene, local sources, and particular foreign, diplomatic reports that placed popular organizations and their youth members at the center of the war. What emerges is a more complex understanding of the production of

---

[41] For more information on how socioreligious difference in Lebanon was institutionalized and is now enshrined in law, see Hanna Ziadeh, *Sectarianism and Intercommunal Nation-Building in Lebanon* (London: Hurst and Company, 2006).

[42] Those popular organizations who were in support of the Lebanese government often use the phrase events, crisis, or war, while those against the government refer to it as a revolution. I often use the term war, not in defense of the government, but to emphasize the role of armed conflict in the events.

[43] For those studies focusing almost exclusively on the 1958 War, see Fahim I. Qubain, *Crisis in Lebanon* (Washington, DC: The Middle East Institute, 1961); Arnold Hottinger, "Zu'ama' and Parties in the Lebanese Crisis of 1958," *Middle East Journal* 15, no. 2 (Spring 1961): 127–140; Fawaz A. Gerges, "The Lebanese Crisis of 1958: The Risks of Inflated Self-Importance," *The Beirut Review* 5 (Spring 1993): 1–24; Irene L. Gendzier, *Notes from the Minefield: United States Intervention in Lebanon and the Middle East, 1945–1958* (New York: Columbia University Press, 1997); 'Abbas Abu Salah, *al-'Azma al-Lubaniyya 'Am 1958: Fi Dawa' Watha'iq Yukshaf 'anha al-Awwal Marra* [The Lebanese Crisis of 1958: In Light of Documents Revealed for the First Time] (Beirut: al-Kursa al-Mashur, 1998); Caroline Attié, *Struggle in the Levant: Lebanon in the 1950s* (London: I.B. Tauris Publishers, 2004); Omri Nir, "The Shi'ites during the 1958 Lebanese Crisis," *Middle Eastern Studies* 40, no. 6 (2004): 109–129; Claude Boueiz Kanaan, *Lebanon 1860–1960: A Century of Myth and Politics* (London: Saqi Books, 2005); Sami Baroudi, "Divergent Perspectives among Lebanon's Maronites during the 1958 Crisis," *Critique: Middle Eastern Studies* 8, no. 1 (Spring 2006): 5–28; and 'Adel Malik, *1958: al-Qassa, al-Asrar, al-Watha'iq* [1958: The Story, the Secret, the Documents] (Jounieh, Lebanon: Dar Sa'ir al-Mashriq, 2011).

a particular type of violent social interaction, sectarian violence, in this very moment in 1958. While Makdisi correctly links the creation of sectarianism to the events of 1860, 1958 was different in that the geography of violence was national (from Tripoli in the north to the Bekaa in the east), violent practices were perpetuated by young people identified as punks, and this violence was justified by populist language akin to the twentieth century. More specifically, 1958 marks a critical juncture in the construction of sectarianism. Young people associated with these groups, once seen as the bedrock for the *sha 'b* and its successes, became thought of as prone to sectarian violence. In an ironic twist, then, the groups themselves, alongside detractors, pundits, and scholars, rendered *futuwwa*, the former spirit of youth agency, as the basis of a social, sectarian malady.

Outline of the Present Work

For one to study youth politics in the modern world, someone, or something, had to create it. Chapter 1 explores the architecture and architects of youth politics in mid-twentieth-century Lebanon. It moves chronologically from the 1920s to 1950s, describing the historical background of multiple popular organizations, and taking an individual group as a means to explore one theme in the construction of youth politics – that is, building a group culture, flair, and feel, and organizational capacity among youth-centric organizations. I argue that these groups were collectively the shapers of a distinct manifestation of popular politics in the Middle East, what I refer to as populism. This trend found its earliest expression with the Lebanese People's Party in the 1920s, continued with youth organizations like the Najjadeh in the 1930s, and culminated with transnational student groups like the Arab Nationalist Youth in the 1950s. Using the source material of these groups, I find that although they were deploying radically different worldviews to win Lebanon, based on the different, competing ideologies of the time – Arab nationalism, Lebanese nationalism, international socialism – there was more continuity than difference between these groups in their early years. They all channeled anger with colonial rule, the complicity of Lebanese elites in this subjugation, and used a discourse of populism to launch public awareness and protest.

With a historical overview of each group established, Chapter 2 discusses the roles that rituals, gatherings, and confrontation played in the rising popularity of these groups during the mid-twentieth century. Through analyzing multiple rituals, ranging from a protest on the streets to a Ping-Pong tournament at the group headquarters, I argue that by gathering, these groups produced a space – symbolic and physical – within the public sphere to practice their identity and recruit new members. However, autonomy was not easily won, as organizations were the site of surveillance and repression by the Ottoman, French colonial, and early independence state. After analyzing multiple types of gatherings and state control over them, Chapter 2 focuses on two episodes of street and state violence: one in the 1930s between the Kata'ib and French security forces, and one in the 1950s between the Progressive Socialist Party and Lebanese security forces. Following these clashes, these groups mobilized a history of violence in yearly events commemorating the battles. All popular organizations had confrontation narratives and rituals, and as a by-product, embedded violence – or at least struggle – within group culture. While being mindful not to essentialize violence within these groups, this point helps to foreshadow how they could conceive violent practices under extreme circumstances and threats.

As of the 1930s, the makeup of popular organizations was principally middle class and male, which was soon to change drastically. Chapter 3 explores the expansion of membership beyond these core demographics during the 1940s and 1950s. I argue that these groups encouraged the political socialization of new groups and categories of people in new places. By setting up organizational outposts throughout the country, establishing wings for marginalized populations, and connecting the group with relevant populations outside Lebanon, these organizations started to incorporate the countryside, young women, and émigrés into national and regional politics. In turn, this chapter finds that these groups expanded the notion of who constituted "youth," and accordingly, played a significant, albeit not exclusive, role in solidifying mass, youth politics in Lebanon and the broader Middle East. And although these groups were building a cosmopolitan base in many ways, they were circumscribed by the national, sociopolitical system (whereby sect determined how, or if, people could participate in official politics) in Lebanon, and linked class, gender, and regional inequalities. In turn, contradictions emerged within groups, including membership distinctions between the middle class, male, urban ideal, and everyone else. Furthermore, competition between these groups played out in terms of overlapping claims of who was – and was not – deemed as backward, or in some cases, "sectarian."

The last two chapters of *Winning Lebanon* take the 1958 War (May–October) as their basis, focusing on the participation of popular organizations in this conflict. Chapter 4 examines what transformed popular organizations from allies to enemies in the late 1950s. On one side of the conflict were those groups against the government and Lebanese President Camille Chamoun. They included the Progressive Socialist

Party, Najjadeh, Lebanese Communist Party, and the Arab Nationalist Youth. In speeches, petitions, and articles, these groups claimed that Chamoun's recent actions in domestic and foreign policy were authoritarian, represented a threat to sovereign Lebanon, and were grounds for armed revolution. On the other side were the Kata'ib and Syrian Social Nationalist Party. They made the point that foreign interference from Syria and Egypt, and its leftist sponsors in Lebanon (most notably, the Progressive Socialist Party), challenged Lebanon's sovereignty, the constitution, and their group. Given that defending Lebanon and its sovereignty was not, at least in the eyes of multiple popular organizations, sectarian, Chapter 4 represents a need to rethink sectarianism among sociopolitical actors in and beyond 1958. Indeed, whether groups had clear sect majorities (the Kata'ib and Najjadeh) or not (the Syrian Social Nationalist Party and Lebanese Communist Party), I argue that their perspectives before the conflict were quite complex, linked to multiple factors, and cannot be reduced to sectarianism alone.

Chapter 5 analyzes the dynamics of the fighting itself, starting in the summer of 1958. First, it takes up the place of ritual in the 1958 War. By focusing on the Kata'ib's shift, from the sidelines to frontlines, I argue that routine practices linked to youth belonging, play, and order were mobilized to perform violence. More broadly, whether it was singing a group anthem at an initiation ceremony before battle or marching in a funeral procession for a fallen fighter, popular organizations of all shades mobilized the youth cultures that were cultivated over past decades to win Lebanon. Chapter 5 also discusses several fronts of the war, including the final battle in Beirut between the Kata'ib and Najjadeh. While some scholars contend this phase was one of sectarian bloodletting, the reality was more complex. Neither side used exclusively sectarian discourse to describe other popular organizations. Instead, they deployed coded language, describing their enemies as maddened punks. This reality leads to *Winning Lebanon*'s main conclusion on sectarianism and sectarian violence. In the course of this conflict, youth or youthfulness, terms with little connection to sect, became linked to sectarian violence, in practice and discursively, a trend that continued beyond 1958. The Epilogue explores this legacy and makes a call for more research on the 1958 War, both as a rupture point in modern Middle East history, and as a site for understanding global, disruptive, youth politics.

1 The Future of Young Men
The Construction and Performance of Youth Politics

Did we not persuade our comrades in the neighborhood to fall under its [the group's] banner and unite and steer the energies of the youth [quwan al-shabab] in its organization and glory?[1]

In April 1937, youth organizer Muhyi al-Din al-Nasuli posed this question in a published appeal. The answer, at least in Nasuli's estimation, was a resounding yes. Those that were united, what he referred to as *al-najjad*, "the helper," were young, educated men located in the mostly Sunni Muslim neighborhoods of Beirut, Lebanon. Nasuli believed these youth, and their youthful energies, would be the drivers of a postcolonial future. They would also make up the recruitment basis of the Najjadeh; a popular organization formally founded in November 1937, which would be led, organized, and cultivated by Nasuli himself.[2]

While Nasuli's appeal signals the beginnings of a particular group at the center of youth mobilization and popular politics in French colonial Lebanon, his call is also significant for its broader, symbolic features. It first echoes ideas that were new to the youth masses of early twentieth-century Lebanon. Most prominent was the role that they, as ordinary (colonial) citizens, could play in building their young nation, however conceived, and community. To Nasuli, "serving your nation," whether in the form of helping the sick, poor, or orphans, was the most "sincere service."[3] This call for mass mobilization was not unlike that professed by another popular organization twelve years earlier: the Lebanese People's Party. On May 1, 1925, International Workers' Day, the executive committee of this newly formed workers' association led a diverse cast of characters to the streets, including young carpenters, barbers, and factory

---

[1] Muhyi al-Din al-Nasuli, *Akhi al-Najjad* [My Najjadeh Brother], *Majallat al-Najjad* no. 1, April 14, 1937. Cited in *Min Qulb Bayrut: Muhyi al-Din al-Nasuli, 1897–1961* [From the Heart of Beirut: Muhyi al-Din al-Nasuli, 1897–1961] (Beirut: Dar al-Nahar li-l-Nashr, 1992), 193.
[2] Suleiman, *Political Parties in Lebanon* (1967), 201–202.   [3] Nasuli, *Akhi al-Najjad*, 193.

workers, for protest in hopes of building a better future for lower-class laborers of Lebanon.[4]

Equally important as Nasuli's endorsement for political socialization was the medium in which it was distributed. This appeal to his "brothers" was part of the first issue of *Majallat al-Najjad* ("the Helper's Journal"), a publication for his newly formed youth movement and its members.[5] The journal was a companion to Nasuli's *Bayrut* ("Beirut"), a newspaper which he owned and served as the editor for since 1936. A growing public sphere, expanding technologies, and lower production costs allowed for the existence of a diverse print culture and niche cultural production. Publications such as *Majallat al-Najjad*, and the reading communities they targeted – at this point in time, largely young men of Beirut's Sunni middle class – constituted a new site for laying out what the young group was and whom it served. The Progressive Socialist Party's *al-Anba'* ("The News"), established fourteen years later, served a similar purpose. One of the first issues in 1951 reported on a separate youth movement that reflected the party's brand of social justice. The movement, ostensibly sponsored by the Progressive Socialist Party, would advocate for health insurance, care for the elderly, and in the words of the *al-Anba'* article, "bread and work for all."[6]

Beyond new ideas and publications, we must also consider the newly forming audience of Nasuli's appeal: young people, or more particularly during the 1920s to 1930s, young men. Nasuli spoke directly to *al-shabab*, technically "the boys," or "the [male] youth" in 1937, instructing that to foster a strong admiration of their homeland they must "love nature" and "become intimate with the trees, birds, stars, rivers, plants, and valleys." By fostering this bond, the helper would "grow up in the throes of [the homeland]," as youth development paralleled national development.[7] Targeting the youth, especially through activities meant to build them, physically and mentally, for the sake of nation building, was also common for another popular organization formed in the mid-1940s. The Tala'i', like the Najjadeh and its counterpart the Kata'ib, sent its boys on trekking expeditions in South Lebanon and Palestine, for the sake of building a community of young, strong, mostly Shi'i, Lebanese men.[8]

Collectively, the material evidence these groups left behind hints to the construction and performance of youth politics and a new brand of

---

[4] *Al-Insaniyya*, May 15, 1925. Cited in Lebanese Communist Party, *Sawt al-Sha'b Aqwa: Safhat min al-Sahafa al-Shiyu'iyya al-'Amaliyya wa-l-Dimuqratiyya 'ala Khamsin 'Ama* [The Voice of the People Is the Strongest: Pages from the Communist, Working, and Democratic Press at Fifty Years] (Beirut: Dar al-Farabi, 1974).
[5] Nasuli, *Akhi al-Najjad*, 193.   [6] *Al-Anba'*, April 6, 1951.
[7] Nasuli, *Akhi al-Najjad*, 193.   [8] *Al-Hayat*, March 19, 1946.

popular politics. Whether it was the Syrian Social Nationalist Party in the 1930s or the Arab Nationalist Youth in the 1950s, all popular organizations cultivated their identities through developing platforms, enacting them in the public sphere, disseminating and distinguishing them in newspapers and pamphlets, and practicing disciplined, masculine youth culture – uttering slogans, wearing club uniforms, singing club songs, and performing activities – in the group on a daily basis. This chapter follows the formation of this collective identity and popular culture through the eyes of several popular organizations, and the young people within them, chronologically from the French mandate era (1920–1943) into the early independence era (1943–1958).

In addition to charting the early history of each popular organization, this chapter uses a particular group to highlight a specific feature emblematic across groups. Whether describing the funding strategies of a group, or youth culture in a group, I draw a range of comparisons between organizations. This is for the sake of adding nuance to the literature on these groups, which often focuses solely on their different, and conflicting, ideologies and sectarian backgrounds.[9] In fact, I argue that putting these groups in conversation with each other allows for an emphasis on their similarities, including similar populist discourses, and comparable styles and performativities meant to sanctify group life and belonging. This was, however, at the very same time that these groups were cultivating radically different visions of their nation for the sake of conceiving Lebanon, representing their Lebanon, and winning Lebanon in their image. This narration of context, biography, and experience in the history of popular organizations not only begins to show why these groups coordinated at times, but also how they could eventually conduct and condone acts of violence against the "other."

Populism as a New Movement and Discourse: The Lebanese People's Party

Millions of young people across the Middle East were forced to come of age during the tumultuous era of the Great War. For Ottoman Bilad al-Sham, the war was particularly traumatic, marked by large-scale instability, death, displacement, and starvation.[10] While many families left their homes, others endured throughout the war, and many more returned to

---

[9] For three examples, see Yamak, *The Syrian Social Nationalist Party* (1966); Suleiman, *Political Parties in Lebanon*, and Entelis, *Pluralism and Party Transformation in Lebanon* (1974).

[10] For more information on the trauma associated with this era in Greater Syria, see Thompson, *Colonial Citizens* (2000); Tylor Brand, "Lives Darkened by Calamity:

what was now French colonial Lebanon after the war. This was the milieu in which populism and its logics – the people against the elites – emerged. For all intents and purposes, its founders were twenty-three-year-old Yusuf Ibrahim Yazbak and thirty-year-old Fuad al-Shamali, the leaders of the Lebanese People's Party (al-Hizb al-Sha'b al-Lubnani).

Yazbak (1901–1982) was born in Beirut to a well-off Maronite family – but not of the traditional *zu'ama'* – that decided to remain in their Beirut home throughout the war.[11] Writing was his passion, and like other urban, educated, young Lebanese men, Yazbak attempted to channel through literary form what he saw as the "horrible conditions ... misery, poverty and injustice" that the people had to experience.[12] He did so in his capacity as a journalist. As early as the age of twenty-one, he wrote for *al-Sahafi al-Ta'ih* ("the Wandering Journalist," founded in 1922) and *al-Ma'rid* ("the Exhibition," another left-leaning paper of the 1920s), all under his pen name al-Shabah al-Baki, "the Weeping Ghost."[13] In these papers, Yazbak spelled out the ideology that would become the basis of the Lebanese People's Party. His first public pronouncement of his worldview came over two years before the group was formed. In a May 1922 article in *al-Sahafi al-Ta'ih*, Yazbak admitted that after observing the state of the world with "an impartial eye," seeing "a large battle between the rich and the poor, the strong and the weak," "I am pure socialist *(ana ishtaraki samim)*."[14] Inspired by the Bolshevik revolution and its anti-colonial credentials, his ideas revolved around how socialism, not ethnic nationalism, was the answer for the trauma of the Great War.[15]

In contrast to Yazbak, the intellectual, Shamali (1894–1939) was the activist.[16] While the latter was born in the Mount Lebanon village of Sehayleh in the Kisrawan Province, some twenty kilometers north of Beirut, he did not spend his youth there.[17] His father worked in

Enduring the Famine of WWI in Lebanon and Western Syria (PhD diss., American University of Beirut, 2014); and Graham Auman Pitts, "'Make them Hated in All the Arab Countries': France, Famine and the Making of Lebanon," in *Environmental Histories of World War I*, ed. Richard P. Tucker et al. (Cambridge: Cambridge University Press, 2018), 175–190.

[11] Kais M. Firro, *Inventing Lebanon: Nationalism and the State under the Mandate* (London: I. B. Tauris, 2002), 142.

[12] Suleiman, *Political Parties in Lebanon*, 58.   [13] *Al-Sahafi al-Ta'ih*, October 14, 1922.

[14] Ibid., May 5, 1922.

[15] Farid Assaf, "*al-Hizb al-Shiyu'i al-Lubnani*" [The Lebanese Communist Party], in *Ahzab Lubnan* [Lebanese Political Parties] DVD series (Seattle, WA: Arab Film Distribution, 2003).

[16] Tareq Y. Ismael and Jacqueline S. Ismael, *The Communist Movement in Syria and Lebanon* (Gainesville, FL: University Press of Florida, 1998), 4.

[17] No sources that I have encountered mention Shamali's sect. Given that the province he is from is almost exclusively Christian, and mostly Christian Maronite, it is most likely that he hailed from a Maronite family.

Palestine and then Egypt, where Shamali finished his schooling and took a job at a tobacco factory in Alexandria at the age of sixteen. At age twenty-two, he joined a union, and at twenty-nine, he became active in the illegal Egyptian Communist Party and founded his own labor union.[18] It appears that these activities led the British to expel Shamali from Egypt. In August 1923, he arrived in Lebanon, where Yazbak, who had a day job at the Passport and Emigration Department of the Port of Beirut, was the immigration officer set to book him.[19]

Yazbak had at his back young, middle-class, socialist-leaning intellectuals. Shamali, though, held the working-class recruits. He founded the General Syndicate of Tobacco Workers in the village of Bikfaya in 1924 and held connections with workers in factories, artisanal guilds, printing presses, and restaurants from across Mount Lebanon to the suburbs of Beirut.[20] Yazbak and Shamali combined their networks to form the Lebanese People's Party in October 1924.[21] The executive committee, made up of a mixed group of mostly young Arab workers and intellectuals, selected Yazbak as the first secretary general. The party operated underground until recognized by the French colonial government on April 30, 1925.[22]

Together, Yazbak and Shamali would go on to do much more than found a worker's party. They constructed a distinct type of, and frame within, popular politics: populism. It would be for and by the young workers and peasants and modeled against the status quo. In Thompson's words, this populist call for change, a product of the "nightmare" of the Great War, "was a revelation that discredited the old order and inspired political action," even if the new order was not yet outlined.[23] Beyond an idealized future, Yazbak in particular set a precedent for a certain type of leadership for popular organizations.

---

[18] Nadhir Jazmati, *Musahama fi Naqd al-Harakat al-Siyasiyya fi Suriya wa-Lubnan: al-Hizb al-Shuyu'i al-Suri, 1924–1958* [Contribution to Understanding Political Movements in Syria and Lebanon: The Syrian Communist Party, 1924–1958] (Damascus: Mutaba'a Ibn Hiyan, 1990), 4–7; and Riad Hassan Moharram, "Fuad al-Shamali: Shuyu'i Lubnani min Misr" [Fuad al-Shamali: A Lebanese Communist from Egypt], February 27, 2014, www.ahewar.org/debat/show.art.asp?aid=402869.

[19] Naziy Jazmati, *al-Hizb al-Shuyu'i al-Lubnani* [The Lebanese Communist Party], in *al-Ahzab wa-l-Harakat al-Shiyu'iyya wa-l-Markisiyya al-'Arabiyya* [The Arab Communist and Marxist Parties and Movements], vol. 1 (Damascus: Arab Centre for Strategic Studies, 2000), 264; and Ismael and Ismael, *The Communist Movement in Syria and Lebanon*, 7.

[20] *Al-Nida'*, October 26, 1980; and Ismael and Ismael, *The Communist Movement in Syria and Lebanon*, 6–7.

[21] Jaamati, *al-Hizb al-Shuyu'i al-Lubnani*, 273–274.

[22] Suleiman, *Political Parties in Lebanon*, 61; and Ismael and Ismael, *The Communist Movement in Syria and Lebanon*, 8–12.

[23] Thompson, *Colonial Citizens*, 30.

Ranging from Antoun Saadeh of the Syrian Social Nationalist Party to George Habash of the Arab Nationalist Youth, these founders were middle-class nouveau intellectuals in their twenties and thirties. They all accessed aspects of a global, secular universalism, which offered multiple answers on how to alleviate poverty and prepare the youth for the future. This universalism, at least in the 1920s under Yazbak's leadership, was *by* the educated and *for* the masses.

"Founded in the service of the workers and peasants defending *their* rights and organizing *their* ranks"; this was the slogan for the party's first newspaper, *al-Insaniyya*, founded in 1925.[24] Meaning "The Humanity" (an appropriation of the name of the French communist daily, *L'Humanité*, operating since 1904), *al-Insaniyya* was not primarily a place for breaking news, but a means to construct a populist discourse and platform. The Leninist vanguard, including Yazbak, Shamali, and the greater executive committee, would save the people, specifically the "peasant workers" – the only individuals who could be members of the party.[25] On International Labor Day, May 1, 1925, the executive committee organized a rally and demonstration in Beirut to reveal the group's platform, including its seven demands for French authorities.[26] They included:

(1) limiting the time of work to eight hours a day
(2) determining a minimum wage
(3) a minimum age [fourteen] that protects workers[27]
(4) education for children and sustenance for elders and injured laborers – the labor owners and social commission [governmental] are accountable
(5) forbidding night work
(6) the decision of the wages commission remains in effect for laborers[28]
(7) revival of economic projects[29]

These seven demands establish that the People's Party was not strictly political in its early days. It was a labor network, attempting to coalesce young (but not too young) workers into one general platform. This

---

[24] *Al-Insaniyya*, May 15, 1925 (emphasis added).   [25] Ibid.
[26] This was not the first time Yazbak had organized a May 1 event; two years earlier in 1923, Yazbak and his colleague at the journal *al-Sahafi al-Ta'ih*, Iskander al-Riyashi, apparently sponsored the first Labor Day celebration in Lebanon. M. S. Agwani, *Communism in the Arab East* (New York: Asia Pub. House, 1969), 14.
[27] The Lebanese People's Party clarified this "minimum age" in the next issue of *al-Insaniyya*. *Al-Insaniyya*, May 24, 1925.
[28] This likely regarded upholding a protection against forced labor without pay. While this was the norm under the Ottomans as regarded infrastructure projects, the French modified the policy slightly, "paying low wages to volunteers and those who owed back taxes." Thompson, *Colonial Citizens*, 82.
[29] *Al-Insaniyya*, May 15, 1925.

platform was populist, choosing economic grievances as a way to channel mass disenfranchisement – political and social – with the current order of things. In the opinion of the Lebanese People's Party, this order, created by the French, and supported by the wealthy Lebanese, did not have the worker's rights in mind.

Apparently, this form of protest worked. Preceding May Day 1925, there were few labor unions in Lebanon (most notably, the General Syndicate of Tobacco Workers, founded by Shamali), as Ottoman and French officials actively restricted the right to organize.[30] After the party's demonstrations and seven demands, two unions were founded for carpenters and barbers.[31] Furthermore, the government supposedly responded to the seven demands of the People's Party. In the same edition of *al-Insaniyya* that included the list of demands, the writer(s) claim that the French government promised it would consider the first of the seven demands on shortening work hours, and study the others, as long as the party did not disrupt "the conduct of business in the country."[32]

Alongside these rather pragmatic demands, the Lebanese People's Party also developed radical critiques of imperialism and its Lebanese surrogates. The writer(s) of *al-Insaniyya* reported in these early days after the Labor Day protests that their actions, and by extension the group itself, were against the "capitalist system" and the "wealthy which eat the fruit of the people's labor" in this "oppressed county."[33] This populist rhetoric became more direct and detailed with time. In the second edition of *al-Insaniyya*, May 24, 1925, the writer(s) stated that the People's Party had received a set of requests from the people. In turn, the party responded to the will of the people to combine these requests into a party program. The program mixed economic platforms – like "energizing industry, agriculture, and business" through tax increases on capitalists and their machinery – with educational, national, and political ones. These included calls to "strengthen national schools [with] free education … for boys and girls," make foreign schools subject to review, "kill the crimes of religious intolerance and sectarianism," and stipulate that "religious men not [serve] in politics."[34] Thus, in addition to constructing an inclusive populist platform and membership (Figure 1.1), in the party's words, as "the true defender of the rigors of workers and peasants," the People's Party was radically secular.[35]

---

[30] For more on Ottoman and French policy regarding unionization, see Thompson, *Colonial Citizens*, 81–83.
[31] Suleiman, *Political Parties in Lebanon*, 61.   [32] *Al-Insaniyya*, May 15, 1925.   [33] Ibid.
[34] Ibid., May 24, 1925.   [35] Ibid., May 15, 1925.

Figure 1.1 A Lebanese Communist Party meeting in 1936 in Baalbek. Lebanese Communist Party, *Nidal al-Hizb al-Shiyu'i al-Lubnani min khilal Watha'iqahu* [The Struggle of the Lebanese Communist Party through Its Documents], vol. 1 (Beirut: Manshurat al-Hizb al-Shiyu'i al-Lubnani, 1971). Courtesy of Bibliothèque Orientale, University of Saint Joseph, Beirut.

This last set of critiques signaled multiple changes to the group. Following the successes of Labor Day, the executive committee decided to expand the group and its ideology. In the summer of 1925, the Lebanese People's Party officially reconstituted as the Communist Party of Syria and Lebanon.[36] Two of its earliest stances were to "support the Syrian revolution" and "strengthen the struggle against imperialism," both of which were referencing the 1925 Syrian Revolt against the French.[37] Predictably, the French government shut down *al-Insaniyya* – after only five issues – and sentenced Yazbak and Shamali to jail in coastal Syria on charges of obstruction of public

[36] This shift in name and ideology is a product of events unfolding in 1924–1925. They include Shamali's attempts to reach out to the Comintern, Joseph Stalin winning out against Leon Trotsky in Russia, and the addition of self-avowed Armenian Communists to the party's executive committee. For more information, see Suleiman, *Political Parties in Lebanon*, 60–63.

[37] Ismael and Ismael, *The Communist Movement in Syria and Lebanon*, 13. For more on the Syrian Revolt of 1925, see Michael Provence, *The Great Syrian Revolt and the Rise of Arab Nationalism* (Austin, TX: University of Texas Press, 2005).

interests.[38] When released in 1928, Yazbak either left the party or was forced out.[39] In 1929, the French outlawed the Lebanese People's Party.[40] And in 1932, Shamali himself was pushed aside, on grounds of collusion with Lebanese Internal Security.[41] Thereafter, the Communist Party of Syria and Lebanon took a new direction, working in lockstep with Joseph Stalin's USSR.

Both Yazbak and Shamali's significance to Lebanon's popular organizations should not be understated. Yazbak reminisced in his 1974 memoir about these contributions:

We [the Lebanese People's Party] were a wonderful entity in terms of quality and a very little thing in terms of size. In terms of quality, we were the vanguard who shook the brains of people. We were bold and initiated fights against all the powerful bodies at all levels, whether rich or rulers, clergy, or traditional leaders. That was our character and our identity in the Lebanese community.[42]

While perhaps boastful, the platforms, plights, and slogans popularized by Yazbak and Shamali's Lebanese People's Party constituted the earliest, most organized, and well-sustained distillation of populism in Lebanon. Like the socialist and anarchist moments of the Eastern Mediterranean in the late nineteenth century, masterfully outlined by Khuri-Makdisi, the populist moment of the early twentieth was not an ideology per se, but a "revolutionary movement" within popular politics.[43] In defense of al-sha'b, and in the face of French colonialism and the zu'ama' patron-client relations that sustained it, this movement became quite compelling for the youth of tomorrow.

Although their populism was unique in its critique of capitalism and its focus on economic demands, others followed Yazbak and Shamali's lead. A decade later, another middle-class intellectual, Antoun Saadeh, made a name for himself by criticizing the Lebanese elite and its colonial supporters. Like Yazbak and Shamali, this landed Saadeh in prison, where he told French officials in 1935 that his Syrian Social Nationalist Party was looking for "elements of honest youth (al-shabab al-nazih) distant from the decadent political corruption" to form the basis of his

---

[38] Jazmati, Al-Hizb al-Shiyu'i al-Lubnani, 265.

[39] For competing explanations, see Ismael and Ismael, The Communist Movement in Syria and Lebanon, 14–15; and Suleiman, Political Parties in Lebanon, 62–63.

[40] Salwa Mansur Jurdak, "The Evolution of Lebanese Party Politics: 1919–1947" (master's thesis, American University of Beirut, 1948), 57.

[41] Ismael and Ismael, The Communist Movement in Syria and Lebanon, 20.

[42] Yusuf Yazbak, Hikayat Awwal Ayyar fi al-'Alam: Thikrayat wa-Tarikh wa-Nisus, 69–74. Cited in Ismael and Ismael, The Communist Movement in Syria and Lebanon, 9.

[43] Khuri-Makdisi, The Eastern Mediterranean and the Making of Global Radicalism (2013), 20.

pan-Syrian nation.[44] Others, like the Kata'ib and Najjadeh, were less ideologically driven, but more activist, holding strikes (sometimes jointly, sometimes separately) to protest the high prices for basic goods and services throughout the final years of French rule. These groups were not socialist or communist, however. They employed different shades of populism to inform their model for national – or transnational – development. At the same time, plights that began with the Lebanese People's Party in the 1920s, including alleviating collective trauma, realizing social change, and readying the youth and poor for the future were foundational for later popular organizations that took shape in the 1930s to 1950s.

Producing and Consuming Collective Identity: The Syrian Social Nationalist Party

For populism to become a movement and discourse with multiple tentacles, disseminating it was as important as the milieu in which it emerged. Throughout the 1920s to 1950s, the main medium for inculcation was the newspaper. Not unlike Benedict Anderson's producers of "national print-languages," and clear in the case of the Lebanese People's Party's *al-Insaniyya*, the newspaper served as a space within the public sphere for popular organizations to cultivate their imagined community.[45] The newspaper served as a place to conceive the group, its ethos, its allies, and its outsiders. It also was a space of consumption, as newspaper advertisements targeted their young, middle-class members, readers, and consumers. The Syrian Social Nationalist Party (al-Hizb al-Suri al-Qawmi al-Ijtima'i), founded in 1932, and its earliest newspaper, *al-Nahda* ("the Renaissance," 1937), demonstrate these trends in the early history of popular organizations.

Like Shamali, Antoun Saadeh (1904–1949) came of age outside Lebanon. Those who left Lebanon during the late Ottoman, Great War or French colonial era had multiple reasons, including forced displacement, fear of execution for anti-government beliefs, or hopes for making a better living than currently attainable in Lebanon or Syria. Khalil Saadeh (1857–1934), Antoun's father, decided to leave his homeland of Bilad al-Sham based on all of these considerations.[46] He first moved to Egypt in 1901,

---

[44] Ahmad Salim al-Ahmad, *Hizb al-Suri al-Qawmi al-Ijtima'i, 1932–1962: Dirasa Tarikhiyya* [The Syrian Social Nationalist Party, 1932–1962: A Historical Study] (Beirut: Dar wa-Maktabat al-Turath wa-l-Adab, 2014), 48.

[45] Benedict Anderson, *Imagined Communities: Reflections of the Origin and Spread of Nationalism*, revised ed. (London: Verso, 2006), 67.

[46] For more information on Khalil Saadeh, see Sofia Saadeh, "Khalil Sa'adeh and Syrian Nationalism in the Aftermath of World War I," in *The Origins of Syrian Nationhood: Histories, Pioneers and Identity*, ed. Adel Beshara (New York: Routledge, 2011), 328–340.

Argentina in 1913, and then Brazil in 1921 where he was joined by his son.[47] The Saadehs, a Greek Orthodox family from Mount Lebanon, were representative of a larger wave of Syro-Lebanese immigration to South America.[48] Outside Bilad al-Sham, and technically displaced, Antoun would work with his father and practice thinking through the beliefs and ideology of what would become the Syrian Social Nationalist Party.

Antoun's father, Khalil, had founded the National Democratic Party (al-Hizb al-Dimuqrati al-Watani) in 1919, which hoped to "attain complete independence" of Greater Syria, "implement democratic rule," promote secularism (inspired by Mustafa Kamal Ataturk of Turkey), and "initiate social reform" to alleviate social inequality – all from Buenos Aires.[49] Khalil also ran several newspapers that served to jump-start these initiatives and bring together Syrian communities in South America, including *al-Majalla* ("the Journal") and *al-Jarida* ("the Newspaper"). His son worked as a commentator for both. In his teens, Antoun wrote articles on Syrian unification (including Lebanon, Syria, and Palestine) in defiance of the mandate system, the paradox of French republicanism and colonialism, what he saw as the misguided concept of Islamic caliphate, and the troubling nature of America's growing imperialist stance.[50] And later, on the cusp of age twenty, he transmitted the idea of displacement, through essays such as "Memory of Homeland and Family."[51]

Antoun Saadeh returned "home" to French-controlled Lebanon in 1929, where he quickly found employment at the American University of Beirut (AUB) as a German and Arabic tutor.[52] AUB's campus in west Beirut was the recruiting zone for Saadeh, who in 1932, with several

---

[47] Ibid., 330–331; Margaret M. Bodron, "Violence in the Syrian Social Nationalist Party" (master's thesis, American University of Beirut, 1970), 14; and al-Ahmad, *Hizb al-Suri al-Qawmi al-Ijtima'i*, 52–53.

[48] For more information on Syro-Lebanese migration to South and North America during the late nineteenth and early twentieth century, see Khater, *Inventing Home* (2001); and Stacey D. Fahrenthold, *Between the Ottomans and the Entente: The First World War in the Syrian and Lebanese Diaspora, 1908–1925* (Oxford: Oxford University Press, 2019).

[49] Saadeh, "Khalil Sa'adeh and Syrian Nationalism in the Aftermath of World War I," 332–335. For more information on the National Democratic Party's platform, see Nuwaf Hardan, *Sa'adeh fi al-Mahjar* [Saadeh in Exile], vol. 1, 1921–1930, Brazil (Beirut: Dar Fikr li-l-Ibhath wa-l-Nashr, 1989), 40–41.

[50] *Al-Jarida*, June 25, 1921; al-Ahmad, *Hizb al-Suri al-Qawmi al-Ijtima'i*, 52–53; and Hardan, *Sa'adeh fi al-Mahjar*, vol. 1, 126–134.

[51] *Al-Majalla*, March 1923.

[52] Jibran Jiraj interview, July 1, 1970. Cited in Bodron, "Violence in the Syrian Social Nationalist Party," 17. Al-Ahmad claims German was one of the nine languages he "perfected" by age twenty-four in Brazil. He also knew English, Latin, French, Spanish, Italian, Portuguese, and Russian. Al-Ahmad, *Hizb al-Suri al-Qawmi al-Ijtima'i*, 53.

students, alumni, and faculty of diverse backgrounds formed what would later be known as the Syrian Social Nationalist Party. Within two years of its founding, around thirty students from AUB (at least sixteen years of age or older, according to party by-laws) were members of the Syrian Social Nationalist Party.[53] And by 1935, the leadership of the Syrian Social Nationalist Party had branched outside of AUB, recruiting 1,600 to join the ranks of the group.[54] Given this growing popularity, French authorities eventually found out about the group, and particularly Saadeh's growing disdain for a separate Lebanese nation-state. Accordingly, the French banned his group and sent him to jail.[55] Saadeh was charged with obstruction of public interests under a French law on youth groups, which forbid student social clubs like Saadeh's "from all political acts and all participation in demonstrations or protests with political nature."[56]

During this first imprisonment of 1936 (Saadeh would be imprisoned two more times over the next two years), he wrote what would become known as *The Birth of Nations (Nushu' al-Umam)*, which served as the ideological basis for the Syrian Social Nationalist Party and its pan-Syrian nation.[57] It was informed by multiple scholarly traditions, ranging from Ibn Khaldun, the great fourteenth-century Arab historian and social theorist, who outlined cycles of history, to the American sociologist Robert M. MacIver, who made a strong case for the fundamental association between a community, the environment, and land.[58] Both gave Saadeh the basis to argue for a prehistoric and eternal, Syrian nation. Nothing of Saadeh's experience in South America was outlined in this book. Yet, individual longing for return and the sociological foundations for an official homeland influenced the Syrian Social Nationalist Party's original platform. The party's founding principles state that Syrians, whether in South America, Syria, Lebanon, or elsewhere, constituted

---

[53] Al-Ahmad, *Hizb al-Suri al-Qawmi al-Ijtima'i*, 62.

[54] Bodron, "Violence in the Syrian Social Nationalist Party," 18–19.

[55] Yamak, *The Syrian Social Nationalist Party*, 56.

[56] *Qarar Raqim 146, Bi-Sha'n Jam'iyyat al-Shaban al-Munsh'a al-Mumarisa al-Il'ab al-Riyadiyya* [Decision #146 Concerning Youth Associations Established for the Practices of Sports] (July 4, 1934), Principle 1. *Records at the Lebanese National Archives Center*. Beirut, Lebanon.

[57] For a digital version of the original Arabic text, *Nushu' al-Umam*, see the Syrian Social Nationalist Party's fan website, www.ssnp.com/?page_id=344. I consulted the original 1938 version: Antoun Saadeh, *Nushu' al-Umam: Kitab al-Awwal* [The Birth of Nations: The First Book] (Beirut: 1938). For an accurate English translation, see Antoun Saadeh, *The Genesis of Nations*, trans. Department of Culture of the Syrian Social Nationalist Party (Beirut: 2004).

[58] Adel Beshara, "Antun Sa'adeh: Architect of Syrian Nationalism," in *The Origins of Syrian Nationhood*, 345–346 and 351.

a nation, without their "natural environment." Only the "Syrian psyche originating in independence" could awaken Syrian nationalism from its slumber.[59]

The collective identity of popular organizations, however, was not the product of ideology alone. In other words, not every member could quote the treatises of their leaders or party principles. Perhaps more immediate in the everyday life of members was browsing through the group newspaper. The Syrian Social Nationalist Party's *al-Nahda* was its first licensed paper, operating between 1937 and 1939. Almost from the beginning, *al-Nahda*, like other newsprint from popular organizations, included advertisements. Ads show both who the *al-Nahda* reader was and how the Syrian Social Nationalist Party sought to cultivate an ideal member.[60] Targeting young male readers in 1937, a product called "Atta Boy" promised a "clean quick shave."[61] In another edition, *al-Nahda* showcased the Artcraft store and its "Town Chiffon" pantyhose.[62] While the former Atta Boy ad confirms male readership, the latter could hint that the Nationalist Party reading public included women as early as 1937. More likely in these early days was the assumption that husbands would buy these items for their wives. Male *al-Nahda* readers could find this hosiery at the Artcraft location on Weygand Street in downtown Beirut or at the nearby ABC department store, which also received an advertisement in the pages of *al-Nahda*.[63]

These ads, and others like them, first demonstrate the middle-class credentials of their readers, although, as other scholars of twentieth-century reading publics in Beirut and Cairo have suggested, newspapers would be read aloud and shared with those outside these groups.[64] More specifically for these readers and observers, the ads indicate that members of the Syrian Social Nationalist Party were not mere political beings, but capitalist consumers – or aspiring consumers – enjoying leisure in Beirut. Finally, ads were meant to give a certain air of "official-ness," which could bring legitimacy and more recruits back to the group. The writer(s) of *al-Nahda*, then, used the authority of the official gazette to craft a certain

---

[59] Antoun Saadeh, *Mabadi' al-Hizb al-Suri al-Qawmi al-Ijtima'i wa-Ghayatuh* [The Principles of the Syrian Social Nationalist Party and It Goals] (Beirut[?]: Syrian Social Nationalist Party[?], 1947), 18 and 26.

[60] For more information on the role of advertisements in creating ideal members of groups, national or otherwise, see Mona L. Russell, *Creating the New Egyptian Woman: Consumerism, Education, and National Identity, 1863–1922* (New York: Palgrave Macmillan, 2004).

[61] *Al-Nahda*, November 13, 1937.   [62] Ibid., November 21, 1937.

[63] Ibid., December 9, 1937.

[64] For more information on illiterate reading publics in earlier periods, see Fahmy, *Ordinary Egyptians* (2011) and Khuri-Makdisi, *The Eastern Mediterranean and the Making of Global Radicalism.*

ideal, and a collective identity, being, and sense of belonging around that ideal.[65]

Moreover, the writer(s) would discuss those outside the ideal in the form of write-ups and investigative reports on other popular organizations. Throughout the first week of December 1937, the Syrian Social Nationalist Party ran a series in the pages of *al-Nahda* critical of other Lebanese and Syrian political parties. The articles left no group or leader unscathed. It referred to Tawfiq ʿAwad, leader of the Lebanese Union Party, as "tactless," and the National Front in Lebanon, and its vague Lebanese nationalism, as no more than a "fussy noise . . . in reaction to the emergence of the Syrian Social Nationalist Party."[66] The articles on the political blocs of Syria were no kinder, as the members of the National Front in Syria were "men that have traditional reactionary culture (*thaqafa taqlidiyya rajʿiyya*)" and only "superficial familiarity" with politics, and the "loose principles" of the National Action League in Syria (a youth organization) were "closer to imagination than the truth."[67]

Yet, the reports on two Lebanese popular organizations, the Kataʾib and Najjadeh, were most pointed. Highlighting the dangerous nature of the Najjadeh on December 1, the writer(s) make several claims. First, its leader, Nasuli, is no more than a parliamentarian insider, posing as a populist, and playing the game of "sectarian politics." Second, its newspaper, *Bayrut*, "was a sectarian newspaper to defend the interests of the Muslim sect." Third and finally, the writer(s) used the term "scout movement" in scare quotes, as Nasuli dressed "a sectarian political movement," the Najjadeh, in scout's clothing. This is all meant to be alarming to the reader of *al-Nahda*, as the Najjadeh marks the proliferation of "destructive sectarian gangs" in Lebanon.[68] The Kataʾib was also part of this current. According to *al-Nahda*, the group was formed solely to combat the popularity of the Syrian Social Nationalist Party and used sport as a cover for their "sectarian face (*wajhan taʾifiyyan*)." In fact, it did not appear to the writer(s) that Kataʾib members actually played sports; all they ever saw were militaristic demonstrations. Its leader, Pierre Gemayel, was part of a "feudal family," and his organization was not for the good of the nation. Instead, like other Lebanese nationalist groups, such as the Lebanese Union Party, with which *al-Nahda* lumped the

---

[65] For the relationship between newspaper writing and authority, see Khuri-Makdisi, *The Eastern Mediterranean and the Making of Global Radicalism*, 43–45; and Kevin W. Martin, *Syria's Democratic Years: Citizens, Experts, and Media in the 1950s* (Bloomington, IN: Indiana University Press, 2015).

[66] *Al-Nahda*, December 1 and 2, 1937.   [67] Ibid., December 3 and 7, 1937.

[68] Ibid., December 1, 1937.

Kata'ib, Gemayel's group was a "foreign manifestation" with "personal goals."[69]

In short, the Syrian Social Nationalist Party used its newspaper not only to project the ideal and togetherness, but the other. These articles made a distinction between their (implicit) popular movement, and the outsider, sectarian parties. Its readers knew and continued to process that the community of Syrian Social Nationalist Party supporters were not sectarian and its pan-Syrian nationalism was not a foreign manifestation based on unfounded principles. And even though the place of sport in the Najjadeh and Kata'ib is difficult to reduce to a cover, the reality behind this argument was not important for the Syrian Social Nationalist Party. Whether to highlight middle-class consumptive experiences, or differences between groups, popular organizations used their cultural production, including newspapers, to project collective identity, accumulate new recruits, and stake their claim as the true representative of the imagined, national whole.

Other popular organizations were not only on the receiving end of distinction making. Nasuli's newspaper, *Bayrut*, for example, reported in 1936 that thirty-three members had withdrawn from the Syrian Social Nationalist Party.[70] That these ex-members left Saadeh's party was more than just a matter of symbolic importance to Nasuli and his emerging Najjadeh. This trend of defection would continue, as the party's founder and leader, Saadeh, left Lebanon again for South America in 1938, before the start of World War II.[71] Where these new recruits would end up, and who or what would draw them in, was of material significance to all active groups in the field of youth and popular politics.

Rituals and Becoming a Member: The Najjadeh Organization

While protesting the status quo, reading advertisements, and criticizing the other were part of the story, so were the routines, styles, and activities that make up the daily life and culture of popular organizations. To shift the focus toward rituals highlights the centrality of youth in the lived historical experience of these groups, whether the group called itself a "party," "organization," "movement," or "club." In these facets of group identity, leaders, regardless of ideological position or vision, were accessing a global grammar of youth in full bloom by the mid-twentieth

[69] Ibid., December 2, 1937.   [70] *Bayrut*, July 30, 1936.
[71] Nuwaf Hardan, *Sa'adeh fi al-Mahjar* [Saadeh in Exile], vol. 2, 1938–1940 (Beirut: Bisan li-l-Nashr wa-li-l-Tuzi'a, 1996), 57–65.

century. This performativity – common in cities across the Eastern Mediterranean in this period – was undergirded by capitalist consumer culture and tastes, and grounded in a certain novelty of being modern and looking the part.[72]

First and of utmost importance, the rank and file of various popular organizations were officially introduced to stylistic practices through the process and spectacle of becoming a member. Here, I use the Najjadeh Organization (Munazzamat al-Najjadeh) as a case study; not because it is particularly unique, but because it has left behind some of the most detailed records on their membership rituals. Notable are a 1944 pamphlet, titled "The Internal Organization for the Troops" (al-Tanzim al-Dakhili li-l-Firaq), and a contemporaneous blank Najjadeh application form.[73] They outline the entire process of belonging to the group, from joining to testing to oathing. But to contextualize these rites of passage, it is best to start with the history of the organization and its founder.

Muhyi al-Din al-Nasuli (1896–1961) was another of Beirut's urban middle class that would go on to play a central role in French mandate-era youth politics. He was born and raised in late Ottoman Beirut, went to primary school in the capital, and eventually studied Economics at AUB.[74] Unlike the intellectual leaders discussed thus far, Nasuli's beliefs were not based on global ideologies and theoretical distillations, but a basic and different goal: creating the model, young citizen. He would succeed, according to his contemporaries, who knew him as the "jewel of Beirut youth."[75] He would eventually take this role into national politics, serving as a member of parliament four times after 1937.[76]

In terms of ideology, Nasuli's was informed by Arab nationalism alongside notions of Sunni Islamic values of piety, kindness, and morality. Similar to his contemporary, and eventual prime minster, Riad al-Solh (1894–1951), Nasuli's secular Arab nationalism linked Arab

---

[72] For more information on Beirut as a global, capitalist, consumptive city, starting in the late Ottoman period, and the forms of social organization that emerged around it, see Tofoul Abou-Hodeib, *A Taste for Home: The Modern Middle Class in Beirut* (Stanford, CA: Stanford University Press, 2017); and Khuri-Makdisi, *The Eastern Mediterranean and the Making of Global Radicalism*. For more on embodiments of modernity and modern living during this period in the Eastern Mediterranean, see Watenpaugh, *Being Modern in the Middle East* (2006).

[73] Najjadeh Party, *al-Tanzim al-Dakhili li-l-Firaq* [The Internal Organization for the Troops] (1944) and Fillable Application Form (?). Najjadeh Party Files, Linda Sadaqah Collection, American University of Beirut.

[74] Milya Malik Khir, *Muhyi al-Din al-Nasuli, 1896–1961* [introduction to Nasuli's *Bayrut* newspaper microfilm] (Beirut: American University of Beirut, Jafet Library Audiovisual Materials, 1971).

[75] Dueck, *The Claims of Culture at Empire's End* (2010), 187.

[76] Khir, *Muhyi al-Din al-Nasuli*.

contributions to civilization, without contradiction, to the daily practice, values, and history of Islam.[77] But also, and like other popular organizations that stressed temperance and morality alongside nationalism, religiosity in the Najjadeh was not about strict doctrine. At least in the 1930s, Nasuli was cultivating *futuwwa*, or "youthfulness," in a group of young, disciplined, practicing Sunni Muslims. This would prepare these men to play a part of a broader, cross-sect Lebanon.

Perhaps more so than Arab nationalism, Nasuli was inspired by scouting. In 1920, Nasuli founded the Muslim Scouts (al-Kashshaf al-Muslim), and in the 1930s, he supposedly met and conversed with British scout founder Robert Baden-Powell at a number of international scouting conferences.[78] He also translated sections of Baden-Powell's 1908 *Scouting for Boys: A Handbook for Instruction in Good Citizenship* for his new youth organization, the Najjadeh. Similarly to Baden-Powell's "scout law," which emphasized being "obedient to every order," Nasuli stressed that the *najjad*, or "helper," should "love [his] superiors and obey them."[79] And in the preface of a 1936 volume dedicated to the Muslim Scouts, Nasuli adapted Baden-Powell's emphasis on physical strength and ability for the sake of nation building, stating that through "recreation and play," a "power [was] awoken" in the scout.[80] This dormant strength would help realize "the man of the nation" (*rajul al-watan*), the Arab nation.[81] To realize this goal, Nasuli created the Najjadeh in late 1937 and would serve as its president throughout the 1930s. It was an entity distinct from the Muslim Scouts. As outlined in a 1944 pamphlet, the Najjadeh served as the "third creation of scout life," meant to indoctrinate "values in the service of each other and the service of society."[82] Separating individuals of eighteen years of age or older toward this service confirmed that one had to be of a certain age and temperament to be "prepared" to forge the nation.[83]

[77] Kamal Salibi, *A House of Many Mansions: The History of Lebanon Reconsidered* (Berkeley, CA: University of California Press, 1988), 209–213. For more information on secular Arab nationalism, both in its Christian and Muslim varieties, see Hourani, *Arabic Thought in the Liberal Age* (1983).

[78] Khir, *Muhyi al-Din al-Nasuli*. A 1936 book dedicated to the Muslim Scouts includes a 1933 note from Baden-Powell, which commends those Muslim Scouts "interested in the Scout Mouvement [sic]" and "cordially wish[es] Good Camping to all[.]" Shafiq Naqqash and 'Ali Khalifa, *al-Haraka al-Kashshafiyya fi al-Aqtar al-'Arabiyya* [The Scout Movement in the Arab Countries] (Beirut: Dar al-Kashshaf, 1936),

[79] Robert Baden-Powell, *Scouting for Boys: A Handbook for Instruction in Good Citizenship* (1908), ed. Elleke Boehmer (Oxford: Oxford University Press, 2004), 44; and Nasuli, *Akhi al-Najjad*, 193.

[80] Naqqash and Khalifa, *al-Haraka al-Kashshafiyya fi al-Aqtar al-'Arabiyya*.   [81] Ibid.

[82] Najjadeh Party, *al-Tanzim al-Dakhili li-l-Firaq*, 3.   [83] Ibid., 18.

So like the Lebanese People's Party and the Syrian Social Nationalist Party, the Najjadeh formed a sense of belonging through principles and platforms, whether the medium was a newspaper, book, public notice, or scouting guide. Yet, ideology should not be overstated in the history of popular organizations. To do so favors worldview, and its place in indoctrination, over the cultural practices of these groups.[84] Indeed, rituals were also a strategy used by leaders in cultivating *futuwwa*. At the same time, to move toward how an individual becomes a member of a popular organization can reconstruct, albeit incompletely, who the young members of popular organizations were aspiring to be and what they would do to get there.

The first step in the process of organizational belonging was filling out an application. Applications were most likely distributed to potential Najjadeh members at the group's main bases of recruitment: the Islamic Makassed College, the American University of Beirut, or the mosques or charitable institutions housed in Sunni urban poor neighborhoods of Beirut, such as Tariq el-Jdideh and Basta.[85] In a Najjadeh application of the early 1940s, the individual, or what the Najjadeh referred to as a "student," was asked basic personal information – their family name, address, marital status, occupation, and education – as well as how long they served and what rank they achieved in the Muslim Scouts.[86] The recording of this scout information was afforded a separate line right in the middle of the application form, suggesting that troop leaders and movement officials alike found it desirable to have members with prior experience in scouting practices and activities.[87]

One aspect of this application that is worthy of investigation is what applicants were not asked: the "sect," or *ta'if*, of the potential recruit. Perhaps this was presumed, given existing Najjadeh membership patterns and recruiting bases in majority Sunni Muslim neighborhoods of the capital. Nonetheless, and counter to the supposed predetermined sectarian nature of this group, the Najjadeh was uninterested with recording this information. So were many other popular organizations; in Kata'ib, Tala'i', and Progressive Socialist Party applications and ID cards, the term *ta'if* is nowhere to be found.[88] This curious omission demonstrates

---

[84] There are only a few secondary studies that provide explanations on the practices and rituals of popular organizations in twentieth-century Lebanon. They include Thompson, *Colonial Citizens*; and Dueck, *The Claims of Culture at Empire's End*.

[85] Dueck, *The Claims of Culture at Empire's End*, 187; and Juha, *Ma'rakat Masir Lubnan fi 'Ahd al-Intidab al-Faransi* (1995), 656.

[86] Najjadeh Party, Fillable Application Form (?).

[87] Najjadeh Party, *al-Tanzim al-Dakhili li-l-Firaq*, 18.

[88] Lebanese Kata'ib Party, Fillable Application Form (?). Lebanese Kata'ib Party Files, Linda Sadaqah Collection, American University of Beirut. Tala'i' Organization

that organizations that were made up of significant majorities from one sect did not always mobilize sectarian identity, nor find it necessary or worthwhile to do such. In other words, sect mattered, but it was not everything for these groups, especially in their early days.

After completing their application, potential Najjadeh members would turn it in to the closest branch office, along with a modest registration fee of 12 Lebanese lira or roughly 5 USD.[89] After members submitted this fee, the director of finance for the organization then recorded, on the back of the application, the day in which it was processed.[90] As these finances were being settled, the applicant would have to go through a review process. As outlined in the 1944 "The Internal Organization for the Troops" pamphlet, a committee of reviewers would first judge "the character of the joining student."[91] If approved, and that process could take up to two weeks, the applicant would assume the rank of a "candidate."[92] As a candidate, the individual must attend all branch activities for a month. This could include more formal affairs, such as review of Baden-Powell's scout's law, or more entertaining, diverting activities, including the playing of sports.

Next, the student had to pass a test, at the level of a novice, to become an official member.[93] The 1944 pamphlet does not mentioned if this test was physical, intellectual, or both, although other organizational exams tested physical prowess (the Kata'ib) or knowledge of party history (the Progressive Socialist Party).[94] Given the Najjadeh's investment in creating a citizen of sound mind and body, the test likely included both drilling and lessons, some social, other religious. If the individual passed the test, the branch would register the candidate in the organization and then hold an official ceremony for the new member in the presence of branch leadership.[95] At what was called a "consecration party" (hafla takris), the new member would say the Najjadeh oath: "I swear by God the great

---

Collection, Membership Cards. 'Amiliyya Islamic Benevolent Society Records, Beirut, Lebanon. I was able to view a Progressive Socialist Party member card thanks to Khalil Ahmad Khalil. Discussion with author, Beirut, Lebanon, November 22, 2013.

[89] Najjadeh Party, Fillable Application Form (?); Le Commerce du Levant, December 29, 1942.

[90] Najjadeh Party, Fillable Application Form (?).

[91] Najjadeh Party, al-Tanzim al-Dakhili li-l-Firaq, 18.   [92] Ibid.   [93] Ibid.

[94] Lebanese Kata'ib Party, Ta'amim 'Adad 46, Ila R'uswa' al-Afriqa wa-l-Firaq fi al-Aqalim [Announcement #46, To the Heads of the Groups and the Teams in the Regions] (October 14, 1940). Kata'ib Museum Collection, Haret Sakher, Lebanon. And even during the Lebanese Civil War, the Progressive Socialist Party authorized members to complete party ullams. These exams were to demonstrate knowledge of party ideology, structure, and history, and its highest scorers were listed in future issues of the party newspaper, al-Anba'. Al-Anba', July 31, 1975, and May 9, 1976.

[95] Najjadeh Party, Fillable Application Form (?).

that I respect the Najjadeh organization and its goals and I am attempting to work by its principles faithfully and loyally."[96] Thereafter, they would receive the uniform and badge, which read *wa-a'iddu*, or "and prepare," a Qur'anic translation and appropriation of Baden-Powell's famous slogan "be prepared."[97]

The spectacle of becoming a member was similar for other popular organizations, including the Kata'ib. This is demonstrated by a later, April 1958 event in the village of Hammana in Mount Lebanon.[98] The leader of the Kata'ib, Pierre Gemayel, visited the party branch, stood by as new members uttered their oath to the Lebanese homeland and Kata'ib, and then presented them with their membership cards.[99] Afterwards, the party band played music, club anthems, and classical Arabic music presumably, celebrating this official moment in group belonging.[100] While other popular organizations do not offer this level of performative detail, that does not mean they did not consecrate individual members. For instance, the Syrian Social Nationalist Party and Progressive Socialist Party include sections on oathing – both the process and what is stated by new members – in their party documents of the 1950s.[101]

In judging the centrality of membership rituals for groups like the Najjadeh, terms like officialization and authentication are most fitting. The process of application, review, training, and the more performative practice of oathing consecrate the individual. These steps represent the passing of responsibilities to the helper, and show faith in the individual's allegiance, strength, ability, and aspirations, all under the Najjadeh collective. Even if other affiliations, such as family, neighborhood, or community held a place in the heart of the *najjad*, the Najjadeh rituals and youth culture placed the party at the center of the young member's life. This symbolic act of oathing, and the material steps that preceded it – learning and training – recognized the group, not the entire sect (or its parliamentary representatives) or locality (the urban *zu'ama'*), as the claimant on that individual. Indeed, to win Lebanon, a basis was crucial, and the rank and file of popular organizations like the Najjadeh was

---

[96] Najjadeh Party, *al-Tanzim al-Dakhili li-l-Firaq*, 19–20.
[97] Dueck, *The Claims of Culture at Empire's End*, 202. This phrase is in the eighth chapter of the Qur'an and used by the Muslim Brotherhood since its earliest days.
[98] *Al-'Amal*, April 7, 1958.
[99] Lebanese Kata'ib Party, *al-Qanun al-Asasi* [Basic Law] (194?). Lebanese Kata'ib Party Files, Linda Sadaqah Collection, American University of Beirut.
[100] *Al-'Amal*, April 7, 1958.
[101] Syrian Social Nationalist Party, *al-Nizam al-Dakhili* [The Internal Structure] (Beirut: Syrian Social Nationalist Party, 1955); and Progressive Socialist Party, *al-Nizam al-Dakhili* [The Internal Structure] (Beirut: Progressive Socialist Party, 1972), 37–39.

authenticated through rituals such as examination, training, and ceremony.

What to Wear, How to Sing: The Kata'ib Organization

Equally important in the youth culture of popular organizations was image making and cultivating a style. After becoming a member and performing membership rituals, the clothes worn, the drills performed, the work completed, and the words sung were the main components of everyday life and popular culture in these youth-centric groups. All popular organizations constructed who they were through a certain interpretation of the global grammar of youth, which included a look, symbols, and slogans. At the very same time, individual groups were cultivating radical discourses and distinct visions for Lebanon. This paradox is perhaps most clear in the case of the Lebanese Phalanx Organization (Munazzamat al-Kata'ib al-Lubnaniyya, or in French, Phalanges Libanaises), or the Kata'ib.

Pierre Gemayel (1905–1984), the founder of the Kata'ib, was born in the village of Bikfaya directly north of Beirut to a modest Christian Maronite family.[102] Like Shamali and Saadeh, Gemayel grew up outside Mount Lebanon in Mansoura, Egypt, of the Delta region during the Great War. He attended a Christian school in Egypt and fostered a passion for history and geography. According to Joseph Abu Khalil, current vice president of the Kata'ib and biographer of Gemayel, this is where he became interested in "historic [read Christian, pre-Ottoman, and pre-Islamic] Lebanon."[103] When his family returned to Lebanon at the end of the Great War, they moved from Bikfaya to Beirut. Gemayel's moves reflected those of many Christians from Mount Lebanon who relocated to the urban core and its suburbs during the late nineteenth and early twentieth centuries.[104] This shift coincided with the emergence of a distinct ideology called "Phoenicianism" or (Christian) Lebanese nationalism. Separate from others of the time, this Lebanese nationalism celebrated the pre-Islamic *and* pre-Arab tradition of what Christians of Mount Lebanon saw as their ancient, cosmopolitan, seafaring forefathers:

---

[102] Jenab Tutunji, "Pierre Gemayel," in *Political Leaders of the Contemporary Middle East and North Africa: A Biographical Dictionary*, ed. Bernard Reich (New York: Greenwood Press, 1999), 202.

[103] Joseph Abu Khalil, *Biyar al-Gemayel: Qisa Rajul wa-Watan* [Pierre Gemayel, Story of a Man and His Nation] (Beirut: Haquq al-Tuba'a Mafuza li-l-Mu'lif, 2002), 14.

[104] For more on Christian and other migrations from Mount Lebanon and elsewhere to Beirut in the late nineteenth to early twentieth centuries, see Fuad Khuri, *From Village to Suburb: Order and Change in Greater Beirut* (Chicago, IL: University of Chicago Press, 1975); and Khater, *Inventing Home*.

the Phoenicians.[105] While not the intellectual founder of this Lebanese nationalism, Gemayel popularized it in Christian Beirut and made a separate Lebanon the crux of national youth development.

He studied pharmacy at the University of Saint Joseph, a Jesuit school in Beirut, and received his degree in France before setting up his own pharmacy in 1930.[106] What he named the "New Gemayel Pharmacy," located near Saifi in downtown Beirut, was as much a meeting place between his friends and neighborhood youths as it was a place for cures and remedies.[107] Besides pharmacy, Gemayel's other passion was sport, particularly football. After playing and refereeing for years, he became the president of the Lebanese Football Federation in 1936.[108] In this capacity he oversaw the formation of a self-funded Lebanese delegation that would attend the 1936 Summer Olympics in Berlin.[109]

During and after Gemayel's trip in his early thirties, he and others describe the importance of this visit in the founding of a new youth movement. A 1943 pamphlet titled "History and Action," made by supporters of the Kata'ib, explains:

He returned from Europe in the summer of 1936 after surveying its different countries, and observing the activities of their youth, their identities, fine training, and their continuing work in the service of their countries, and seeing the stark comparison between the two youths, their youth and our youth.[110]

The pamphlet then demonstrates the differences between European and Lebanese youth through the use of descriptive couplets:

There [in Europe] organization and here [in Lebanon] chaos
There life and here death
There action and here laziness
There everything for the homeland and here everything for foreigners.[111]

---

[105] For more on the ideology of Phoenicianism, see Salibi, *A House of Many Mansions*; and Asher Kaufman, *Reviving Phoenicia: In Search for Identity in Lebanon* (London: I.B. Tauris & Co Ltd, 2004).

[106] Suleiman, *Political Parties in Lebanon*, 233.

[107] Samir Khalaf, *Heart of Beirut: Reclaiming the Bourj* (London: Saqi Books, 2006), 199.

[108] Jean Aoun and Joseph Abu Khalil, *Al-Sheikh Pierre: Tarikh fi Sur* [Sheik Pierre: History in Pictures], trans. Joyce Badran and Darine Karkafy (Beirut: Mehanna Group, 2007), 9.

[109] For more information on Gemayel's 1936 visit to Berlin, along with other cities in Europe, see Dylan Baun, "Lebanon's Youth Clubs and the 1936 Summer Olympics: Mobilizing Sports, Challenging Imperialism and Launching a National Project," *The International Journal of the History of Sport* 34, no. 13 (2017): 1347–1365.

[110] *Al-Kata'ib al-Lubnaniyya: Tarikh wa-l-'Amal* [The Kata'ib: History and Action] (November 1943), 4. Lebanese Kata'ib Party Files, Linda Sadaqah Collection, American University of Beirut.

[111] Ibid., 4.

Gemayel's self-discovery was often reduced to the following question, repeated in some form in many Kata'ib iterations of its origin story: If structure and discipline are ordering the youth in Europe, why not here?[112] Gemayel's realization culminated with the Kata'ib. Its first formal meeting was held November 8, 1936.[113]

Like Yazbak, Shamali, and Saadeh, Gemayel was a populist. He took issue with the implicit zu'ama'-colonial pact, conceiving of his group as "above parties and politics."[114] What was distinct, and more similar to Nasuli, was Gemayel and the Kata'ib's dedication to youth development in the form of scouting, training, and, most decisively, marching and military garb. Along with his trip to Germany, these traits led many government officials or commentators of the time to label it a fascist organization. These claims for the Kata'ib or other popular organizations are not baseless. Whether it was the Kata'ib's uniforms, Nasuli's critique of "moral chaos" in Lebanon's public sphere, or the Syrian Social Nationalist Party's outlawing of Jewish members, some of these groups adapted fascist discourses and practices.[115] However, as other scholars of quasi-fascist, paramilitary, youth organizations from Egypt to Syria have proven, these groups did not seek to implement racialized national socialism.[116]

This is not to say Gemayel was not interested in fascism. He expressed as much both before and after his 1936 visit to Berlin, championing the "blind obedience (al-ta'a al-'amiyya) and a foresight to the greater good" that he witnessed across Europe.[117] Yet, like other middle-class leaders of popular organizations, he was accessing universalist language and global youth styles, part of the air of the times, prefaced on a certain solution:

[112] For examples of this line of reasoning, voiced by Gemayel over the years, see al-Bashir, February 6, 1938. Cited in Juha, Ma'rakat Masir Lubnan fi 'Ahd al-Intidab al-Faransi, 685; and Robert Fisk, Pity the Nation: the Abduction of Lebanon, 4th ed. (New York: Thunder Mouth Press/Nation Books, 2002), 65.

[113] Jean Charaf, Tarikh Hizb al-Kata'ib al-Lubnaniyya [The History of the Lebanese Kata'ib Party], vol. 1, 1936–1940 (Beirut: Dar al-'Amal li-l-Nashr, 1979), 69–70.

[114] Ibid., 68.

[115] Thompson, Colonial Citizens, 193; and Suleiman, Political Parties in Lebanon, 101.

[116] For similar arguments, see Watenpaugh, Being Modern in the Middle East; Gotz Nordbruch, Nazism in Syria and Lebanon: The Ambivalence of the German Option, 1933–1945 (New York: Routledge, 2009); and Israel Gershoni and James Jankowski, Confronting Fascism in Egypt: Dictatorship versus Democracy in the 1930s (Stanford, CA: Stanford University Press, 2010). This point necessitates some additional explanation as it relates to Antoun Saadeh's stance on Jews. Given growing Jewish support of Zionism after 1948, Saadeh argued that Jews had no place in the [illegible] Syrian nation. However, his arguments were much more a stand against Zionism and colonialism – which in his estimation sought to separate Greater Syria – than a sustained policy against Jewish people.

[117] Bayrut, September 16, 1936.

"generic fascism."[118] In the Lebanese context, this meant that strong, disciplined, and docile young men were the means to end colonialism and the foundation for a strong Lebanese (separate and Christian) nation.[119] In the end, arguing for historically grounded ideological adaptation, over blind adoption, is meant to contextualize the centrality of muscular practices and masculine ideology in the history of not only Gemayel's Kata'ib, but all groups in the field of youth politics, quasi-fascist or otherwise, in the 1930s to 1940s.

To capture how the global grammar of youth permeated through popular organizations, it is critical to explore popular culture. To start with the words shouted, slogans are useful vectors for analyzing popular culture, as they are short, easy to memorize, and pervasive in the source material consumed by members, ranging from newspapers to ceremonies. The Kata'ib experimented with several different slogans in the early days. One read "the Lebanese Kata'ib from the people and to serve the people."[120] This slogan exhibits how youth-centric organizations in the mid-twentieth century employed populist discourse in short form, with the *sha'b* as an abstraction, to boost their credentials. However, the slogan's ambiguity, not grounded in any specific aspect of the Kata'ib ideology, led it to be superseded by other slogans. "In the Service of Lebanon" and "God, Nation, and Family," for example, needed no interpretation or specification. These slogans are still used today, alongside long-standing others from various groups. They include the Lebanese Communist Party's slogan, "We will get what we want: a free and happy people," or the Syrian Social Nationalist Party's "Freedom, Duty, Organization, and Strength."[121]

Another oral practice in the realm of popular culture was *al-nashid*, or "the anthem." All organizations had songs, and lyrically, they represented a call to action, reflected aspects of the group's ideology, and used imagery, often dealing with land and nature, to stake their claim as guardian of the nation's physical glory.[122] Take, for instance, the Kata'ib anthem, "Come on, Kata'ib Youth" (*Haya Fata al-Kata'ib*):

---

[118] Watenpaugh, *Being Modern in the Middle East*, 255–256.
[119] For more on Gemayel's comments and sympathies, and the need to contextualize them, see Baun, "Lebanon's Youth Clubs and the 1936 Summer Olympics," 1353–1355.
[120] *Al-'Amal*, December 31, 1939.
[121] *Sawt al-Sha'b*, January 7, 1944; and *al-Nahda*, November 12, 1937.
[122] For other group anthems, see al-Ahmad, *Hizb al-Suri al-Qawmi al-Ijtima'i*, 74; *Sada al-Ansar* (Najjadeh), May 30, 1944; and Ghassan Ahmad 'Issa, *Munazzamat al-Tala'i' fi Lubnan min khilal Watha'iquha al-Asliyya, 1944–1947* [The Vanguard Organization of Lebanon through Its Founding Documents] (PhD diss., Lebanese University, 1992), 131–132.

Come on, Kata'ib youth, to the highest and the duty
For the era of non-partisanship
Come on, Kata'ib youth

We are the smile of the time and the greenery of hope (*khudrat al-amal*)
We were the fortress (*siyaj*) of the nation in the incident [violent event of 1937]
Our motto is action (*al-'amal*)
And immersed in the parts, come on, Kata'ib youth.[123]

The anthem uses lushness and fortifications to symbolize the Kata'ib defense of beautiful Lebanon. Moreover, it calls the male youth to participate and act in this defense.

The lyrics of anthems, however, speak more so to ideological indoctrination. To investigate the style and sound of group songs helps clarify the role that youth played in shaping the collective identities of these groups. While most official anthems were replicas of the Lebanese national anthem, other songs mixed "Arabesque" styles with militaristic chants (i.e., call and response). Like demonstrated in the Kata'ib chant, "On the Rock We Drill," or the Progressive Socialist Party's "The Popular Army," blending classical Arabic tones, similar to those popularized in the 1960s by Umm Kulthum or Fairuz, was a way to relate to the majority of members, young people, within these groups.[124] Kata'ib youth, or other members of popular organizations, were not just sites of ideological exploitation. Rather, they went to the cinema, played games, and listened to music. Combining familiar sounds was a way to tap into these sentiments, while instilling a sense of order and discipline alongside them.

If slogans and songs were part of a larger process of creating a style for the Kata'ib, clothing was the most visceral aspect of this process. In the earliest days of the group, every member would wear a long sleeve button-up shirt, a tie, slacks, shoes, and spats. Depending on the occasion, including marches, a Kata'ib youth might don a sash, gloves, or even a bayonet.[125] Fostering a look was evident with other groups too, as popular organizations pulled from a global repertoire of styles for the

---

[123] Farid Assaf, "*al-Kata'ib al-Lubnaniyya*" [The Lebanese Kata'ib Party], in *Ahzab Lubnan.*

[124] See "Anashid Hizbiyya" [Party Anthems], www.kataeb.org; or Progressive Socialist Party, *Anashid al-Hizb al-Taqaddumi al-Ishtiraki* [Anthems for the Progressive Socialist Party] (Beirut: Progressive Socialist Party, n.d.).

[125] Jean Charaf, *Tarikh Hizb al-Kata'ib al-Lubnaniyya* [The History of the Lebanese Kata'ib Party], vol. 3, 1946–1952 (Beirut: Dar al-'Amal li-l-Nashr, 2009); and Aoun and Abu Khalil, *al-Sheikh Pierre.*

sake of collective identity. While the Najjadeh or Tala'i' member would be seen in similar clothing to the Kata'ib, most other popular organization members, ranging from the Lebanese People's Party down to the Arab Nationalist Youth, wore white shirts, black suits, and sometimes ties, meant to reflect their dandy, middle- and working-class members.[126]

In addition to the look, "physical action" (al-'Amal, the name of the Kata'ib's newspaper starting in 1939), whether in sport or work, was part of the image-making process. Regarding sport, the performance of training and activity were ways Kata'ib leaders connected with the youth. As explained in a letter from the organizational center to branch leaders in the 1940s, physicality would be taught through long nature walks, summer retreat camps, and sport, including football, wrestling, boxing, running, jumping, and cycling.[127] Clearly the Najjadeh was not the only group attempting to cultivate a love for the outdoors in the youth. Kata'ib guides would take the shabab on yearly camping trips in villages across Mount Lebanon, presumably where life skills and physical strength were conditioned.[128] While of course trying to order youth energies, the Kata'ib leadership understood that young people also had other distractions, as detailed in another 1940s statement. It explains that to be a Kata'ib youth did not mean giving up hobbies, including visiting cafes or playing.[129]

In terms of work, and most important for their populist image, it was social care. In the same letter to branch leaders of the 1940s, the organizational center laid out a plan for this type of service. It included restoring roads, revamping the tourist industry, and working in the countryside to benefit peasant job opportunities and well-being.[130] This included the practice of afforestation, as showcased in Kata'ib events recognizing International Tree Day in the 1930s to 1940s.[131] Regarding aspects of communal health, one Kata'ib event is worth mentioning. In 1939, specifically during the earliest phase of World War II, the group distributed essential medicine at low costs. As Gemayel was a pharmacist by training, he had access to drugs, but only at their high prices, which were not subsidized by the French colonial government. After shouldering

---

[126] For an example, see Lebanese Communist Party, Nidal al-Hizb al-Shiyu'i al-Lubnani min khilal Watha'iqahu [The Struggle of the Lebanese Communist Party through Its Documents], vol. 1 (Beirut: Manshurat al-Hizb al-Shiyu'i al-Lubnani, 1971).

[127] Lebanese Kata'ib Party, Li-Taka Hayatana Hayat 'Amal wa-Quwwa wa-Nishat [For Adapting in Our Life a Life of Action, Strength, and Activity] (?). Lebanese Kata'ib Party Files, Linda Sadaqah Collection, American University of Beirut.

[128] Charaf, Tarikh Hizb al-Kata'ib al-Lubnaniyya, vol. 1, 208.

[129] Lebanese Kata'ib Party, Ila al-Shabab (1940), 5.

[130] Lebanese Kata'ib Party, Li-Taka Hayatana Hayat 'Amal wa-Quwwa wa-Nishat.

[131] Charaf, Tarikh Hizb al-Kata'ib al-Lubnaniyya, vol. 3; and al-Kata'ib al-Lubnaniyya, 15.

some of the costs himself, he sent out trucks with the Kata'ib emblem, carrying medicine at reduced prices in "an attempt to break the monopoly" of state, pharma materials.[132] Alongside these price-cutting measures, he made care more accessible to the people. As noted in an *al-'Amal* announcement in late 1939, the Kata'ib "guarantee[d] regular clinic services" every day at the Kata'ib headquarters, hosting doctors who specialized in surgery, women's health, childcare, ear, nose, and eye issues, and internal, gastrointestinal, and general medicine.[133]

Like in the other aspects of platform and performativity, similarities between these groups abound in the realm of social care. In 1946, on a group trip in Haifa, Palestine, Tala'i' members teamed with doctors to treat the poorest members of the town.[134] And in 1952, the Arab Nationalist Youth opened a "people's clinic" in Amman, Jordan, where "they treated the inhabitants of the [Palestinian] refugee camps without receiving any fees."[135] Indeed, the Kata'ib did not own health promotion and well-being. In fact, others expanded beyond Lebanon's borders as a part of their populist agendas.

Making Money at Home and Abroad: The Tala'i' Organization

This chapter has thus far explained how individual leaders came to a particular ideology, spread group ideas and practices through the public sphere, and catered to the political and social engagement of young men, which was followed by individual members joining, reading, singing, and caring. Nevertheless, ideology and popular culture help less when considering how popular organizations actually built their group and retained a stream of young men in the group. For this, we must take up financial support, bureaucratic structure, hierarchy, and networks; both within and outside the organization.[136] For one, the Najjadeh was plugged into a broader network of socialization for young Sunni Muslims, including the scout club (the Muslim Scouts), youth organization (Najjadeh Organization), and school (the Makassed primary school and

---

[132] Charaf, *Tarikh Hizb al-Kata'ib al-Lubnaniyya*, vol. 1, 287.

[133] *Al-'Amal*, December 31, 1939.   [134] *Al-Hayat*, March 19, 1946.

[135] Walid Kazziha, *Revolutionary Transformation in the Arab World: Habash and His Comrades from Nationalism to Marxism* (New York: St. Martin's Press, 1975), 25.

[136] In this task, I am benefited by the work of social movement scholars, particularly those scholars who work on resource mobilization and networks. For more on social movement theory, and its particular subfields, see Steven M. Buechler, *Understanding Social Movements: Theories from the Classical Era to the Present* (Boulder, CO: Paradigm Publishers, 2011).

college).[137] This was the case for the Kata'ib as well, which held strong connections with other parallel institutions in Beirut, including the French Scouts du Liban and the University of Saint Joseph, where Gemayel and many other Kata'ib leaders received their degrees.[138] Another popular organization that made use of existing educational and social ties to build and finance the group was the Vanguard Organization (Munazzamat al-Tala'i') or Tala'i'.

The leader of this group, Rashid Baydun (1889–1971), was born into a long line of Shi'i merchants.[139] Although Baydun would later go on to represent South Lebanon in parliament (1937–1946), he lived most of his life in Beirut.[140] This was representative of many other Lebanese Shia, whose families hailed from south and east Lebanon, but would settle in the villages-cum-suburbs just southeast of the city center, such as Ghobeiry, al-Chiyah, and Ras al-Naba'a during the late nineteenth and early twentieth centuries.[141] Yet, unlike many of these rural, internal migrants, Baydun came to wealth by way of his merchant relatives from Damascus.[142] Accordingly, and unlike other leaders of popular organizations, he was from the landowning class, the zu'ama' so vehemently criticized by populists during the mandate period and beyond. But unlike Kamal Jumblatt, another za'im turned populist, Baydun's family wealth and status was relatively new in Lebanon. This non-inherited wealth made it easier for Baydun to distinguish himself as nouveau riche, much like Yazbak and Saadeh before him.

His father, Yusuf, had established a school for girls in Damascus in the early 1900s. The son then followed his father's footsteps, enrolling in an Ottoman school in Beirut, and becoming a teacher, schoolmaster, and philanthropist thereafter.[143] While Christians had their French-sponsored private schools, and Sunni Muslim institutions of learning were tolerated by the French, young Shi'i Muslims were without comparable, separate education in the 1920s.[144] To solve this crisis of marginalization and social

---

[137] Dueck, *The Claims of Culture at Empire's End*, 207.

[138] Juha, *Ma'rakat Masir Lubnan fi 'Ahd al-Intidab al-Faransi*, 679; and Dueck, *The Claims of Culture at Empire's End*, 207.

[139] Hussein Maki, *Rashid Baydun: Qawl wa-Fi'l* [Rashid Baydun: Sayings and Actions] (Beirut: Matabi' al-Masri, 1967); and Evelyn Early, "The Amiliyya Society of Beirut: A Case Study of an Emerging Urban Za'im"(master's thesis, American University of Beirut, 1971), 92.

[140] Baydun would also serve Beirut on and off from 1947 to 1968. For more information on Baydun and his parliamentary career, see Maki, *Rashid Baydun*.

[141] For more information on Shi'i migratory patterns toward Beirut during the period, see Khuri, *From Village to Suburb*, 24–32.

[142] Early, "The Amiliyya Society of Beirut," 92.   [143] Maki, *Rashid Baydun*, 15.

[144] For more information on the plight and development of Shi'i education, see Roschanack Shaery-Eisenlohr, *Shi'ite Lebanon: Transnational Religion and the Making of National Identities* (New York: Columbia University Press, 2006), 56–58.

mobility, Baydun served throughout his life in a charitable organization called the ʿAmiliyya Islamic Benevolent Society (al-Jamʿiyya al-Khiriyya al-Islamiyya al-ʿAmiliyya – or the ʿAmiliyya Society). Founded in 1923 in Beirut by Rashid's brother, Muhammad Baydun, ʿAmiliyya had as its main objective the enlightenment of Shi'i youth across Lebanon.[145] Serving as president from 1925 until his death, Rashid used this institution, and its funds, to build a primary school (1929), secondary school (1932), and college (1947), collectively known as the ʿAmiliyya school in the Ras al-Nabaʿa neighborhood of southeast Beirut.[146]

Similar to how Nasuli leveraged organizations (the Muslim Scouts) and institutions (the press and his newspaper, *Bayrut*) as the basis for the Najjadeh, Baydun used his school and political career as a springboard for the Talaʾiʿ. In mid-June 1944, Baydun recruited some young men, presumably associated with the schools he founded, who were dedicated to "struggle in the cause of the independence of Lebanon and its freedom."[147] This origin story reflects the Talaʾiʿ's distinct Lebanese nationalist roots. They were somewhere in between the Kataʾib and Najjadeh, conceiving Lebanon as separate, but neither Phoenician, pre-Arab, nor Sunni Arab. More simply, Talaʾiʿ ideology was an attempt to write the population it served, Shi'i youth, into the body politic on the cusp of Lebanon's full independence from the French.

For the Talaʾiʿ, being Lebanese meant serving as an example for the entire youth of the country and leading its destiny, with Baydun as its driver, into the future. As indicated in its basic laws, the group would "organize the youth and unite their ranks."[148] Like the Kataʾib and other popular organizations, the Talaʾiʿ sought to unite through a certain style of dress. Young members wore khaki long pants and long-sleeved shirts, white spats, black shoes, ties, field service caps (or a side cap), and badges.[149] The badge had "the sword of ʿAli" (*dhu al-faqqar*) on it, a reference to this important figure in Shi'i Islam.[150] Around 1947, the sword badge was accompanied by the Talaʾiʿ slogan: "Freedom, Life, and Equality" (*hurriya hayat wa-musawa*).[151]

[145] Early, "The Amiliyya Society of Beirut," 92.

[146] Aman Atiyyah, "Development of Shi'ite Education in Lebanon" (master's thesis, American University of Beirut, 1972), 150; and Maki, *Rashid Baydun*, 17.

[147] Maki, *Rashid Baydun*, 52.

[148] Talaʾiʿ Organization Collection, *al-Qanun al-Asasi wa-l-Dakhili* [Basic and Internal Laws] (194?). ʿAmiliyya Islamic Benevolent Society Records.

[149] For descriptions and pictures of Talaʾiʿ garb, see Early, "The Amiliyya Society of Beirut," 102; Maki, *Rashid Baydun*; and Talaʾiʿ Organization Collection, Miscellaneous Pictures, ʿAmiliyya Islamic Benevolent Society Records.

[150] Talaʾiʿ Organization Collection, *al-Qanun al-Asasi wa-l-Dakhili*.

[151] Talaʾiʿ Organization Collection, Membership Cards.

The presence of national, secular language alongside Shi'i religious symbols may at first appear contradictory. But Baydun's group was attempting to place religion, which was familiar to its young members, within the umbrella of Lebanese nationalism.[152] This was dissimilar from the Lebanese People's Party and Syrian Social Nationalist Party, which mobilized populism and anti-sectarianism alone to forge a path forward for the youth. But like their Maronite and Sunni counterparts in the Kata'ib and Najjadeh, Tala'i' members sought to square national affiliation with sect recognition.

One of the Tala'i''s specific goals in helping Shi'i youth was to "fight illiteracy and ignorance."[153] "Ignorance," or al-jahl, referred to the supposed state of mind of many Tala'i' recruits. They were homeschooled Shi'i men, in their twenties, often unmarried, and from village environs very different from Beirut. Filled out membership cards speak to this demographic reality.[154] They also provide a window into the Tala'i''s strategy of monitoring and erasing illiteracy. On the form, branch leaders would either mark the joining individual as "literate" (muta'allim) or "illiterate" (ummi).[155]

One young man who was labeled muta'allim was Ahmad. Ahmad, who joined the Tala'i' in 1947, was born and raised in Taybe, two hours south from the capital in which he currently lived. Fortunate for Ahmad, his current residence, in the neighborhood of Mousaytbeh, was only a fifteen-minute walk to the headquarters of the Tala'i' and affiliated center of learning, 'Amiliyya, both of which were located in the Ras al-Naba'a neighborhood. Ahmad was a pupil at the 'Amiliyya secondary school, practicing his reading and writing. If the education of Shi'i youth was a priority for Baydun, Ahmad was the proof. This was a long-term investment though, indicated by the picture included alongside Ahmad's membership form (Figure 1.2). It is not the young adult Ahmad, twenty-three years old, but child Ahmad.[156] This picture exists because Ahmad was part of a three-tier youth network of Shi'i youth socialization, including the affiliated 'Amiliyya primary and secondary schools, the scout organization, and the youth group.[157]

---

[152] For more on the Shi'i fight to legitimize their religion and social group as part of the Lebanese community, see Lara Deeb, *An Enchanted Modern: Gender and Public Piety in Shi'i Lebanon* (Princeton, NJ: Princeton University Press, 2006); Shaery-Eisenlohr, *Shi'ite Lebanon*; and Weiss, *In the Shadow of Sectarianism* (2010).

[153] Tala'i' Organization Collection, *al-Qanun al-Asasi wa-l-Dakhili.*

[154] Tala'i' Organization Collection, Membership Cards.   [155] Ibid.   [156] Ibid.

[157] The 'Amiliyya Scouts were established after the Tala'i' in 1947, in reverse order to Nasuli's Muslim Scouts (1920)-Najjadeh (1937) connection. Ministry of Planning in Lebanon, *Ralil al-Nawadi al-Thaqafiyya wa-l-Riyadiyya fi Lubnan* [Directory of Cultural and Sports Clubs in Lebanon] (Beirut: 1968). *Records at the Lebanese National Archives*, Beirut, Lebanon.

Figure 1.2 1947 Tala'i' membership card for Ahmad. Courtesy of Ghassan Ahmed 'Issa and the 'Amiliyya Islamic Benevolent Society, Beirut, Lebanon.

This system of catering to the youth points to another similarity across popular organizations. Each group utilized ancillary networks and stakeholders, at home and abroad, to build the organization and fund it. More broadly, organizational development can be considered the bedrock for collective identity; as integral for group existence and popularity as ideology or popular culture. The money that went into making the Tala'i' came from multiple sources. They included private sources – the Baydun family or other 'Amiliyya Society supporters – and state contributions.[158] In a seven-month period in 1944, the Tala'i' was the recipient of 75,725 Lebanese lira or almost 35,000 USD.[159] These donations would be used to pay for uniforms, reserve public spaces for festivals, fund the education of members, rent a building for its headquarters, and most likely, to pay the salaries of the some eighty or so leaders of the group.[160]

As the Tala'i' expanded, it tapped resources beyond Lebanon's borders. Most important would be the many Shia of Lebanon who settled in West Africa during the gold- and diamond-mining boom of the 1930s. It was common that these workers would send home the money they made

[158] For more information on the financial structure of the 'Amiliyya Society and Tala'i', including private and government support, see Early, "The Amiliyya Society of Beirut," 68–79.
[159] Tala'i' Organization, Funds for 1944. Cited in 'Issa, *Munazzamat al-Tala'i' fi Lubnan min khilal Watha'iquha al-Asliyya*, 380; *Le Commerce du Levant*, December 19, 1944.
[160] Tala'i' Organization, Leadership List, 1944–1947. Cited in 'Issa, *Munazzamat al-Tala'i' fi Lubnan min khilal Watha'iquha al-Asliyya*, 381.

to their families and affiliated associations (i.e., the mosque, the school, the village).[161] Baydun then went on a number of funding trips to Africa, the first of which was set up by Kamel Mroueh (1915–1966) in 1938.[162] Mroueh was a geography instructor at ʿAmiliyya and would later become the owner of *al-Hayat* ("the Life") newspaper. According to one interlocutor, Mroueh had extensive family connections to wealthy Shia in West Africa and told Baydun that if he wanted money for his school, this is how he could obtain it.[163] At age twenty-two and forty-eight, respectively, Mroueh and Baydun traveled across West Africa in the summer of 1938 for five months, supposedly "enduring" a total of 60,000 kilometers.[164]

The trip was so financially successful that Baydun would return to Africa two more times, first in 1948 so the Talaʾiʿ could be on the receiving end of these monetary flows. From April to October of that year, Baydun traveled from Senegal, to Guinea, to the Ivory Coast, to Nigeria, and finally to Sierra Leone. At each location, Baydun would presumably meet with a community, tell them – or update – about the ʿAmiliyya-Talaʾiʿ enterprise, what it could do for their families in Lebanon, and ask for financial assistance. This 1948 visit was a "big success," thanks to the "generous donation" of these wealthy Shiʿi expatriates.[165] Upon his return from Sierra Leone, at an ʿAshura festival in November, Baydun recalled not only the triumphs of the trip, but also the difficulties of traveling across Africa:

We traveled through lonely deserts and long distances visiting distant villages looking for [Shiʾi] immigrants ... [.] We traveled 400 kilometers a day through jungles full of lions and poisonous insects, crossing rivers with dangerous crocodles [sic]. All this made us more determined.[166]

Although technically part of the pejorative "Orient" itself, Lebanese like Baydun deployed their own stereotypes of the exotic, far away Africa. But

---

[161] For more information on Lebanese settlement in West Africa during the early twentieth century, see Fuad Khuri, "Kinship, Emigration, and Trade Partnership among the Lebanese of West Africa," *Africa Journal of the International African Institute* 35, no. 4 (1965): 385–395.

[162] For more information on this 1938 Africa trip, see Kamel Mroueh, *Nihna fi Afriqiyya: al-Hijra al-Lubnaniyya al-Suriyya ila Afriqiyya al-Gharbiyya Madiha, Hadirha, Mustaqbala* [Us in Africa: The Lebanese Syrian Migration in West Africa, Past, Present, and Future] (Beirut: al-Makshufa, 1938).

[163] Karim Mroueh, conversations with author, June 5, 2018. Beirut, Lebanon.

[164] Early, "The Amiliyya Society of Beirut," 75; and Maki, *Rashid Baydun*, 29. Pictures of this trip show Mroueh and Baydun posing with the former's family and friends. Kamel Mroueh Foundation Collection, Beirut, Lebanon.

[165] Maki, *Rashid Baydun*, 76.

[166] ʿAmiliyya files. Cited in Early, "The Amiliyya Society of Beirut," 75. For more information on Baydun's 1948 Africa trip, see Maki, *Rashid Baydun*, 76–78.

this framing device is more than African Orientalism.[167] It linked a story to the capital received, spicing up the financial mechanics of organizational development. Additionally, that Baydun's survival was in jeopardy throughout this journey confirms the importance of the mission: to raise money to build the organization of Tala'i'.

Baydun had received approval from the president of Lebanon, Bishara al-Khuri (1943–1952), to make this 1948 trip. When visiting a particular diasporic community, he would show a letter of support from the president, a way to make official the mission, raise his credentials, and solicit more donations.[168] Khuri and Baydun were actually good friends, and Baydun leveraged this relationship for the sake of the organization. From 1943 until the Tala'i' ceased to officially exist in 1949, 'Amiliyya and Tala'i' received yearly funding from the government.[169] Therefore, in addition to building transnational networks, local official support was critical for the development of this organization. This was not the same for other popular organizations. With Saadeh in political exile throughout most of the 1940s, the Syrian Social Nationalist Party depended on transatlantic networks to spread ideas, platforms, and funds. The Progressive Socialist Party tapped more into local, communal donations, in the face of a hostile Khuri government in the 1950s. Hence, although the relations between group and state varied – depending on ideology, practice, and context – funds mattered a great deal in fueling the machine.

Codifying and Distinguishing the Organization: The Progressive Socialist Party

The arguably less exciting side of being in a popular organization, compared to joining the group, playing games, or even solving the problem of illiteracy, was attending weekly branch meetings. In the case of the Progressive Socialist Party (al-Hizb al-Taqaddumi al-Ishtiraki), the routine parameters for such meetings were detailed in their al-nizam al-dakhili, or "internal (organizational) structure." The nizam, officially sanctioned through an executive council meeting on May 4, 1954, did not stop at outlining the process of reading minutes, motioning for new measures, secret ballot, and approval of proposals. At over 100 pages long, the nizam included procedures ranging from the promotion process for branch leadership to the system by which the party collected

---

[167] See Edward Said, *Orientalism* (New York: Vintage Books, 1978). On the first trip in 1938, Mroueh "othered" Africa. For one, his book *Nihna fi Afriqiyya* included pictures of well-dressed, "civilized" Mroueh, alongside naked, "uncivilized" African women. Mroueh, *Nihna fi Afriqiyya*, 24.
[168] Maki, *Rashid Baydun*, 76.   [169] Early, "The Amiliyya Society of Beirut," 76.

donations, membership fees, and considered exemptions.[170] It was part of a set of texts that instituted organizational life for the group, including basic laws, or *al-qanun al-asasi*, the charter (*al-mithaq*), and group principles (*mabadi'*). This group, however, is by no means unique for its rigor. All popular organizations created and made use of this set of texts for the sake of developing their organizational structure. For the Progressive Socialist Party, these features of bureaucratic life served to distinguish its collective identity and ideology from other groups.

While the majority of leaders, notwithstanding Baydun, were of the urban professional strata, Kamal Jumblatt (1917–1977), the founder of the Progressive Socialist Party, was born into a prominent Druze family from Moukhtara of the Chouf District in Mount Lebanon.[171] His father, Fuad Jumblatt, was the head of the Jumblatt clan in the early twentieth century, which afforded him a position as a *za'im* in late Ottoman politics. When Jumblatt was four, his father was assassinated, and his mother, Sitt Nazira, became the holder of the Jumblatt estate and his manager of sorts.[172] In his twenties, he followed his mother's political advice. This included joining the pro-French National Bloc under President Emile Eddé (1936–1941), and holding posts in President Bishara al-Khuri's first-term cabinet in 1943.[173] But by the late 1940s, Jumblatt outgrew his mother's tutelage, both leaving the National Bloc and criticizing the Khuri government.[174] This was partly informed by his wants to create his own distinct political movement and build populist credentials outside the *zu'ama'* and Jumblatt name.[175]

Like Saadeh and Gemayel, Jumblatt's beliefs were shaped in part by experiences outside Lebanon. Upon finishing his schooling at St. Joseph

---

[170] Progressive Socialist Party, *al-Nizam al-Dakhili*, 17–20. Although the publication date reads 1972, the administrative council of the party approved the *nizam* that I consulted in 1954. Ibid., 3.

[171] For more information on the Jumblatt family, from its prominence in the eighteenth century to its marginalization in the nineteenth, see Salibi, *A House of Many Mansions*; Makdisi, *The Culture of Sectarianism* (2000); and Hady Zaccak, *Kamal Jumblatt: al-Shahid wa-l-Shuhada* [Kamal Jumblatt: Witness and Martyr], DVD (Beirut: Friends of Kamal Joumblatt Association, 2015).

[172] Fathi 'Abass Khalaf Mahanna al-Jabburi, *Nasha'a al-Hizb al-Taqaddumi al-Ishtiraki wa-Muwaqafahu al-Dakhiliyya wa-l-Kharajiyya, 1949–1975: Darasa Tarikhiyya* [The Origins of the Progressive Socialist Party and Its Internal and External Positions, 1949–1975: A Historical Study] (Moukhtara, Lebanon: Dar al-Taqaddumiyya, 2009), 39.

[173] Richani, *Dilemmas of Democracy and Political Parties in Sectarian Societies* (1998), 35.

[174] Eyal Zisser, *Lebanon: The Challenge of Independence* (New York: I.B. Tauris & Co Ltd, 2000), 133.

[175] For more on this line of reasoning, see Yusri Hazran, "Lebanon's Revolutionary Era: Kamal Junblat, the Druze Community and the Lebanon State," *Muslim World* 100 (January 2010): 157–176.

College in Antoura, Mount Lebanon, he left to study at the Sorbonne in Paris for one year toward degrees in sociology and psychology.[176] During this time, he met, read, engaged, and joined the ranks of the French social thinkers – from Durkheim to Halbwach – of the day.[177] Thereafter, he returned to Lebanon for training as a lawyer at the University of Saint Joseph in Beirut.[178] Jumblatt's experiences abroad and his reading of World War II, which showcased the worst of humanity, fashioned his specific version of populism. To him, a postwar "revolution in human life" necessitated the building of a new society.[179] To this end, he called for seven essentials in this society. They point to Jumblatt's earliest ideological distillations and reflect a delicate balance between socialism, nationalism, and democratic humanism:

(1) the adoption of principles from the French Revolution, specifically its foundations in individual rights
(2) the place of associations and institutions in nation building
(3) the nation as guarantor of security and justice
(4) a new theory on property and taxes
(5) using this new theory to tie humans to the land
(6) equality for all
(7) collective identity in society[180]

In the context of Lebanon, Jumblatt argued that a society built on these seven things would both cancel out sectarianism and create a moral unification between Lebanon and its Arab neighbors.[181] He stressed that this was only a symbolic unification, as he saw Lebanon as a separate entity, equal and connected with its neighbors.[182]

To realize this seven-point platform – oddly similar in number to the Lebanese People's Party's original seven demands – Jumblatt formed the Lebanese Social Movement (al-Haraka al-Ijtima'iyya al-Lubnaniyya) in the late 1940s. Set up to operate outside parliamentary politics, the group quickly decided that an official political party was a better direction, forming the Progressive Socialist Party in 1949.[183] Not unlike the

---

[176] Progressive Socialist Party, *Rub' Qarn min al-Nidal* [A Quarter Century of the Struggle] (Beirut: Progressive Socialist Party, 1974), 123.

[177] Jumblatt references several French social thinkers in his earliest writings and lectures, including Kamal Jumblatt, *Nahu Sigha Jadida li-l-Dimuqratiyya al-Ijtima'iyya wa-l-Insaniyya 1945* [Toward a New Formula for Humanist and Socialist Democracy 1945] (Moukhtara, Lebanon: Dar al-Taqaddumiyya, 2004); and Kamal Jumblatt, *Kayfa Nabni al-Mujtama' al-Muqbil* [How Do We Build the Future Society?] (1947), in Kamal Jumblatt, *Fi Maraqf al-Umam* [In the Service of the Nations] (Moukhtara, Lebanon: Dar al-Taqaddumiyya, 2007).

[178] Progressive Socialist Party, *Rub' Qarn min al-Nidal*, 123.

[179] Jumblatt, *Kayfa Nabni al-Mujtama' al-Muqbil*, 44.   [180] Ibid., 51–63.

[181] Progressive Socialist Party, *Rub' Qarn min al-Nidal*, 109–111.   [182] Ibid., 120.

[183] Ibid.; Richani, *Dilemmas of Democracy and Political Parties in Sectarian Societies*, 37.

Lebanese People's Party and Syrian Social Nationalist Party, the leadership of Jumblatt's group was diverse: lawyers, sheikhs, publishers, professors, accountants, all of different sect backgrounds.[184] This was mirrored in the rank and file, as in its first year, 50 percent of the party's 300 members were Christian.[185]

The founding of the Progressive Socialist Party, and its focus on the individual as the crux of a healthy society, was not only the product of postwar French thought. Equally influential were Jumblatt's multiple trips to India in the 1950s. His first visit was in the winter of 1951. While romanticizing this trip to the "far Orient" should be avoided, its itinerary is worth mentioning: by car from Lebanon, through Syria, Iraq, Iran, Afghanistan, and Pakistan, not to mention a sixteen-hour train ride across India from Delhi to West Bengal and Calcutta. This path appears to have colored the letters Jumblatt sent home, where he talked as much of the beauty of the country, open road, plants, and nature as he did about his experiences with young socialist counterparts and yogi masters.[186]

Besides visiting Gandhi's village and engaging with his "socialist brothers" in countless discussions, one experience that Jumblatt discusses at length was during a tour of Calcutta. As he was paraded around the city, he came across a statue of Queen Victoria in fine condition; a clear vestige of British colonial rule in India. Seeing this statue in independent India left a strong impression on Jumblatt, who realized these socialists, and Indians writ large, were not a vengeful people. Instead, as he explains in a letter home, Indians held a "deep humanitarian national [feeling]" (bi-qawmiyya insaniyya 'amiqa).[187] Jumblatt also spoke at length after his 1951 trip on what Sri Atmananda, a yogi master from the Pamba River region of South India, taught him about individual "experimental knowledge"; to become enlightened you have to gain the "experience of oneself for oneself."[188]

From his time in France to India, Jumblatt distinguished his group from the field by its focus on individualism. Unlike almost all other popular organizations, which emphasized uniformity, subsuming the individual for the sake of the collective alone was anathema to the Progressive Socialist Party's identity. The slogan of the Lebanese Social

---

[184] For descriptions of the other leaders of this group, see Richani, *Dilemmas of Democracy and Political Parties in Sectarian Societies*, 37; and al-Jabburi, *Nasha'a al-Hizb al-Taqaddumi al-Ishtiraki*, 42–46.

[185] Richani, *Dilemmas of Democracy and Political Parties in Sectarian Societies*, 70.

[186] *Al-Anba'*, December 8, 1951. Cited in Kamal Jumblatt, *Rihla ila al-Hind: Liqa' al-Hakim Shri Atmananda* [Trips to India: Meeting with the Doctor Sri Atmananda] (Moukhtara, Lebanon: Dar al-Taqaddumiyya, 2011), 33–35.

[187] *Al-Anba'*, November 30, 1951. Cited in Jumblatt, *Rihla ila al-Hind*, 39–40.

[188] Zaccak, *Kamal Jumblatt*.

Movement, which Jumblatt founded, read, "[n]o collectivism, no chaos, just democratic organization."[189] Jumblatt's experiences, and the formation of this group after World War II, played a role in this difference. However, to reduce ideological construction to experience alone misses a major aspect unfolding in the field of popular organizations. So far in this chapter, I have argued that popular organizations were more similar than different in their performativity, ranging from joining to singing in the group, and populist platforms. In this context of continuity, Jumblatt leveraged the tools meant to build an organization, including party documents, infrastructure, and meetings, to distinguish the party's organization and its culture from others. This distinction making is demonstrated in the sources of the group, which dedicate much space to the group's bureaucratic structure, the institutionalization of everyday party life, and the connection of these developments to the collective identity and ideology of the group.

Difference was first read by members, if they could or chose to, of course, in the form of the textual mechanisms for party duties and organizational life, including the organization of leadership. The Progressive Socialist Party's 1952 constitution, or *dustur*, names all eighteen commissioner posts of the group. Eight focused on the group's national platform: justice, interior affairs, financial and economic affairs, legislation, electoral affairs, Arab affairs, popular mobilization (*al-ta'bi'a al-sha'biyya*), and foreign affairs. The rest were centered on bettering the individual, particularly the youth, as part of the Progressive Socialist Party's future society. They included student, sports, and youth affairs, education, knowledge (*al-mu'arif*), labor, economic growth (*al-ta'mir wa-l-iqtisad*), health and environment, social affairs, science, women's affairs, and perhaps most notable, self-affairs (*al-shu'un al-dhatiyya*), or issues dealing with individual personhood and morality.[190]

Whereas the *dustur* conveyed the overarching structure for individualism, the *mithaq* was the place to prove to a member why the party was something unique and worth joining. The charter states that the party works to "focus humanist entities and institutions on the fullest humanitarian ideals."[191] Focal to this and other aspects of the *mithaq* was the concept of social engineering, a product of Jumblatt's ideas. Phrases like the "construction of humans" and "build society" for the sake of "social tranquility, justice, prosperity, peace, and freedom" were meant to

---

[189] Progressive Socialist Party, *Rub' Qarn min al-Nidal*, 120.

[190] Al-Jabburi, *Nasha'a al-Hizb al-Taqaddumi al-Ishtiraki*, 72.

[191] Progressive Socialist Party, *Mithaq al-Hizb al-Taqaddumi al-Ishtiraki* [The Charter of the Progressive Socialist Party] (Beirut: Dar al-Ahad, 195[?]), 61.

confirm the organization's unique dedication to individual human rights.[192]

Constructing identity, and linking it to an organizational capacity that would help realize that ideal, also unfolded in the textual for popular organizations with member obligations, often outlined in the *nizam*. Some were quite bureaucratic, such as logistics for party meetings. Others were based on behavior, what was titled "good conduct and reputation." This was not only measured by dedication to tenets, completion of duties, or knowledge of the organization and its history. It was also based on morals. Progressive Socialist Party members could not exhibit drunkenness, gambling, or pickpocketing.[193] While it may seem peculiar that a secular, sociopolitical organization had stipulations dealing with vice, all popular organizations in one way or another preached temperance. For instance, in the 1943 Kata'ib-affiliated pamphlet "History and Action," the writer(s) stresses that members could not display bad habits, whether gambling, drunkenness, or debauchery.[194] In its *nizam*, the Progressive Socialist Party added that members must avoid "immortality and sticking with gangs," and this was especially deplorable if one was "addicted" (*sifat al-idman*) to these things.[195] This last tenet targets the party's youth, seeking to keep the youngest members in line as embodiments of "good" *futuwwa*. Dedication to the cause of societal and nation building, regardless of whether the individual or society was at the middle, left little room for distraction.

The Progressive Socialist Party included mechanisms in their internal structure to ensure the rules were not broken. These were laid out in two long sections of the *nizam* titled "[...] Resignation, Separation, and Expulsion" and "Irregularities, Punishments, Objection, Crimes, and Referral to the Courts."[196] As stipulated, if any requirement was violated, the member would be "separated immediately" by presidential decision – two years for honor code violations, lengthier punishments for more treasonous behavior.[197] Of course, other popular organizations had codified expulsion rules and would even report to the masses when these rules were violated. In its official newsletter, the Syrian Social Nationalist Party would announce multiple expulsions often for "conduct and behavior" against the interests of the group, and sometimes urged members to "boycott the expelled members."[198] In both subtle forms (occurring behind closed doors or by word of mouth as sanctioned in the *nizam al-dakhili*), and its more obvious forms (in a newsletter), this documentation

---

[192] Ibid., 61–62.   [193] Progressive Socialist Party, *al-Nizam al-Dakhili*, 33.
[194] *Al-Kata'ib al-Lubnaniyya*, 14.
[195] Progressive Socialist Party, *al-Nizam al-Dakhili*, 59.   [196] Ibid., 39–44 and 58–62.
[197] Ibid., 34.   [198] *Al-Nashra al-Rasmiyya*, June 30, 1947, and August 15, 1947.

of disciplinary action was key to creating, in the words of Foucault, "docile bodies" in the popular organization.[199] Members knew that moral behavior was central to their identity in the group, but also their individual membership, which would be terminated if they strayed from the party's established path.

In sum, these texts created boundaries, not only within but between groups. Distinction making was not exclusive to name calling, like in the case of the Syrian Social Nationalist Party 1937 diatribe, or clothing, chants, and slogans, clear in the case of the Kata'ib. The Progressive Socialist Party shows that othering could also be bureaucratic. In their texts, this popular organization emphasized the uniqueness of its humanist claim. More implicit was that other models of organization ran counter to its sense of being. This is where Pierre Bourdieu's concept of distinction helps conceptualize this process within popular organizations, ranging from songs to stipulations. Not unlike Bourdieu's art aficionados that use the crude, lay observer to cultivate their own subculture, all popular organizations created distinction between their group and other similar sociopolitical groupings for the sake of claiming that they represented Lebanon and had the youth of the nation by their side.[200]

Leveraging Ties within and beyond the University: The Arab Nationalist Youth

The final group to be introduced is the Arab Nationalist Youth (al-Shabab al-Qawmi al-'Arabi). It formed in the summer of 1951 and was closely linked to the field of student politics at the American University of Beirut. This was not unlike other popular organizations. Recall that Saadeh worked at AUB and Najjadeh members also frequented the campus. Moreover, the founders of the Kata'ib and Progressive Socialist Party both attended the University of Saint Joseph, pulling recruits from this institution in their early days. And even groups that were not founded or particularly active on university campuses, like the Tala'i' or Lebanese People's Party, were made up of young workers and middle-class students. This continuity points to the last theme to be examined in the field of popular organizations, which is how they leveraged ties within institutions of higher learning as a basis for organizing and recruitment both within and beyond the university. In the case of the Arab Nationalist Youth, it built off of, and rose exclusively out of, AUB politics

---

[199] Michel Foucault, *Discipline and Punish: The Birth of the Prison*, trans. Alan Sheridan (New York: Vintage Books Edition, 1979), 135–169.
[200] Bourdieu, *Distinction* (1984), 6–7.

Figure 1.3 George Habash at his graduation from AUB medical school in 1951. Courtesy of Wikimedia Commons.

and a particular student organization called Jam'iyyat al-'Urwa al-Wuthqa ("the Indivisible Bond Association") or 'Urwa. George Habash (1925–2008, Figure 1.3), the founder of the Arab Nationalist Youth and president of the 'Urwa in the late 1940s to early 1950s, first made use of the campus and group to spread his mission throughout the region: regain Palestine through violent, revolutionary action.

Habash was born in Lydda, Palestine – about halfway between Tel Aviv and Ramallah – to a family of successful food merchants. Given this type of work, Habash's family moved around often, and worked between Jaffa, Jerusalem, Ramallah, and Amman.[201] In 1944 at the age of nineteen, he was accepted to the College of Medicine at AUB. During his schooling at this predominantly liberal arts institution, Habash developed various interests, including Arab literature, culture, music, arts, sports, and politics.[202] His studies were disrupted in 1948, when he decided to return to his hometown of Lydda and serve in the Arab Liberation Army as

[201] Kazziha, *Revolutionary Transformation in the Arab World*, 17; and Fuad Matar, *Hakim al-Thawra: Sira Jurj Habash wa-Nidalahu* [The Doctor of Revolution: Biography of George Habash and His Struggle] (Beirut: Dar al-Nahar, 2008), 13.
[202] Matar, *Hakim al-Thawra*, 13.

a medical assistant in the war for Palestine. In his position, Habash bore witness to the atrocities of the Arab depopulation of Palestine. In a later account, he described seeing "[t]hirty-thousand people [in Lydda] walking, crying, screaming with terror[,] women carrying babies on their arms and children clinging to [them], with the Israeli soldiers pointing weapons at their backs . . ."[203] Through these experiences, Habash cultivated both his future profession as a medical doctor and leader of a resistance group.

Beyond this trauma, his political ideals were shaped by the synergy that existed between students, professors, and student groups at AUB. Founded in 1918 on AUB's campus, what was first known simply as an Arab literature association (*jam'iyya adabiyya 'Arabiyya*) became the 'Urwa in 1923.[204] Like other popular organizations, it came of age under European colonial rule and the creation of the British and French mandates. However, it had a different membership profile, common at AUB: Arab, non-Lebanese, young men from across the region, but often having family ties to Palestine.[205] The 'Urwa benefited from the regional nature of the campus, and the growing disorder in the wake of the Ottoman collapse, to bring a new form of student activism, sustained against mandatory and state authorities across the Arab world.[206] While it is unclear exactly when Habash joined the 'Urwa, his first major post in the group was on the administrative board.[207]

A major influence for Habash was Constantine Zurayk (1909–2000), the 'Urwa faculty advisor during the mid-to-late 1930s and ideologue for a new, militant brand of Arab nationalism.[208] His most famous essay was

---

[203] Yezid Sayigh, *Armed Struggle and the Search for State: The Palestinian National Movement 1949–1993* (Washington, DC: Institute for Palestine Studies, 1997), 71–72.

[204] Amjad Dhib Ghanma, *Jam'iyyat al-'Urwa al-Wuthqa: Nash'atuha wa-Nashatatuha* [The Indivisible Bond Society: Its Birth and Activities] (Beirut: Riad El-Rayyes Books, 2002), 38–40. Interestingly enough, Ghanma argues that Muhyi al-Din al-Nasuli inspired the formation of the 'Urwa, but this author cannot confirm that through other secondary literature. Nevertheless, members of the Nasuli family were well-represented in the 'Urwa during the early days. Ibid., 41.

[205] As of 1940, out of the some 1,800 AUB students from the Arab Middle East, 21 percent were Palestinian and 13 percent Iraqi. These were the two largest Arab demographic groups at AUB after Lebanese and Syrian students (61 percent). Stephen B. L. Penrose, *That They May Have Life: The Story of the American University of Beirut, 1866–1941* (Beirut: American University of Beirut, 1970), 331–333. These demographics continued into the 1948–1949 school year, as there were more Palestinian (462) than Syrian (346) and Iraqi (320) students. *Al-'Urwa*, February 1949.

[206] For information on the 'Urwa, and AUB politics during the interwar period, see Makram Rabah, *A Campus at War: Student Politics at the American University of Beirut, 1967–1975* (Beirut: Dar Nelson, 2009), 23–26; and Anderson, *The American University of Beirut* (2011), 119–130.

[207] Ghanma, *Jam'iyyat al-'Urwa al-Wuthqa*, 171.

[208] For more information on Zurayk, see Constantine Zurayk, *The Meaning of the Disaster*, trans. R. Bayly Winder (Beirut: Khayat's College Book Cooperative, 1956), vii–viii; and

Ma'na al-Nakba, or "The Meaning of the Disaster," published in the wake of the 1948 War. Following a lengthy discussion of both the meaning and immediate solutions to the disaster, Zurayk calls for a "longtime violent Arab struggle" against the enemy: the Zionist state.[209] This struggle was not, however, just the duty of Arab heads of state and their militaries. Instead, "thousands of their young men (*bil-aluf min sha-babha*)," Zurayk declared, must "repel attack and assault . . . defend[ing] our existence from subjugation and imperialism."[210] In addition to the 'Urwa, Zurayk and his ideas would serve as guiding texts for groups beyond the campus of AUB. One particular group that formed in 1935, was the Society of the Red Book (Jama'at al-Kitab al-Ahmar – named after another famous work of Zurayk), also known as the "Secret Arab Movement" (al-Haraka al-'Arabiyya al-Sirriyya).[211] While separate from the 'Urwa, it recruited heavily from the student organization Zurayk advised at the same time at AUB.[212] Additionally, the secret society had branches outside Lebanon, including in Syria, Palestine, and Iraq.[213] These dynamics within the 'Urwa mirror an important trend for popular organizations. Following the creation of groups like the Society of the Red Book, scholars and students at AUB would continue drawing on student activism within campus to form the ranks of broader political organizations beyond. This was not unlike how Nasuli and Baydun used schools and scout organizations as feeders for their groups. Operating inside and outside smaller, established circles of youth politics became central to the growth and success for all popular organizations.

Before Habash took control of the 'Urwa, the organization was quite heterogeneous, made up of cadres of existing clubs and groups active on AUB's campus. These included the likes of popular organizations discussed in this book thus far, such as the Lebanese Communist Party, Syrian Social Nationalist Party, and Najjadeh.[214] While these groups were sympathetic to regional and extra-Lebanese causes, Habash was distinct in his drive to center organizational development around the

---

'Aziz al-'Azmah, *Qustantin Zurayq: 'Arabiyyun li-l-Qarn al-'Ishriyyin* [Constantine Zurayk: Arabs for the Twentieth Century] (Beirut: Mu'assasat al-Darasat al-Filistiniyya, 2003), 5–6.

[209] Constantine Zurayk, *Ma'na al-Nakba* [The Meaning of the Disaster] (Beirut: Dar al-'Alim li-l-Malayin, 1948), 3. For an accurate English translation, see Zurayk, *The Meaning of the Disaster*.

[210] Zurayk, *Ma'na al-Nakba*, 80.

[211] Shifaq Juha, *al-Haraka al-'Arabiyya al-Sirriyya: Jama'at al-Kitab al-Ahmar, 1935–1945* [The Secret Arab Movement: The Society of the Red Book] (Beirut: al-Furat, 2004).

[212] Rabah, *A Campus at War*, 24.   [213] Juha, *al-Haraka al-'Arabiyya al-Sirriyya*.

[214] Kazziha, *Revolutionary Transformation in the Arab World*, 20.

Arab-Israeli conflict. In particular, he advocated for student engagement in armed struggle against the state of Israel, stressing the necessity of training with weapons.[215] The president of AUB, Stephen Penrose (1948–1954), may have been unaware of this brewing transformation. Nevertheless, he "respected the goals which [the 'Urwa] worked for" and was prepared to help the organization in any way possible.[216] The following year, Habash won the presidency of the 'Urwa and served until his graduation in 1951, solidifying the group's new direction.[217]

Equally consequential to the founding of the Arab Nationalist Youth was Habash's affiliation to another student faction within the 'Urwa called "The Youth for Vengeance," or Shabibat al-Tha'ir (referred to as the Shabiba). The Shabiba was founded by Habash and two other medical students at AUB, Wadie Haddad (from north Palestine and a similar class background as Habash) and Ahmad al-Khatib (from a family of humble means in Kuwait).[218] They led the central organ of the 'Urwa from 1949 to 1951, heeding Zurayk's call to "struggle with heart, hand, and tongue," fomenting "vigilance and militancy" within its core ranks.[219] Like Zurayk's Society of the Red Book, the Shabiba recruited 'Urwa members at AUB, while telling AUB officials they were not a student group.[220]

Habash built upon this inside-out trend in the summer of 1951. Haddad, Khatib, and other Shabiba/'Urwa members met Habash at a cafe close by AUB in the Raouché neighborhood of west Beirut after graduation.[221] They agreed they wanted another venue to continue their political activism beyond their college degrees. To this end, they founded the clandestine Arab Nationalist Youth, which would be based in Beirut, at least to start. Similar to the earlier Society of the Red Book, it was meant to operate as a transnational organization, forging links with similar student groups in Syria, Iraq, and Egypt.[222] Within a year, Habash

[215] Ghanma, *Jam'iyyat al-'Urwa al-Wuthqa*, 171; and Matar, *Hakim al-Thawra*, 56.

[216] Ghanma, *Jam'iyyat al-'Urwa al-Wuthqa*, 172.

[217] Hani al-Hindi and 'Abd Ilila al-Nasurawi, *Harakat al-Qawmiyyin al-'Arab: Nashataha wa-Tatwarha 'abr Watha'iqha, 1951–1967* [The Arab Nationalist Movement: Its Foundation and Development according to Its Documents, 1951–1967], vol. 1 (and vol. 4 2004) (Beirut: Jam'iyyat al-Haquq Mahfutha al-Abhath al-'Arabi, 2001), 77–78.

[218] Kazziha, *Revolutionary Transformation in the Arab World*, 19; and Rabah, *A Campus at War*, 25.

[219] Zurayk, *Ma'na al-Nakba*, 80; and Rabah, *A Campus at War*, 26.

[220] Rabah, *A Campus at War*, 25.

[221] Matar, *Hakim al-Thawra*, 71; Kazziha, *Revolutionary Transformation in the Arab World*, 21; and al-Hindi and al-Nasurawi, *Harakat al-Qawmiyyin al-'Arab*, vol. 1, 79.

[222] For more information on the Arab Nationalist Youth and Ahmad al-Khatib's role within it, see Abdel Razzaq Takriti, "Political Praxis in the Gulf: Ahmad al-Khatib and the

pursued expansion opportunities in both Jordan and Syria, leaving the Beirut cell to the leadership of Muhsin Ibrahim (a school teacher from South Lebanon, not educated at AUB) and al-Hakam Darwaza (a Palestinian and AUB drop-out).[223] This was not a mere passing of the baton, but a signal that the Arab Nationalist Youth was more than a middle-class movement. In fact, its Beirut leadership would reflect the masses of disenfranchised Palestinians and Arabs.

While not a student organization, from the beginning the Arab Nationalist Youth maintained close ties with the 'Urwa, the faculty at AUB (who would attend Arab Nationalist Youth events), and other young, educated people in Beirut. Regarding the latter, recruits for the movement would include those men attending the Makassed College and the University of Saint Joseph in Beirut, where an Arab Nationalist Youth cell was founded in 1953.[224] Therefore, Habash chipped away at the existing recruitment bases of other popular organizations, including the Najjadeh and Kata'ib. Moreover, Habash's leveraging strategy, not unlike Baydun's 'Amiliyya-Tala'i' transnational Shi'i networks, helped expand this organization. Also, and similar to the Progressive Socialist Party and Syrian Social Nationalist Party, mechanisms to govern the group and disseminate its identity were essential to the growth of the Arab Nationalist Youth.

One of these tools was the Arab Nationalist Youth's first newspaper, *al-Tha'ir* ("the Vengeance"). Launched on November 20, 1952, its slogan was "Back to Palestine" (*al-'Awda ila Filistin*).[225] One article in particular, "This Is the Solution," reflects multiple trends surrounding the Arab Nationalist Youth. The article focuses on developments in the Arab-Israeli conflict since the loss of Palestine; first and foremost was the international support for the Zionist enterprise at the expense of displaced Palestinians. The writer(s) of *al-Tha'ir* argue they will not accept "half-baked solutions" from the United Nations Security Council, which merely perpetuate the "recklessness of Zionism." Instead, members of the Arab Nationalist Youth will "stand up for the concept of violent, extreme revenge" put into action by the "highly organized loyal national youth battalions."[226]

Movement of Arab Nationalists, 1948–1969," in *Arabic Thought against the Authoritarian Age: Towards an Intellectual History of the Present*, eds. Jens Hanssen and Max Weiss (Cambridge: Cambridge University Press, 2018), 94–98.

[223] Kazziha, *Revolutionary Transformation in the Arab World*, 25 and 73.

[224] Matar, *Hakim al-Thawra*, 70; al-Hindi and al-Nasurawi, *Harakat al-Qawmiyyin al-'Arab*, vol. 1, 88; and Kazziha, *Revolutionary Transformation in the Arab World*, 30.

[225] Kazziha, *Revolutionary Transformation in the Arab World*, 30; and al-Hindi and al-Nasurawi, *Harakat al-Qawmiyyin al-'Arab*, vol. 1, 94.

[226] *Al-Tha'ir*, November 20, 1952. Cited in al-Hindi and al-Nasurawi, *Harakat al-Qawmiyyin al-'Arab*, vol. 4, 547.

On one level, the messages of this article in *al-Tha'ir*, which originated from the Shabiba-led 'Urwa, were now being spread to the members of this distinct movement. On another level, the particular language used marks the beginnings of a new populist discourse. In another 1954 article, *al-Tha'ir* writer(s) called for "the execution of every traitor conspiring with the [Zionist] enemy," citing that the Lebanese "ruling class and its inaction encourages our enemy the Jew in its conspiracy!"[227] Like the Lebanese People's Party, the enemy of the people in the eyes of the Arab Nationalist Youth are the elites. But in this historical context, the *zu'ama'* are not only sponsored by colonialism, but Zionism.

In short, what facilitated this new brand of youth militancy, beyond historical context, was the group's use of institutions of higher education, campus politics, and semiautonomous student organizations around AUB. Furthermore, even after the 'Urwa was disbanded in 1955 – ironically enough, under the AUB presidency of Zurayk – the Arab Nationalist Youth maintained relationships with another club off campus: the Arab Cultural Club (al-Nadi al-Thaqafi al-'Arabi).[228] Members of this group, with their transnational makeup and interest in reclaiming Arab greatness, would serve as another recruitment base for the Arab Nationalist Youth. Both within and beyond the gates of AUB, in the "open and free city of Beirut," the Arab Nationalist Youth continued to cultivate a base of operations.[229] The early success of Habash's group, however, was not just a product of network building. In Chapter 2, we will explore the role that gatherings, such as joint Arab Cultural Club-Arab Nationalist Youth events, play in these groups' rising popularity.

But at this point, it is worth mentioning what a certain degree of autonomy allows for: membership and organizational growth. By 1956, Habash held the first organizational conference of what would be referred to as the Arab Nationalist(s) Movement (Harakat al-Qawmiyyin al-'Arab) after 1958.[230] The transnational group held this meeting in either Beirut or Amman, the group's new de facto headquarters.[231] At this meeting, the movement established its official policy and announced

[227] *Al-Tha'ir*, February 11, 1954. Cited in al-Hindi and al-Nasurawi, *Harakat al-Qawmiyyin al-'Arab*, vol. 4, 548.
[228] Anderson, *The American University of Beirut*, 130. This club was formed in 1944. For more information on its origins, see Ghanma, *Jam'iyyat al-'Urwa al-Wuthqa*, 153–154.
[229] Matar, *Hakim al-Thawra*, 13.
[230] Muhammad Barut, *Harakat al-Qawmiyyin al-'Arab: al-Nash'a, al-Tatawwur, al-Masa'ir* [The Arab Nationalist Movement: Origins, Development, Fate] (Damascus: al-Markaz al-'Arabi li l-Dirasat al-Istratijiyya, 1997), 68–70.
[231] While Barut notes that the conference was in Beirut, Matar mentions Amman. Given that Habash lived in Amman at the time, and his strong connections to Beirut, either is likely. Barut, *Harakat al-Qawmiyyin al-'Arab*, 70; and Matar, *Hakim al-Thawra*, 14.

leadership councils, including a new one based in the Occupied Territories.[232] Thereafter, the strategy of off campus/on campus networks, stretching back to Zurayk's 'Urwa-Society of the Red Book linkages, and through Habash's Shabiba-Arab Nationalist Youth-Arab Nationalist Movement connections, was mimicked and expanded by Arab nationalists across the Arab world. Members of the Arab Nationalist Movement, often unrecognized by the host government of their respective Arab country, would meet in the designated Arab Cultural Club (often loosely affiliated to a university) to congregate, network, and propagate ideas.[233] By the late 1950s, branches of the Arab Nationalist Movement had sprung up from Bahrain and Yemen in the Arabian Peninsula to Egypt and Morocco in North Africa.[234] How the Arab Nationalist Movement expanded, leveraging existing communal ties and groups, was not exactly new. But where it spread, and the militant populist discourse that was its basis, was a sign for things to come in the field of youth and popular politics in the 1950s and beyond.

Conclusion: Similar Performativity, Distinct Worldviews

These seven popular organizations constitute a sampling of the field of youth and popular politics during the first half of the twentieth century in Lebanon. Some of their leaders were born at the turn of the century (Yazbak, Shamali, Nasuli, and Baydun), some closer to the Great War (Saadeh and Gemayel), and others thereafter (Jumblatt and Habash), all coming of age in quite different historical contexts. Some of the groups were more textual and intellectual, ranging from the Lebanese People's Party to the Arab Nationalist Youth. Others did not often engage in theoretical debates, as their ethos was predicated on "doing," whether it was the Najjadeh's building of the moral young citizen or the Kata'ib's emphasis on strength, action, and muscular politics.

However dissimilar in specific form and context, these groups matter to the history of modern Lebanon and the twentieth-century Middle East because they constructed populist discourses, constituted the populist moment, and were central to youth politics. To varying degrees, they were all anti-elite, anti-colonial, and stood in defense of the sha'b. And while some were more youth-centric than others (e.g., the Tala'i', a youth organization, versus the Progressive Socialist Party, a political party with a youth component), all popular organizations embraced youth culture, structured under the group, and catered to issues central to young people,

---

[232] Sayigh, *Armed Struggle and the Search for State*, 74.
[233] Suleiman, *Political Parties in Lebanon*, 158.   [234] Matar, *Hakim al-Thawra*, 14.

whether encouraging literacy or activism. All of these groups were also shaped in part by French colonialism and the *zu'ama'* that had once supported it. Alongside the wars, famines, and forced migrations of the first half of the twentieth century, popular organizations embodied a similar ethos of forward thinking and modernity, moving away from, not toward, what they perceived as the backwardness of earlier ages. These historical processes gave the organic intellectuals that served as the leaders of these organizations a platform to become popular and followed.

In short, popular organizations became quite powerful because they produced something new and intriguing to young people: a populist agenda, however ambiguous, against the established order, and a novel vision of communal relations based on duty, strength, and social care. Given these characteristics, Thompson argues that what I call popular organizations can be considered subaltern movements, "for they opposed the power of mediating elites, seeking to substitute the direct loyalty of citizens to the nation for old patron-client ties."[235] Equally fitting would be the term social movements, formed outside established political circles, but, especially by the 1940s to 1950s, developing their platforms and policies in conjunction with elite politics.

This does not mean that these groups were equally successful in their populist plights. These groups can be broken into two categories based on staying power. Less effective were the Lebanese People's Party, Najjadeh, and Tala'i'. These three groups faced a number of crises throughout the 1940s and 1950s, based primarily on the direction of the group and state authorization – or rejection – of that path. For what became known as the Lebanese Communist Party, the issue was whether the group was an intellectual or workers' party, a question that lingered since the days of Yazbak and Shamali. For the Najjadeh, especially after independence in 1943, the issue was whether the organization would accept complete Lebanese sovereignty or favor some form of geographic union with other, Arab nation-states. Finally for the Tala'i', the group decided to disband when the government asked it to in 1949.[236] An established politician in his own right by the late 1940s, Baydun instead decided to focus his efforts on his own parliamentary politics, on one hand, and the 'Amiliyya Society's younger scout movement, on the other. These groups

---

[235] Thompson, *Colonial Citizens*, 193. She makes the claim for mandate-era groups, but I find that it can extend beyond this period.

[236] *Marsum 'Adad 10691, Hul al-Munazzamat wa-l-Jam'iyyat Shabu al-'Askariyya bi-Istathna' al-Jam'iyyat al-Riyadiyya al-Sarfa* [Decree # 10691, The Dissolution of Paramilitary Organizations and Associations with the Exception of Pure Sports Associations] (July 20, 1949). *Records at the Lebanese National Archives.*

and their leaders did not resurface until the 1950s, particularly in the context of the 1958 War.

More successful were the Syrian Social Nationalist Party, Kata'ib, Progressive Socialist Party, and Arab Nationalist Youth. Saadeh, Gemayel, Jumblatt, and Habash, who all spent considerable time outside their homeland, and were all intellectuals and/or activists of the postwar era, received wider support in their different constructs of sovereignty based on geographic, nationalist, or transnational causes. Saadeh's and Jumblatt's visions were more expansive, anti-imperialist, and ardently secular, drawing young, intellectually minded men away from more mainstream Arab and Lebanese nationalist causes. Gemayel and Habash were more exclusionary. At most, the Kata'ib was tacitly accepting of imperial designs, or at least fitting them into the group's own historical narratives of a separate, Christian Lebanon. This was appealing to the Christian masses, fed up with elite politics and colonial rule, but still supportive of the causes that Christian and French elites championed in mandate Lebanon. On the other hand, the Arab Nationalist Youth was against all that did not prioritize popular armed struggle against Israel. This militant populism was not invented by Habash – if anything, Zurayk was the founder – but popularized by him in the 1950s, and then adapted by the Palestinian Liberation Organization and "Lebanese Left" in the 1960s and beyond.

Regardless of trajectory, these groups all added a new identification for their youth. Their rank and file members were no longer just from a certain neighborhood, a certain sect, or a certain nation, but from a certain organization with certain ideas and practices. Along the way, these groups became concretized social forms, ranging from workers' associations to youth organizations, with membership rules, slogans, and songs. Performed day after day, month after month, year after year, these rituals became a matter of what it meant to be a member of a particular group. Hence, neither by chance or diffusion alone, these groups formed distinct and overlapping popular cultures that were lived on a daily basis.

Moreover, all groups widened their organizational capacity during the mandate and early independence period as well. Indeed, building an organization and creating networks were key elements to the construction of youth politics. At this point, however, youth as an experience and state of being was gendered masculine. Young men made up the mass majority of members in these groups. These young men residing in Beirut, who were products of changes in the public sphere that ranged from publication to popular music, were almost exclusively of the middle class. These demographics would change, however, as popular organizations began to forge a new, mass, youth politics in the mid-to-late twentieth century – beyond the city, male membership, and exclusively Lebanese youth. Each popular organization would eventually sanction branches across the country and link sympathetic men and women from both inside and outside the country. All the while, they continued to use mechanisms for organizational structure, ranging from laws to tests, to develop the organization and nurture *futuwwa*.

Accordingly, I find that these groups were quite similar, particularly in terms of performativity. At the same time, when faced with the task of how to stand out, popular organizations stressed their different ideologies (whether socialism, Lebanese nationalism, pan-Syrian nationalism, Arab nationalism, or democratic humanism) against the other. Whether stressing the greatness of a group's worldview or criticizing a trait of another group, this theme of distinction making will prove critical to understanding the production of sectarian violence, performed and propagated in part by these groups, in mid-twentieth-century Lebanon. But for now at least, into the early 1950s, the competition between these groups was often subtle and mostly rhetorical, not physical. Even in the midst of bouts of name calling, popular organizations fostered a collective culture of youth engagement that would represent the most politically active generation in the Middle East up to that point. And for that reason alone, in the form of populist discourses, leveraging media, singing songs, dressing up, and building an organization of young people, their role in popular politics should not be understated.

2   Producing Space
Celebrations of Organizational Life and Death

On September 30, 1956, the Kata'ib Party – no longer just a youth organization – held its first general conference at Hotel Beit Mary in the mountains just east of Beirut. At this gathering, the party laid out its official national and foreign policy platforms. They included the Kata'ib's continued dedication to the 1943 Lebanese National Pact, especially its view of Lebanon as interconnected "between East and West," and the place of the Arab League as a tool for "understanding and balance between [League] members."[1] These recommendations, in and of themselves, are not remarkable; the Kata'ib had been practicing Lebanese nationalism in writing and action for the past two decades. What is of particular significance is the official gathering itself. A grand event it was, at a picturesque resort overlooking the capital at 2,500 feet above sea level, for the sole purpose of meeting to declare and record these platforms.

A little less than a year after this official gathering, the Kata'ib profiled another, very different event in the pages of their newspaper. In a regular column of al-'Amal simply titled "Athletics" (al-Al'ab al-Riyadiyya), the writer(s) reported on George Basil, a Kata'ib member and ostensibly "the first Lebanese hero of Ping-Pong." They lamented the decision of the president of the Lebanese Ping-Pong Federation, who did not choose Basil to represent Lebanon at the upcoming Ping-Pong World Games in Stockholm. "How may the hero of Lebanon," the writer(s) questioned, "not be a member of the team … prohibit[ing him] from glory and victory?"[2] The writer(s) and readers alike may have found Basil unique in his abilities, but most likely not in his training. The Kata'ib had been hosting weekly Ping-Pong tournaments and training sessions at its headquarters, Bayt al-Kata'ib ("the Kata'ib home"), since it opened in the 1940s.

---

[1] Lebanese Kata'ib Party, *Tawsiyat al-Hizb al-Kata'ib al-Dimuqratiyya al-Ijtima'iyya al-Lubnaniyya min Mu'tamir al-Awwal ila Mu'tamir al-Thamin 'Ashir* [Recommendations of the Lebanese Social Democratic Kata'ib Party from the First Conference to the Eighteenth Conference] (Beirut: Manshurat Dar al-'Amal li-l-Taba'a wa-l-Nashr, 1993), 5.

[2] *Al-'Amal*, March 13, 1957.

The process of motioning and arriving at policy platforms at a yearly Kata'ib conference may appear less exciting than its Ping-Pong tournaments, or what popular organizations referred to as "sports parties" (*haflat riyadiyya*). Moreover, young, rank-and-file Kata'ib members likely did not receive invitations to the yearly conference anyways, nor have the opportunity to experience resort life at Hotel Beit Mary. Yet, the two events were equally critical to the Kata'ib mission, which included boosting its bureaucratic credentials in the eyes of state officials alongside its popular appeal among the young masses. Gatherings, the focus of this chapter, were organized by the heads or branch leaders of popular organizations and reinforced overlapping commitments for the individual member, linked to strength, discipline, knowledge, and routines. And although in different ways, convening for the sake of physical and intellectual training both brought material and cultural capital back to the center. In other words, gatherings authenticated the organization, and the space in which the organizer gathered its members, as the producer of both order *and* fun.

It is in the realm of gatherings in mid-twentieth-century Lebanon that we see additional similarities between popular organizations. Regardless of their distinct, conflicting worldviews, events for the community of members were integral to shaping the collective identities and performativities of popular organizations. In part, gatherings were built into the DNA of these groups. As outlined in Chapter 1, the group first sets to cultivate an identity for its young members, disseminate it in multiple forms – ranging from articles to advertisements – and build an organization to order the youth. Along the way, the group makes distinctions between its people and the "other" for the sake of projecting a certain uniqueness. Last, but certainty not least, the group physically gathers to realize and practice all of these things.

Cultivating an identity, organizing the group, and meeting does not, however, help address the question of how popular organizations captivated and owned "the street." To capture the rise in popularity of these groups in the mid-twentieth century, I find it useful to focus on the concept of social space as developed by Henri Lefebvre and its relationship to the public sphere.[3] Lefebvre argues that any spatial practice, like a gathering, is not simply a "moment," but a *"process"* that is "lived directly before it is conceptualized," followed by the "primacy of the conceived over the lived."[4] In short, a spatial practice produces a social space not merely through its occurrence, but by the meaning, or meanings, that are given

---

[3] Much of the theoretical and empirical foundations of this chapter are adapted from the article, Dylan Baun, "The Gemmayzeh Incident of 1949" (2017).

[4] Henri Lefebvre, *The Production of Space*, trans. Donald Nicholson-Smith (Oxford: Blackwell Publishers Ltd, 1991), 34.

to that spatial practice and connected space.[5] By space, I am referring to both the neighborhoods, streets, and buildings that popular organizations frequent and the importance they bestowed to them. In tandem, symbolic meaning and physically occupying social space contributed to the broader acceptance of popular organizations in the public sphere and afforded them a certain autonomy. Groups then leveraged this space to facilitate their growing popularity. Leasing a flat for a headquarters, hosting lectures at a member's home, throwing a festival for a holiday (religious or otherwise) at a popular cinema, marching in the streets of downtown Beirut, and staging a protest constituted the array of practices of the spatial project that I examine in this chapter.

Although fluidity, more so than exclusivity, colored the relationship between most of these sociopolitical formations until the 1958 War, one group's spatial project could challenge the existence of others. Hence, these groups not only competed for potential recruits, but for a space in the social fabric for their distinct vision. Additionally, the state, government officials, and the *zu'ama'*, whether during the colonial or postcolonial period, were also fighting for the public sphere – albeit not as effectively.[6] Therefore, confrontation among popular organizations and between popular organizations and the state was not uncommon. While contentious politics were not new in the Eastern Mediterranean, sustained mobilization and subsequent storytelling is what distinguishes popular organizations from other earlier associations and social movements. Indeed, several popular organizations memorialize their battles with the state. This chapter then concludes with a discussion of what the Kata'ib and Progressive Socialist Party call their "blood baptism" (*ma'mudiyat al-dam*) and how these groups celebrate it. These battles over space and symbolic meaning uncover the significance of gatherings, violent or otherwise, in the popular cultures and growing popularity of these groups.

Homebodies: The Headquarters as a Space for Learning, Playing, and Belonging

The first social space popular organizations in Lebanon sought to produce and occupy during the mid-1900s was a basis for operations. A "headquarters" in the capital Beirut often served as this physical base.

---

[5] For more information on Lefebvre's understanding of spatial practice, see ibid., 287–291. For another application of Lefebvre in the Arab city, see Leila Hudson, *Transforming Damascus: Space and Modernity in an Islamic City* (New York: Tauris Academic Studies, 2008).

[6] Of course, members of the *zu'ama'* in part made up the state, but not all state officials, especially during the early independence period, were from the landed elite.

In the beginning, group leaders would often use their homes or personal offices as the administrative center and a place for gathering. In the earliest days of the Progressive Socialist Party, for example, Kamal Jumblatt made his west Beirut apartment in Zuqaq al-Blat the space for holding frequent meetings.[7] Similarly, Antoun Saadeh of the Syrian Social Nationalist Party either hosted events at his downtown office or at the houses of other members.[8] Organizational growth in the 1940s to 1950s proved vital in the decision to lease or buy a building for the sake of expanding group operations.

The first headquarters of the Kata'ib was Pierre Gemayel's pharmacy in Saifi, a neighborhood close to downtown Beirut. There was a room in the back of the pharmacy exclusively for the gathering of Kata'ib members.[9] Whether to separate his business and political endeavors or the need for more space, Gemayel decided that the group had to move in early 1937.[10] After a stint at a "modest" apartment just east of downtown, and then the former Ministry of Finance building on Damascus Street downtown, the Kata'ib found its permanent residence in 1947: a large abandoned building near the Beirut port, which once served as a military barracks for the French (Figure 2.1).[11] This space for gatherings and meetings, like those before it, would be called Bayt al-Kata'ib, the "Kata'ib home."

Muhyi al-Din al-Nasuli's Muslim Scouts also called their Beirut headquarters a *bayt* when it was acquired in 1924. Celebrating this gathering place in a 1930s volume, supporters compared the organization to a family, noting "Every family needs a home ... and the scouts as a united family" need a home: Bayt al-Kashshaf, or "the Scout home."[12] The successor to the Muslim Scouts, the Najjadeh, continued this precedent, referring to their own headquarters in the Basta Tahta neighborhood as Bayt al-Najjadeh. Another group that imagined its organization in a home was

---

[7] Khalil Ahmad Khalil, discussion with author, Beirut, Lebanon, November 22, 2013.

[8] Hisham Sharabi, *al-Jamr wa-l-Ramad: Thikrayat Muthaqqaf 'Arabi* [Embers and Ashes: Memoirs of an Arab intellectual] (Beirut: Dar Nelson, 1998), 84 and 219–220.

[9] Charaf, *Tarikh Hizb al-Kata'ib al-Lubnaniyya*, vol. 1. (1979), 68.

[10] By late 1937, Pierre Gemayel reported that the Kata'ib had a membership of 8,000. While it is difficult to support this number, it would help explain why Gemayel and other Kata'ib founders expanded from a room in the pharmacy to a separate building. Lebanese Kata'ib Party, *Connaissance des Kataeb: Leur doctrine et leur poltique nationales* [Knowing the Kata'ib: Their Doctrine and National Politics] (Beirut: 1948), 83.

[11] Charaf, *Tarikh Hizb al-Kata'ib al-Lubnaniyya*, vol 1., 72–73. For more information on the Kata'ib's earliest search for a "home," see Sayyid al-Laham, *Musua'a Hizb al-Kata'ib al-Lubnaniyya min Biyar al-Mu'sas ila Biyar al-Shahid* [Encyclopedia of the Lebanese Kata'ib Party; From Pierre the Founder to Pierre the Martyr], vol. 1, *Bidayat al-Ta'sis wa-l-Intilaq, 1936–1942* [Beginning of the Founding, 1936–1942] (Beirut: Dar al-Ittihad al-Thaqafa al-'Arabi, 2007), 95–99.

[12] Naqqash and Khalifa, *al-Haraka al-Kashshafiyya fi al-Aqtar al-'Arabiyya* (1936), 15.

Figure 2.1 The headquarters of the Kata'ib, Bayt al-Kata'ib, located just east of downtown Beirut. Picture taken by author during field-based research in Beirut, June 2018.

the Tala'i'. Within two years of its founding, Rashid Baydun picked a building in the Ras al-Naba'a neighborhood of Beirut as the new headquarters for his youth organization. Bayt al-Tala'i' was the first meeting place for the group outside the walls of the 'Amiliyya primary school, which Baydun also oversaw. And much like the Kata'ib and Najjadeh, this new home would only be a short walk to the neighborhoods in which members and potential recruits resided and the affiliated schools they attended.

It is worth considering other terms that the Kata'ib, Najjadeh, and Tala'i' could have used instead of *bayt* to assign meaning to their space, including center (*markaz*), office (*maktab*), headquarters (*maqar*), base (*qa'ida*), residence (*khan*), or even building (*bina'*). These were terms that other organizations deployed, especially those that did not conceive of themselves as scout, sports, or exclusively youth organizations. The Progressive Socialist Party, Lebanese Communist Party, and Syrian Social Nationalist Party, for example, called their headquarters a *markaz*. However, *markaz* was a word that did not match the intention of groups like the Kata'ib, Najjadeh, and Tala'i'. The appropriation of the word *bayt* was a means to replace the actual family of the youth with the family of the club, and sanctify a space for that family.

Regardless of terminology, the headquarters was the space in which a host of events were held and spatial practices were performed. These would include lessons, meetings, physical competitions, parties, and lectures. The lecture presented an opportunity for group and community members alike – if the lecture was open to the public, that is – to gather for the sake of cultivating a distinct identity and occupying a space. In early 1948, Saadeh of the Syrian Social Nationalist Party gave a series of lectures on pan-Syrian nationalism that are known, quite fondly by members, as the "Ten Lectures." It began as a "cultural seminar," exclusively for members interested in the affairs of the party's cultural wing and held at the home of Saadeh.[13] Eventually, these lectures became his ideological gestures on the Syrian nation, open to the greater public, attended by hundreds and likely held at the party's larger administrative offices.[14] As Hisham Sharabi, party member and eventual professor at Georgetown University, recalls in his memoir, these types of "parties" were all-inspiring to attendees, who "derived self-confidence" from Saadeh.[15] Sharabi and others were drawn to the man, party ideas, and continued to attend gatherings at the *markaz* sponsored by the organization. Likewise, Saadeh "drew his own confidence in the Party" from the rank and file alongside their financial contributions; as Sharabi remembers, each attendee would donate one lira to organizational upkeep.[16]

The lecture as a spatial practice may have played the largest role in the culture of the Arab Nationalist Youth. This is in part due to its origination on a university campus, as the successor to other student clubs. Well before Habash became the president of the ʿUrwa al-Wuthqa in 1949, the movement used lectures, reading groups, and conferences on campus to "strengthen the Arab heritage and language."[17] By 1950, the ʿUrwa instituted a weekly meeting series, held Saturday afternoon on campus, known as "the Cultural Seminar" (bi-l-Halqa al-Thaqafa). Each week at these meetings, twenty-five to thirty members of the group would meet at West Hall on the campus of AUB to "study a book, an address on nationalism [or] experiences of other struggles."[18] The organizers of these meetings included Ahmad al-Khatib, Wadie Haddad, and

---

[13] *Al-Nashra al-Rasmiyya*, January 15, 1948.
[14] Yamak, *The Syrian Social Nationalist Party* (1966), 64.
[15] Sharabi, *al-Jamr wa-l-Ramad*, 221. For an accurate English translation of Sharabi's memoir, see Hisham Sharabi, *Embers and Ashes: Memoirs of an Arab Intellectual*, trans. Issa J. Boullata (Northampton, MA: Olive Branch Press, 2000).
[16] Sharabi, *al-Jamr wa-l-Ramad*, 220–221.
[17] Anderson, *The American University of Beirut* (2011), 130.
[18] Matar, *Hakim al-Thawra* (2008), 54.

Habash, the original members and founder of the Arab Nationalist Youth.[19]

While West Hall at AUB served as the physical space for the ideological development of what would become the Arab Nationalist Youth, the Arab Cultural Club served as an important ally and meeting place. The club's first headquarters was on Bliss Street, parallel to AUB.[20] Members of the club served on committees of the Arab Nationalist Youth and vice versa. The club and movement also organized joint lectures that were held nightly and attended by members of both groups.[21] While some lectures would be given by distinguished intellectuals, others would be free forums for political parties and movements, including the Arab Nationalist Youth, to "display their programs."[22] The Arab Cultural Club's agenda clearly connected to that of the Arab Nationalist Youth and gave a particular symbolic meaning to that space. This was embodied in the decision to make the club's headquarters a volunteer base during the 1948 War.[23] As described in Chapter 1, groups like the Arab Cultural Club provided a springboard for the Arab Nationalist Youth as it grew outside the walls of AUB's campus. It would be misguided, however, to consider this group as Habash's proxy for radical indoctrination. The club would also hold weekly classical music practice sessions, art gallery exhibitions four to five times a month, and music parties, almost nightly.[24] Indeed, all popular organizations mixed learning and entertainment both within the base and beyond it.

Perhaps most exciting for the organization's youngest members were sports parties. To allow boys to run free, sports and training were sometimes held outside the headquarters. In sports fields across the country, Progressive Socialist Party youth would conduct "training in miscellaneous sports" meant to foster the "taming of the youth (tarwid al-shabab)."[25] And uniformed men in the Syrian Social Nationalist Party would participate in summer "nationalist camps" occupying public space in villages, playing games, drilling, and reaping the "results of training."[26] Nevertheless, sports parties often made their way back to the organizational center. In the spring and summer of 1947, for instance, the Kata'ib held a sports party every

[19] Al-Hindi and al-Nasurawi, Harakat al-Qawmiyyin al-'Arab, vol. 1 (2001), 80.

[20] Arab Cultural Club, Masira al-Khamsin 'Am: al-Nadi al-Thaqafi al-'Arabi, 1944–1994 [A Fifty-Year Journey: The Arab Cultural Club, 1944–1994] (Beirut: 1994), 29.

[21] Arab Cultural Club, al-Nadi al-Thaqafi al-'Arabi khilal 35 'Am, 1944–1979 [The Arab Cultural Club at Thirty-Five Years, 1944–1979] (Beirut: 1980).

[22] Arab Cultural Club, Masira al-Khamsin 'Am, 31–32.

[23] Ibid., 33; and Arab Cultural Club, al-Nadi al-Thaqafi al-'Arabi khilal 35 'Am.

[24] Arab Cultural Club, Masira al-Khamsin 'Am, 31–33.

[25] Progressive Socialist Party, al-Nizam al-Dakhili (1972), 11–12.

[26] Al-Nashra al-Rasmiyya, June 1948.

Thursday at Bayt al-Kata'ib. During this evening of sports and games, onlookers would pack into the headquarters to watch boxing, wrestling, and fencing.[27]

Sports and sports parties were a diversion in the lives of youth members; an escape from the stresses of school, work, or family. But popular organizations could also gain a lot from them. This is why the party announced these activities, published information on sports, and placed pictures of sports events in their newspaper and leaflets.[28] While a 1953 edition of the Syrian Social Nationalist Party's *al-Aswaq* ("the Markets") included the results from recent sports parties (i.e., who won and lost), a 1947 edition of *al-'Amal* pictured the ring that was set up in Bayt al-Kata'ib for matches, and the wrestling champions that audience members watched.[29] Convening sports parties set the groups as producers of structure and play, and the one that offered a space in which both skills could be enriched. The participation, experience, and meaning ascribed to the gathering in turn worked to boost the popularity of the group.

The foray into spatial practices thus far shows that popular organizations leveraged the headquarters and sanctified this physical location as a place to learn organizational ideas, play games, foster collective identity, and encourage community engagement. At the same time, each group had to find ways to distinguish *its* events in order to attract young recruits to its space. This is why ideology matters in space claiming. For Sharabi of the Syrian Social Nationalist Party, Saadeh's boldness was what attracted him to return to the party headquarters. After a particularly famous lecture in 1947, Sharabi and his friends left with "joyful and confident hearts," as Saadeh's words on the causes of Syrian nationalism (against the Lebanese state) and Palestinian nationalism (against Israel) "continue to echo in [Sharabi's] ears."[30]

Not unlike Sharabi, 'Abbas Khalaf of the Progressive Socialist Party was drawn to Jumblatt's ideology. Khalaf explains that Jumblatt "came up with new concepts, new ideas, leftist but not communist, socialist but democrat, socialist and humanitarian ..."[31] Khalaf would become an

---

[27] *Al-'Amal*, July 20, 1947.

[28] Sports reporting in newspapers was not exclusive to popular organizations, but played into growing excitement, since the late nineteenth century, around playing sports, learning about physicality, and watching games in the modern Middle East. For more information, see Murat Yıldız, "Mapping the 'Sports *Nahda*': Towards a History of Sports in the Modern Middle East," in *Sports, Politics, and Society in the Middle East*, ed. Danyel Reiche and Tamir Sorek (Oxford: Oxford University Press, 2019), 11–40.

[29] *Al-Aswaq*, April 23, 1953; and *al-'Amal*, March 4, 1947.

[30] Sharabi, *al-Jamr wa-l-Ramad*, 89 and 86.

[31] 'Abbas Khalaf, interviewed by author, Beirut, Lebanon, December 12, 2013.

important figure of the Progressive Socialist Party in the 1950s. While his words could be read for distinction making alone, an important question arises as it pertains to the current inquiry: How would 'Abbas learn what distinguished the ideology of the Progressive Socialist Party? The answer would be through conversations with friends, lessons, and lectures, all of which were attached in some way or another to the headquarters of the group. For these reasons, Khalaf, as the current head of the Friends of Kamal Jumblatt Association, a group that teaches current youth about Jumblatt and his legacy, holds a weekly lecture series in Jumblatt's honor at their headquarters in Beirut.[32]

Beyond Club Quarters: Public Events, Public Protest, and Public Politics

Gatherings beyond the headquarters, like the Kata'ib General Conference of 1956 at the resort of Beit Mary or the Arab Nationalist Youth's lectures at the Arab Cultural Club, indicate that popular organizations were not content with a semiautonomous, insulated space. Rather, the project of these groups extended beyond protected place into the public sphere. In order to facilitate extra-organizational gatherings, groups had to establish links between hotels, clubs, charities, orphanages, and governmental officials. And in some cases, groups would appropriate public spaces, whether at cinemas or in the streets, to boost popularity, sometimes in accordance with government officials and sometimes in defiance of the state.

The Lebanese Communist Party, like the Kata'ib, conducted official party business beyond the walls of its headquarters. Over the course of three days in 1944, 200 communist delegates of Lebanon congregated to officially separate the Lebanese Communist Party from the Syrian Communist Party. Although the leader of the party, Khalid Bakdash (1912–1995), united the two parties in the 1930s, he believed their split – coordinated by him, of course – made sense by 1944, as Lebanon and Syria were on the way to becoming fully separate, independent entities. Bakdash held this conference to authenticate the landmark division and establish platforms, programs, and new leaderships for each party.[33] The chosen venue was a school in Mousaytbeh, the same

---

[32] Friends of Kamal Jumblatt Association, *Nadwa al-Arba'a' 'ala Khata Kamal Junblatt, 2010–2011* [Wednesday Lecture in the Footsteps of Kamal Jumblatt, 2010–2011] (Beirut: Rabata Asdiqa' Kamal Jumblatt, 2011).

[33] For more information on the congress that Bakdash convened to finalize this separation, see Ismael and Ismael, *The Communist Movement in Syria and Lebanon* (1998), 33–38.

neighborhood in Beirut that housed the party headquarters. A nearby canteen would be the host for unofficial events, including tea parties.[34]

These types of precedent-setting events were for group officials and invited guests only, not branch leaders or the rank and file. On one level, this was the result of spatial limitations and hierarchy. Simply put, not every individual mattered, or was expected to be given a voice in high affairs. On another, more subtle level, these grand events gave the organization a certain celebrity status among individual members. Discussions about these conferences would unfold during the following weeks and months at branches across the country, often in the form of public reviews of annual conferences and the implementation of the measures agreed upon at the conferences. Conference actions would even penetrate the coffee shops and households of members. In the case of the Lebanese Communist Party, the 1944 conference proceedings could be purchased for a small price of 25 piasters, and sayings and slogans coined at the grand events were published in organizational leaflets and newspapers.[35]

Popular organizations also leveraged public spaces and gathering places for less formal events. This included using a park or pitch for a sports festival, occupying a cinema for a rally, strolling across neighborhoods for a march, or tapping into existing cultural spaces to commemorate religious holidays. In September 1943, for instance, the Najjadeh organized a series of lectures around the holy month of Ramadan at the Center for Muslim Orphans (Dar al-Aytam al-Islamiyya) in the Beirut neighborhood of Zarif, only a short walk, or march, from Bayt al-Najjadeh in Basta Tahta. The speakers and topics grew in significance as the holiday came to a close. The first talk was given by none other than Constantine Zurayk, professor at AUB, faculty advisor to the ʿUrwa, and proponent of the Najjadeh's Arab nationalist outlook. The second speaker was the director for announcements and publications at the Arab Library, and the keynote speaker was "His Excellency Ahmed Ramzi Bek," Consul General of the Kingdom of Egypt.[36]

Beyond demonstrating the Najjadeh's networks of recruitment, from college to orphanage, this gathering shows the group's organizational capital in late 1943. It was able to secure and host professors, librarians, and important, external figures. Even more, this event hints at how popular organizations held public gatherings, outside their established spaces, with the goal of normalizing their presence at the center of larger,

---

[34] *Sawt al-Shaʿb*, January 1, 1944.   [35] Ibid., January 22, 1944.

[36] *Ahadith Ramadan* [Events of Ramadan] (September 1943). Najjadeh Party Files, Linda Sadaqah Collection, American University of Beirut.

national festivals – in the Najjadeh's case, a religious one. Another group that was grounded in practices of piety was the Tala'i'. On the Mawlid, or the Prophet Muhammad's birthday, in 1946, "some of the teams of the Tala'i'" would "take a tour," or march, to commemorate the Prophet. As detailed in a notification, likely sent to leaders and members alike, the gathering and march was meant to celebrate "Arabs in general," "Muslims in particular" that sought to "please God," and "the complete freedom and brotherhood of Lebanon."[37]

The short announcement encapsulates the Tala'i''s ethos: the religious duty of young Muslims and cultural duty of Arabs are inextricably linked to the national duty of Lebanon. This spirit was written onto public space through the course of the parade route. The notice outlined that the route started at Bayt al-Tala'i', the Tala'i' home and headquarters in Ras al-Naba'a. It then moved north through the Basta neighborhood and toward downtown with stops at the old mosque and Martyr's Square, an important symbol for the independence of Lebanon. Teams of the Tala'i' would then turn back east toward their neighborhoods of support, including al-Nasra and Ras al-Naba'a, before returning to Bayt al-Tala'i'.[38] While not mentioned in the public memo for this march, other records indicate that young members would sing the "Tala'i' anthem" (nashid Tala'i') during festivals and meetings, and that its talented musical group would follow during these festivals.[39] Public religious festivals, with young men front and center, were more so a spatial practice for groups associated with religious schools, like the Tala'i' and Najjadeh. The latter held a similar Mawlid celebration in 1947 outside the same mosque that the Tala'i' marched by a year earlier.[40] Groups as different as the Kata'ib or Progressive Socialist Party may march, hold a protest, or rally nearby in downtown Beirut. However, the old mosque did not have the same symbolic meaning for these groups.

Another common gathering for popular organizations, with equally powerful spatial dynamics, was the public "speech party," or hafla khitabiyya. Sometimes these events would be held in multiple places, with marches, music, and games in between, and in other instances, they

---

[37] Tala'i' Organization, Biyan 'Umda al-Di'aya wa-l-Nashr bi-Thikra al-Mawlid al-Nabawi al-Sharif, 1946 [Statement of the Director of Announcement and Publication for the Remembrance of the Birthday of the Righteous Prophet, 1946]. Cited in 'Issa, Munazzamat al-Tala'i' (1992), 343.

[38] Ibid.

[39] Tala'i' Organization, Ittifaqiyya li-Tadrib Ba'd al-Tala'i'yyin al-Taba'iyyin lil-Fariqa al-Musiqiyya [Agreement to Train Those Who Play in the Tala'i' Band] (1946). Cited in 'Issa, Munazzamat al-Tala'i', 325.

[40] Al-Iyman, February 10, 1947. Najjadeh Party Files, Linda Sadaqah Collection, American University of Beirut.

would be held in one, fixed open space with a penultimate speech from party leadership. In 1953, the Progressive Socialist Party announced a speech party that would be held outside in the coastal Beirut neighborhood of Manara.[41] Even though Jumblatt's party was formed in Beirut in 1949, with its first official office opening in Beirut in April 1950, its membership coverage did not extend much outside the villages of the Chouf Mountains, an hour southeast of Beirut.[42] According to one study, over 67 percent of the members of the Progressive Socialist Party in 1949 hailed from the greater Mount Lebanon region, which encompassed the Chouf District and other mainly Druze and Christian villages.[43] Hence, this gathering to celebrate the founding of the party was quite important to their acculturation in the capital.[44] The speech party's headliner was Jumblatt, who spoke on how "we [in the party] represent freedom and true democracy in Lebanon."[45] While Jumblatt was comfortable with this discourse, he may not have been in Manara. Choosing this location as the space for a grand event was then a deliberate strategy of the Progressive Socialist Party, a means to open up a new ideological space for popularity in the capital. The event was successful in this goal, as up to 25,000 attended the festival, marking the normalization of the Progressive Socialist Party and Jumblatt in Beirut.[46]

While many speech parties were held out in the open, another popular option was to rent, or simply inhabit, one of some twenty-three cinemas in Beirut for this gathering.[47] Cinemas were appealing to popular organizations for two reasons. First, they held an important place in the life of many young Beirutis. Like other middle-class, spatial practices, such as sports, music, and lectures, for a popular organization to hold a gathering at a cinema was part of a broader attempt to place group culture within the confines of existing youth activities. Second, while cinemas in Beirut faced state regulations (licensure, events held there, content of films), they were not state property. Given this legal opening, cinemas were, in the words of Thompson, "volatile public spaces," and ripe for popular organizations to claim.[48]

Cinema Roxy, one of the most popular, was coveted by groups as divergent in ideology as the Kata'ib, Najjadeh, Tala'i', and the Lebanese Communist Party. In fact, these four and other groups joined

[41] *Al-Anba'*, May 1, 1953.
[42] Progressive Socialist Party, *Rub' Qarn min al-Nidal* (1974), 133.
[43] Richani, *Dilemmas of Democracy and Political Parties in Sectarian Societies* (1998), 70.
[44] Al-Jabburi, *Nasha'a al-Hizb al-Taqaddumi al-Ishtiraki* (2009), 115
[45] *Al-Anba'*, May 8, 1954
[46] Al-Jabburi, *Nasha'a al-Hizb al-Taqaddumi al-Ishtiraki*, 115.
[47] Khalaf, *Heart of Beirut* (2006), 203 and 253.
[48] Thompson, *Colonial Citizens* (2000), 197–210.

forces in the "Union of Lebanese Parties Resisting Zionism" (Ittihad al-Ahzab al-Lubnaniyya li-l-Mukafaha al-Sihyawniyya). The Union chose Roxy to host a 1944 joint "popular meeting."[49] The diverse background of the Union, and what leaders of these popular organizations said, including "protesting Zionism, its supporters," and the Balfour Declaration, likely resonated with their audience.[50] Equally powerful, however, was the setting of this cinema gathering, signaling the appropriation of this section of the public sphere by popular organizations. In a much earlier speech party, noted in Chapter 1, the Lebanese People's Party gathered at Theater Crystal to commemorate International Workers' Day, May 1, 1925. At this event, the executive committee of the party, including Yusuf Yazbak and Fuad al-Shamali, spoke to men and young boys from the theater's stage. They recited the party's "seven demands" for better labor conditions, and called for a demonstration to force French officials to implement the demands.[51]

According to the Lebanese People's Party's newspaper, al-Insaniyya, Theater Crystal, and the 1925 speech party, was the starting point of the protests, turning into and linking up with larger labor strikes across the city. The Lebanese People's Party employed this strategy again in the context of the 1929 parliamentary elections, using gatherings to persuade members and sympathizers to vote for "working-class lists" over those of the elite, pro-capitalist, colonial-sponsored candidates.[52] These mobilizations show a crucial feature of spatial practice. Popular organizations often moved across physical and symbolic boundaries, from cordoned, indoor spaces to outdoor, public venues. In both cases of open and closed gatherings, popular organizations produced a space for their acceptance, one that young members would most likely return to, whether the headquarters or a particular street corner or neighborhood within the group's main sphere of influence.

Some public events were organized in coordination with the state, such as Tala'i' festivals, many of which were attended by President Bishara al-Khuri. Others, including the Lebanese People's Party's 1925 cinema gathering, were in protest of the status quo. Whether state officials attended or outlawed a particular event depends on the historical context, the intention of the gathering, and the group's relationship to the state within that given context. But for some groups, their gatherings were

---

[49] Sawt al-Sha'b, October 28, 1944; and 'Issa, Munazzamat al-Tala'i', 246.
[50] Sawt al-Sha'b, October 28, 1944.
[51] Al-Insaniyya, May 15, 1925. Cited in Lebanese Communist Party, Sawt al-Sha'b Aqwa (1974).
[52] Walter Z. Lacquer, Communism and Nationalism in the Middle East (London: Routledge & Kegan Paul, 1956), 141.

often met with state hostility. In addition to the Lebanese People's Party, this was surely the case for the Arab Nationalist Youth. The 'Urwa, led by Habash from 1949 to 1951, frequently organized protests on AUB's campus that ended in confrontations with campus police and state security forces. One particular demonstration in the fall of 1951, only a few months after the Arab Nationalist Youth was founded, merits further explanation.

The events centered around the British occupation of Egypt. Following the British refusal to terminate their protectorate rule in 1951, protests spread across Egypt and the broader Arab world.[53] In Lebanon, officials blocked any type of gathering concerning events in Egypt. And as AUB was known by students, administrators, and the broader public as a hotbed for activism on regional issues, the government sent security, police, and gendarmerie forces to the main gate of AUB, essentially putting the campus on lockdown. Thereafter, a woman named Asmaa, member of the 'Urwa and host of the weekly meeting series that Habash helped found, the "Cultural Seminar," called for demonstrations against this action.[54] On a particular day in late October 1951, the group decided to start its protest at the smaller medical gate of AUB, in an effort to take security forces by surprise. Then Asmaa, in what appears to be a surprise to other students, "threw herself on the security officers."[55] Galvanized by the act, protesters stormed security forces outside the gate and a clash ensued that resulted in several injuries.

According to Hani al-Hindi, founding member of the Arab Nationalist Youth, these protests "left a wide reverberation in Lebanon and the Arab world."[56] While maybe self-inflated, these events did mark the emergence of their physical – not just ideological – struggle against the forces that either promoted imperialism or were complicit in it, here the Lebanese state. This willingness to confront the status quo without fear is one novelty of popular organizations in the mid-twentieth century. This courage, coupled with its reinforcement through storytelling, in part built the popularity of these groups. This event also represents an instance in which multiple spatial practices, including lectures, open-air speech parties, and demonstrations interconnected. Together, they punctuated a violent, defining moment in the growing popularity of a particular popular

---

[53] For more information on this crisis, see Wm. Rodger Louis, *The British Empire in the Middle East, 1945–1951: Arab Nationalism, the United States, and Postwar Imperialism* (Oxford: Oxford University Press, 1986), 573–604.

[54] For more information on these protests and Asmaa, see al-Hindi and al-Nasurawi, *Harakat al-Qawmiyyin al-'Arab*, 88–89; and Matar, *Hakim al-Thawra*, 13–14.

[55] Al-Hindi and al-Nasurawi, *Harakat al-Qawmiyyin al-'Arab*, 89.   [56] Ibid.

organization; a moment, story, and space that the Arab Nationalist Youth claimed it won.

Containing Youth Politics, Monitoring Organizational Life

To focus on how popular organizations produced space and then assigned meaning to it, whether it be through a lecture, a sports party, or a protest, is not to consider this an inevitable process. It was contingent and contentious, as the state had its own space-claiming project: to establish continuity, build institutions, and garner loyalty. Yet, the state, as developed by Lebanese officials and their earlier Ottoman and French counterparts, took little interest in encouraging youth politics and spectacles. At least during the 1920s to 1950s, they rarely sponsored countrywide youth organizations or cultural gatherings in celebration of young people.[57] This was at the same time that popular organizations were successfully fostering affiliation through gatherings. Thus on balance, these groups were gaining popularity at the expense of the state, and even the *zu'ama'*, although the latter will be discussed in Chapter 3. In response, state officials adopted a heavy-handed approach, drafting ambiguous laws to monitor these groups, controlling the public spaces they frequented, and, as will be clear in the subsequent section, engaging in state violence in an attempt to contain these groups.[58]

In the legal realm, the French High Commissioner first blocked extragovernmental activity emanating from youth circles by extending the 1909 Ottoman Law of Association.[59] This law barred "the forming of [all] political associations," with no definition of what constituted a political association.[60] As pertains to popular organizations in particular, the French later instituted a 1934 law that legalized "youth sports associations" – which many of our groups could, or may want to, classify as – while strictly

---

[57] This disinterest in the politics of youth spectacles likely has to do with the investment of state officials in elections. Throughout the French mandate, and continuing on to the early independence period, the state relied on local and general elections as the means through which to produce knowledge and spatial realities. For more on this point, see Baun, "The Gemmayzeh Incident of 1949," 103–104.

[58] A similar dynamic is evident when considering the state's decision to take a heavy-handed approach toward schools, whether private or public. For an example from the French mandate period, see Nadya Sbaiti, "If the Devil Taught French: Strategies of Language and Learning in French Mandate Beirut," in *Trajectories of Education in the Arab World: Legacies and Challenges*, ed. Osama Abi-Mershed (New York: Routledge, 2010), 59–84.

[59] This 1909 law followed the 1908 Young Turk Revolution and was likely meant to curtail all political activism in the Arab provinces thereafter.

[60] *Qanun al-Jam'iyyat* [The Law of Association] (August 13, 1909), Principle 4. *Records at the Lebanese National Archives*, Beirut, Lebanon.

forbidding them "from all political acts."[61] To uncover subversive activity, the French colonial state required that a building have licensure in order to be considered an official headquarters. If the group followed the law as laid out (i.e., publicly apolitical and presenting no threat to the state), it was not difficult to obtain a license.[62] But given the deliberate ambiguity of what constituted political behavior, the state could, in theory, disintegrate groups and seize their spaces at a moment's notice with these laws as cover.

The Interior Ministry of early independence Lebanon did not discard these laws, but built upon them and adopted others. Under the active 1909 Ottoman Law of Public Gatherings, groups holding public events, like all public gatherings discussed in this chapter, had to submit a document forty-eight hours beforehand. The document had to include the place, day, and hour of the event, in addition to the "intended purpose," and the names of the event organizers.[63] Moreover, in the late 1940s, the government passed Decree # 10691, or "the Dissolution of Paramilitary Organizations and Associations with the Exception of Pure Sports Associations," which included a list of the affected groups: the Najjadeh, Kata'ib, and Tala'i'.[64] Whether it was a private speech, public lecture, the organizations themselves or their spaces, anything that the government deemed threatening could be easily rejected on grounds of security and disbanded accordingly.

Irrespective of these measures, popular organizations were clearly fighting for and occupying space. Stated differently, the groups at the center of this study are unique because they sustained themselves and succeeded – at different levels – under state control, whether they followed the rules often, sometimes, never, or the state did not implement or apply these laws to all popular organizations.[65] This point is important to understanding the

---

[61] *Qarar Raqam 146, Bi-Sha'n Jam'iyyat al-Shaban al-Munsh'a al-Mumarisa al-Il'ab al-Riyadiyya* [Decision #146 Concerning Youth Associations Established for the Practice of Sports] (July 4, 1934), Principle 1. *Records at the Lebanese National Archives.* For more information on how some group leaders used sports as a cover for anti-colonial political agitation, see Baun, "Lebanon's Youth Clubs and the 1936 Summer Olympics" (2017).

[62] *Qarar Raqam 20, Bi-Sha'n Aqfal al-Amakin Allati Ta'qd fiha Ijtima'at Jama'at aw Jam'iyyat ghayr Murakhkhas biha* [Decision #20 Concerning the Closure of Places Which Hold Unlicensed Gatherings, Groups, or Associations] (January 22, 1936), Principle 2. *Records at the Lebanese National Archives Center.*

[63] *Qanun al-Ijtima'at al-'Umumiyya* [Law on Public Gatherings] (1909), Principles 2, 4, and 5. *Records at the Lebanese National Archives Center.*

[64] *Marsum 'Adad 10691, Hal al-Munazzamat wa-l-Jam'iyyat Shabu al-'Askariyya bi-Istathna' al-Jam'iyyat al-Riyadiyya al-Sarfa* [Decree #10691 The Dissolution of Paramilitary Organizations and Associations with the Exception of Pure Sports Associations] (July 20, 1949). *Records at the Lebanese National Archives Center.*

[65] Khuri-Makdisi makes a similar point when investigating Ottoman and Egyptian law of the late nineteenth century regulating the theater. Khuri-Makdisi, *The Eastern Mediterranean and the Making of Global Radicalism* (2013), 77.

different paths by which these groups could become popular. For some, popularity hinged on their acceptance by the state, including the Tala'i', as well as the Najjadeh and the Kata'ib at various points of their early histories. These groups often took pride in state approval and worked to foster another layer of affiliation to the Lebanese state.

For others, their growth was secured through their activism against the state, like that of the Lebanese People's Party during the 1920s, the Syrian Social Nationalist Party during the 1930s, the Progressive Socialist Party in the 1940s, and Arab Nationalist Youth during the early 1950s. All four of these groups and their leaders were banned and jailed under these laws, forcing their groups to go underground at multiple points throughout the 1920s to 1950s. Notwithstanding the Progressive Socialist Party, all would emerge again during the 1958 War, seeking relevance in the physical battle for or against the state. Equally important for populist bona fides, and especially in the case of the Kata'ib and Progressive Socialist Party, was the narrative; that is, the way in which protest, state repression, and violence against the organization was remembered and spatialized.

To Confront the State: The Blood Baptism and Memorializing Violence

On March 1, 1937, the Syrian Social Nationalist Party held a gathering in the village of Bikfaya just outside of Beirut. The occasion was Saadeh's thirty-third birthday. After receiving the proper paperwork for the event, the mayor of the town forbade it. According to one party member, this was because the French High Commissioner offered him promotion if he did so. Ignoring the mayor, and by extension, the colonial power's wishes, the party held the festival in the town square. It ended with a clash between Syrian Social Nationalist Party members and security forces, leading to several injuries.[66] Two days later Saadeh was arrested after he referred to the French-backed Lebanese state, in an official statement, as "aggressive," and its existence, a "corrupt entity."[67]

A year after this clash and Saadeh's release from jail, the Syrian Social Nationalist Party held its first festival to remember Bikfaya and Saadeh's birthday. At this particular event on March 1, 1938, Saadeh gave a speech, calling the Bikfaya clash a "test of tests for the Syrian Social

---

[66] 'Abdullah Qubrasi, 'Abdullah Qubrasi Yatathakar: Ta'sis al-Hizb al-Suri al-Qawmi al-Ijtima'i wa-Bidayat al-Nidal ['Abdullah Qubrasi Recalls: The Founding of the Syrian Social Nationalist Party and the Beginning of the Struggle], vol. 1 (Beirut: Mu'assisa Fikr al-Abhath wa-l-Nashr, 1982), 191.

[67] Al-Ahmad, Hizb al-Suri al-Qawmi al-Ijtima'i (2014), 93.

Nationalist Party and its national efforts," and celebrating those who "stood up in Bikfaya" for the "national renaissance."[68] This practice would extend well beyond Saadeh's untimely death in 1949. On July 8 of that year, Saadeh was executed by a firing squad following a swift Lebanese military tribunal, what is also known as the "Gemmayzeh incident" (hadath al-Gemmayzeh) or "Saadeh affair" (qadiyat Saʿadeh).[69] Indeed, as recent as 2010, there was a celebration, and publication, remembering Saadeh and his life, including the events of Bikfaya and Gemmayzeh.[70]

The Syrian Social Nationalist Party's commemoration of Yawm al-Bikfaya ("the Day of Bikfaya") epitomizes three trends in the history of popular organizations in mid-twentieth-century Lebanon. First, the story focuses on a spatial practice, a public gathering outside club quarters, common in the everyday life of young members. Second, is that, through the act of storytelling, the group gives meaning to the physical space where the confrontation originally took place, and the event itself that marks the group's greater triumph, even in the midst of tragedy and loss. The pervasiveness of these types of actions and stories cemented both the populist credentials of popular organizations and their popular support. Lastly, to consider the commemoration of contentious spatial practices, and the physicality of state responses, allows for a discussion of the place of violence within popular organizations. Two groups with similar bloody sagas, revered by members as "the blood baptism," or maʿmudiyat al-dam, are the Kataʾib and Progressive Socialist Party.

For the Kataʾib, the organization's baptism by blood began with its dissolution. With a nudge from the High Commissioner, French-backed Lebanese officials released a decree on November 18, 1937, that banned the Kataʾib, the Najjadeh, and another group called the White Shirts for their "paramilitary trend."[71] The government decree clarified that these groups' meetings and demonstrations "disrupted general security," which was punishable under the 1934 law governing youth politics.[72] The Kataʾib had planned a march to celebrate its one-year anniversary that month, and took to the press after the ban to voice disgust with this decision. This was before the Kataʾib had its own licensed newspaper,

---

[68] Ibid., 93–94.

[69] For more information on the Gemmayzeh incident, see Baun, "The Gemmayzeh Incident of 1949"; and Beshara, Outright Assassination (2010).

[70] Syrian Social Nationalist Party, Antun Saʿadeh, 1904–1949 (Beirut: Syrian Social Nationalist Party, 2010).

[71] ʿAl Juridu al-Rasmiyya, November 22, 1937. Cited in Juha, Maʿrakat Masir Lubnan, vol. 2 (1995), 573–574.

[72] Ibid.; Qarar Raqam 146.

al-'Amal, so it broadcasted critical messages in *al-Bashir* ("The Omen"), a newspaper sympathetic to its founding.

In a November 21 Kata'ib statement printed in *al-Bashir,* the group linked the government dissolution to the organization's platform and growing support in Lebanon. The state did not allow the Kata'ib to participate in political events, according to the statement, because the group raised "national feelings in all the population, irrespective of doctrinal or religious differences," sentiments that would challenge colonial governance.[73] Its popularity was confirmed by letters from Kata'ib branches and areas of support across the country, included in the same edition of *al-Bashir.* One such letter was from the president of the Falougha branch in Mount Lebanon, named Maron, who wrote that "the Kata'ib dissolution is the irritant of the youth *(haij al-shabab).* Full concern. Dignity for the Kata'ib, dignity for Lebanon."[74]

This popular support appears to have afforded the Kata'ib a certain space to criticize the government. Never before had the Kata'ib, or its leader Gemayel, so vehemently and openly protested the French government. In the context of this dissolution though, the Kata'ib reassured its supporters among the "national Lebanese youth" that it would "eliminate every attempt to make the lives of the Lebanese and their capabilities booty in the hands of the invaders and a tool of imperialism."[75] Alongside these harsh words, the organization set out to meet in Martyr's Square, downtown Beirut, to protest its breakup on November 21, 1937. What ensued was a clash between Kata'ib members, security forces, the French army, and even French Senegalese troops. Government reports of the clash are scant, with sympathizers of the Kata'ib claiming they witnessed "the infamous police sticks in the face of the unarmed Lebanese youth."[76] Although it is unclear who attacked whom first, the results are well known: two Kata'ib members were killed, one Senegalese troop died, and, Gemayel, targeted as the protest organizer, was injured and incarcerated.[77]

The same supporters who wrote to *al-Bashir* rebuking the "unjust" dissolution of the Kata'ib now protested the imprisonment of Gemayel, and were joined by the broader Lebanese press and the Maronite religious establishment.[78] This pressure led the colonial government to release

---

[73] *Al-Bashir,* November 21, 1937.   [74] Ibid.   [75] Ibid.   [76] Ibid., November 23, 1937.

[77] For accounts on the events of November 21, 1937, often from the side of the Kata'ib, see Charaf, *Tarikh Hizb al-Kata'ib al-Lubnaniyya,* vol. 1., 155–157; Entelis, *Pluralism and Party Transformation in Lebanon* (1974), 53–54; Juha, *Ma'rakat Masir Lubnan,* vol. 2, 573–576; Meir Zamir, *Lebanon's Quest: The Road to Statehood 1926–1939* (New York: I. B. Tauris & Co Ltd, 1997), 234–235; and Dueck, *The Claims of Culture at Empire's End* (2010), 213.

[78] *Al-Bashir,* November 21, 1937; and Dueck, *The Claims of Culture at Empire's End,* 213.

Gemayel, who thereafter was referred to as *sheikh al-shabab*, or "leader of the youth," by his supporters.[79] In the following days, Gemayel donned a bandage on his head where he was struck by the police, cementing his image as a youth activist, agitator, and defender of the people.[80] Indeed, his release symbolized that although the government tried to block their gatherings, Kata'ib youth had won the space to exist, and, at least to Kata'ib supporters, that Gemayel had won the youth.[81]

After 1937, there are several references to what would later become enshrined as the "blood baptism."[82] But the first official, public celebration was not until November 21, 1944, a year after Lebanon's independence. Starting at 7:30 a.m., Kata'ib members arrived at the headquarters for the day's festivities. After organizing the ranks, a march began, launched from Bayt al-Kata'ib near the port, moving toward downtown, winding down streets through the sounds of cheering onlookers. This processional had its most symbolic stop at Martyr's Square, the site of the clash between the Kata'ib and colonial forces. At this hallowed ground, the Kata'ib saluted government dignitaries – the prime minster, deputy prime minister, governor of Beirut, and other important state officials – before moving onto the next destination, Cinema Roxy. This gathering was a music party, where in addition to the national and Kata'ib anthems, the party band played a song titled "A Piece of November 21," an homage to the blood baptism. Later in the afternoon, government representatives and Kata'ib members returned to Bayt al-Kata'ib for a speech party by Kata'ib leader, and hero of 1937, Gemayel himself.[83]

Even today, the blood baptism is celebrated by Kata'ib members. During a research visit in Beirut during 2013, I was invited to attend a Kata'ib festival. At this gathering, Amin Gemayel, the current leader of party and son of Pierre Gemayel, instructed Kata'ib members that in the face of today's crises, whether the Syrian Civil War or the issue of Hezbollah's arms, they must remember the day in 1937 when Pierre the founder "shed blood" in defense of the nation.[84] Between 1937 and 1943, while still under total French rule, publicly celebrating the blood baptism

[79] *Al-Bashir*, November 24, 1937.

[80] See pictures in Charaf, *Tarikh Hizb al-Kata'ib al-Lubnaniyya*, vol. 1.

[81] Although the Kata'ib functioned similarly after Gemayel's release, legally speaking, the party was under official ban until 1943. Entelis, *Pluralism and Party Transformation in Lebanon*, 54.

[82] What the Kata'ib first referred to as a "useful ordeal" – not a blood baptism – was taken up in a 1939 Kata'ib speech and a November 21, 1942, edition of *al-'Amal*, including a picture of the clash. Elias Rababi, *al-Shabab fi al-Miydan* [The Youth in the Field] (February 5, 1939), Lebanese Kata'ib Party Files, Linda Sadaqah Collection, American University of Beirut; and *al-'Amal*, November 21, 1942.

[83] *Al-'Amal*, November 28, 1944.

[84] Notes from field-based research in Beirut, Lebanon, November 24, 2013.

was a dangerous enterprise. But in 1944 and beyond, it has become an open celebration, validating the Kata'ib as a key player in Lebanon's postindependence politics.

The Progressive Socialist Party's blood baptism is an equally important hallmark in the culture of the organization. The roots of the event, referred to as "the day of Barouk" (Yawm al-Barouk), began in early 1951, two years after the party had been founded. Party sources claim that the group faced government repression for both its growing popularity and its humanist, populist, and anti-status quo – especially anti-Bishara al-Khuri – platforms.[85] In response, the party published statements chastising the government. One such release was penned by the party's Ministry of Interior, who claimed the government had "use[d] all methods to limit the activities of the Progressive Socialist Party."[86] And only a couple of days before the incident in the Chouf village of Barouk, the party started its own newspaper, al-Anba'. From its very first issue, it highlighted what it saw as government inactivity and corruption, and urged its readers of the "necessity of sacrifice" in the face of the "hostile forces" of the state.[87] This conflict, not unlike others between the government and popular organizations, was a result of the group's spatial expansion, from the region of Mount Lebanon to the Beirut neighborhood of Manara. The government's reaction was predictable; it perceived this group as a challenge to its authority and sought to neutralize it.

Tension came to a head on March 18, 1951. On this date, the Progressive Socialist Party was to hold a festival in the village of Barouk, meant to draw attention to the anti-Khuri candidates it would support in upcoming parliamentary elections, most notably Jumblatt. Security forces were dispatched to the festival. Government reports claim these forces were met by armed protesters.[88] Progressive Socialist Party reports assert that security forces fired shots from rooftops first in order to justify an assault.[89] Regardless of who provoked whom, shots were fired, with multiple injuries on both sides, and the death of two officers and three party members.[90] Thereafter, authorities arrested over fifty Progressive

[85] Progressive Socialist Party, Rub' Qarn min al-Nidal, 149; and al-Jabburi, Nasha'a al-Hizb al-Taqaddumi al-Ishtiraki, 93.
[86] Al-Nahar, January 13, 1951. Cited in Progressive Socialist Party, Rub' Qarn min al-Nidal, 149.
[87] Al-Anba', March 16, 1951. Cited in al-Jabburi, Nasha'a al-Hizb al-Taqaddumi al-Ishtiraki, 93.
[88] Zisser, Lebanon (2000), 198–199; and al-Diyar, March 20, 1951.
[89] Al-Jabburi, Nasha'a al-Hizb al-Taqaddumi al-Ishtiraki, 93–94.
[90] Al-Diyar, March 20, 1951; Progressive Socialist Party, Rub' Qarn min al-Nidal, 151; and Zisser, Lebanon, 198.

Socialist Party members from Barouk and other branches across the country.[91]

One of the more notable arrests was Eli Makrazal, the editor in chief of al-Anba'.[92] In the face of attempts to silence it, however, the party continued to use this paper to criticize the government. Two weeks after the clash, al-Anba' declared "we [the party] will win and defeat the forces of injustice and evil [the government]."[93] And a month after the elections that confirmed Jumblatt as a parliamentarian, a June 8 article went further, referring to the government as the embodiment of "hypocrisy, toxicity, terror, and laziness."[94] In the face of inaction and violence, the article declared that Yawm al-Barouk, or what was immediately called the "blood baptism," was significant because it showed that the people were "in favor of our ideas and the growth of our renaissance" and understand the "meaning of heroism, vitality, and struggle."[95]

A year later, in the lead-up to the one-year anniversary of the clashes, al-Anba' announced the scheduled remembrance for Yawm al-Barouk, "a day," according to the call, "that proves that the people can struggle and win."[96] Then on March 18, 1952, Jumblatt led a mixed driving and walking procession from the village of Sawfar to Barouk (20 kilometers south) and then Barouk to Maaser al-Chouf (10 kilometers south). He was accompanied by thousands of Progressive Socialist Party members and supporters, as well as the Druze religious establishment. The procession visited the homes of the three martyrs of Barouk. At every stop, Jumblatt paid his respects at a shrine to the martyr, and visited the homes of the fallen to console their family members.[97] To traverse across these villages, alongside critiques of the government, was an attempt to claim these public spaces as Progressive Socialist Party spaces.

In the very same edition of al-Anba' that profiled this gathering, Jumblatt wrote a column remembering the martyrs and how their courage gave future members a "freedom of belief" that forced the Khuri regime to accept the party.[98] This column was accompanied by a cartoon (Figure 2.2), which showed several fallen martyrs on the ground, an individual lamenting, gun salutes for the martyrs, and a triumphant man at the top of the mountain of Barouk, waving the party flag. This practice of visualizing Yawm al-Barouk continued beyond this first remembrance, where in 1953, al-Anba' included a cartoon with the faces of the three martyrs,

[91] Al-Jabburi, Nasha'a al-Hizb al-Taqaddumi al-Ishtiraki, 94.

[92] Progressive Socialist Party, Rub' Qarn min al-Nidal, 151. As Jumblatt was a candidate for parliament, the government likely did not want to go so far as to arrest him.

[93] Al-Anba', March 30, 1951.

[94] Ibid., June 8, 1951. Cited in Progressive Socialist Party, Rub' Qarn min al-Nidal, 152.

[95] Ibid.   [96] Al-Anba', March 14, 1952.   [97] Ibid., March 21, 1952.   [98] Ibid.

انصهر الجبل يوم الباروك في حرارة العطاء، وعظمة الاستشهاد قلماً وسعولاً

يوم الباروك يومنا، وفي كل يوم لنا نصر

Figure 2.2 *Al-Anba'*, March 21, 1952. The caption reads: "The mountain of Yawm al-Barouk melted in the heat of tenderness and greatness of martyrdom ... pen and pick [the party slogan]" and "Yawm al-Barouk is our day and in all days for our victory." Courtesy of Jafet Library, American University of Beirut, and Dar al-Taqaddumiyya, Moukhtara, Lebanon.

over the mountain, with a caption that they died "for the cause of freedom."[99]

99 Ibid., March 22, 1953.

After the first celebration in 1952, the site of the clash in Barouk was turned into a shrine for the martyrs. This space would become hallowed ground for the Progressive Socialist Party, a place where the party would hold speech parties and multiple party festivals, including its founding celebration in May 1952.[100] This episode of violence was then celebrated yearly, for example, with a 1958 festival and lecture by Jumblatt and other members on the significance of the event.[101] Their blood baptism was framed not only as the beginning of the party; it was also the moment that exposed a cruel government and gave the party mass support.

Apparent in both Progressive Socialist Party and Kata'ib memory making are the themes of struggle and victory. The struggle began over access to a particular space, whether a public march through the capital or an electoral party in a small village. Each story ends with victory, one that went beyond the event and group to encompass a national mobilization. For the Kata'ib, its blood baptism made the 1943 independence movement possible. In what Juha refers to as "the popular revolution," the joint command of the Kata'ib and Najjadeh was at the center of street mobilization against sustained French rule, which was technically ended on November 22, 1943.[102] For the Progressive Socialist Party, Yawm al-Barouk set the foundation for the "White (or bloodless) Revolution" of 1952.[103] Alongside eventual president Camille Chamoun (1900–1987), Jumblatt formed the National Socialist Front (al-Jabha al-Ishtirakiyya al-Wataniyya), a front that allowed for a national, cross-sect oppositional mobilization, toppling the regime of President Khuri.[104] Through memorializing these group events, and linking them to national politics, these groups normalize repertoires of mobilization that give meaning to the physical spaces they claimed and appropriated. In fact, these markers, and frequenting them in the form of yearly gatherings, remind their supporters and others that they won in the past, they are still relevant now, and are here to stay.

Equally important is how the mere existence of narratives of violence, whether those of the Kata'ib, Progressive Socialist Party, Syrian Social

---

[100] Ibid., April 25, 1952.   [101] Ibid., March 15 and 22, 1958.

[102] Juha, *Ma'rakat Masir Lubnan*, vol. 2, 821. While Lebanon today celebrates November 22, 1943, as Independence Day, French troops did not officially leave Lebanon and Syria until 1946. For more on the 1943 Kata'ib-Najjadeh independence movement, see Zisser, *Lebanon*, 68–82; Traboulsi, *A History of Modern Lebanon* (2007), 104–108; and Baun, "Lebanon's Youth Clubs and the 1936 Summer Olympics," 1347–1348.

[103] Progressive Socialist Party, *Rub' Qarn min al-Nidal*, 165.

[104] For more information on the 1952 Revolution, see Michael Hudson, *The Precarious Republic. Political Modernization in Lebanon* (New York: Random House, 1968), 105–108; el-Khazen, *The Breakdown of the State in Lebanon 1967–1976* (2000), 18–19; and Zisser, *Lebanon*, 220–240.

Nationalist Party, or other popular organizations, helps conceptualize these groups' practices of violence. Whether through attending a gathering, or viewing a cartoon that recalls the date and its martyrs as "important," confrontation is ritualized. Violence is then considered a necessary stage of development, built into group consciousness. This is not unique from other Independence Day gatherings across the colonized Global South, which memorialize and disembody violent historical events. Nevertheless, at least in the 1950s, popular organizations in Lebanon had not yet won what they were celebrating: the realization of their vision for Lebanon.

So while I reject that these groups were somehow more prone to violence than others because of their populist, nationalist, or youthful origins, these violent contexts, and celebrating the spaces in which battles were fought, are inextricably tied to their later practices of violence. When threat was perceived, like in the later 1958 War, leaders within these groups were afforded the ability to mobilize violence, and in particular, a history of violence, in the form of a gathering or strength training, in order to defend what they saw as necessary. The enemy may change – from an abstract entity, to the state, to other popular organizations – as could the discursive framing or mobilization. But the message was quite similar: defend our organization and its vision, like those in the earlier confrontations, to ensure it is not lost.

Conclusion: The Growth and Staying Power of Popular Organizations

Although the state discouraged these alternative sources of political and social authority, sometimes showing force to block their activities, the majority of popular organizations survived attacks on their existence. This chapter has argued that a way to understand this endurance, as well as their growing popularity, is through a consideration of how popular organizations produced space both within and beyond the public sphere. Whether through a weekly meeting or a yearly celebration, these groups occupied multiple types of places, and inscribed meaning onto them. Whatever meaning that may be – space for play, order, both – spatial practices created the possibility for a certain staying power. Therefore, in the face of varying levels of surveillance and repression, popular organizations successfully leveraged the little autonomy they had to create a base of operations.

Furthermore, their engagement in public spectacles signaled different things to different audiences. To those who participated, they helped foster collective identity and associate a group with particular streets, neighborhoods, and places. To those who observed from the outside, spatial practice at best inspired potential recruits and at least worked to normalize a group's presence in certain spaces. At the same time, the officialization of most groups by the late 1950s equated to their participation in state and local elections. Indeed, five of these popular organizations had become established political parties, namely, the Lebanese Communist Party, the Syrian Social Nationalist Party, the Najjadeh Party, the Kata'ib Party, and the Progressive Socialist Party. Popular organizations were thus successfully incorporated into state machinery, something the government preferred over extra-institutional opposition. This also meant that the government had now accepted them as relevant actors in social space, confirming their existence and ceding that they beat the status quo, as the Kata'ib did in 1937 and the Progressive Socialist Party did in 1951.

The popular organizations that did not become political parties were the Tala'i' and Arab Nationalist Youth. While the latter preferred operating as an underground resistance movement with no central headquarters, the Tala'i' decided to disband on its own volition. This does not signal, however, that the messages (Shi'i participation in the nation) or gatherings (lectures on the necessity of armed struggle to reclaim Palestine) of these groups disappeared. Even if certain groups faded into the background, the members that they recruited remained ideologically invested in some way. Therefore, although the Tala'i' and Arab Nationalist Youth/Movement are hard to track into the late 1950s, the populations that they represent – Shi'i Lebanese and non-Lebanese Arabs – and spaces they occupy, will continue to be important to popular and official politics in the late 1950s, including during the 1958 War.

So on balance, our popular organizations turned political parties and social movements, won the right to exist, and in some cases, thrive in mid-twentieth-century Lebanon. Through action and narrative, then, they grew as other earlier associations had perished. This was not only, however, because of their ability to produce space. As Chapter 3 explores, it was because they incorporated new categories of youth into their ranks by the 1950s in their goal to win Lebanon in their image. This included those individuals from humble, rural backgrounds, the urban poor, émigrés, and perhaps most crucial to the growing popularity and vitality of these groups, women.

3 Broadening the Base
The Poor, the Countryside, Women, and Abroad

On May 19, 1946, the Tala'i' held a special gathering for the following two purposes: to celebrate the two-year anniversary of its youth organization and to accept a gold medal of merit from President Bishara al-Khuri. The president attended the event, which included a march by the young Tala'i' men, music performed by the Tala'i' band, games played on a public field, and a speech by its leader, Rashid Baydun.[1] All were in the name of the Tala'i''s efforts in "organizing and leading the youth ... and its duty in the service of Lebanon and its independence," words from the government directive that bestowed the award.[2] The gathering took place in the streets of Beirut near Bayt al-Tala'i'. Nonetheless, in the words of a Tala'i' announcement leading up to the celebration, the event was a national one, and hence, everyone would be welcomed "without exception."[3] In the two years since its founding, the Tala'i' had established seven branches in Lebanon, from Hermel in the north to Bint Jbeil in the south, and one in Palestine.[4] To encourage members outside of Beirut to attend, the organization sent buses the night before from "any village" that would transport them to the capital, presumably free of charge.[5]

On April 5, 1949, the 'Urwa, the Arab Nationalist Youth affiliate, sponsored a different kind of gathering. It was not to celebrate their own achievements, but the contributions of Arab women. In line with "Arab Women's Day," the student movement hosted three women speakers and three male speakers. AUB alums, like Muhyi al-Din al-Nasuli, and rising women's activists, like the writer 'Afaf Baydun, gave speeches to 'Urwa members on "women's rights and their advancement (*al-huquq al-mar'a wa nahdataha*)."[6] This was not a first for the 'Urwa, as

---

[1] For more information on this event and award, see 'Issa, *Munazzamat al-Tala'i'* (1992), 181–185.
[2] Maki, *Rashid Baydun* (1967), 60.
[3] Tala'i' Organization, *Ta'mim li-l-Tala'i'yyin – Mahrijan al-Firaq al-Nithamiyya* [Notice for the Vanguards – Festival of the Founding Teams] (May 1946). Cited in 'Issa, *Munazzamat al-Tala'i'*, 338.
[4] Tala'i' Organization Collection, Map. 'Amiliyya Islamic Benevolent Society Records.
[5] Tala'i' Organization, *Ta'mim li-l-Tala'i'yyin*.   [6] *Al-'Urwa*, May 1949.

its journal, *al-ʿUrwa* ("the Bond"), had served as a space to discuss "the women's issue" (*qadiyat al-marʾa*) since the 1920s.[7] Yet, it was only in 1950, that a woman, Fahima Hakim, was voted in as a member of the ʿUrwa administrative council.[8] George Habash and Hani al-Hindi, founders and early members of the Arab Nationalist Youth, were at the center of these developments, serving on the editorial board for the journal that reported the women's day event in the first place.

These two examples from the early independence period reinforce the centrality of gatherings in the history of popular organizations. As demonstrated in Chapter 2, whether it was a lecture or a hybrid sports-speech party, events projected the collective identity of a group and produced a space in which that identity – and acceptance of it – could be cultivated. More importantly for this chapter, aspects of these two celebrations, including the focus on women or drawing in members outside Beirut, emphasize the roles that popular organizations played in the political socialization of new groups of young people. This inclusive push, however, did not unfold without contradiction. This becomes clear when looking closer at what was said at the ʿUrwa women's lecture and who was not present at Talaʾiʿ's national celebration. In reality, the Talaʾiʿ did not bus individuals from all villages in Lebanon, including those Sunni and Christian ones in the northwest of the country. Talaʾiʿ members were exclusively Shia, and hence did not have a branch office in the northwest.[9] In the second example, the review of the ʿUrwa event adds that speakers at Arab Women's Day not only stressed how women ought to be treated, but also the morals and character "a woman must follow."[10] Indeed, whether rural populations, women, or others were the focus for popular organizations, empowerment and duty, inclusion and control, and diversity and circumscription were never far apart.

This chapter analyzes how these groups grew by incorporating new categories of youth into the body politic. I find that these overtures of popular organizations, detailed in the pamphlets, newspapers, letters, and memoirs of these youth-centric groups, were crucial, albeit not exclusive, to the ushering in of an era of mass, youth politics in modern Lebanon and beyond. More specifically, these groups actively broadened the definition of who could be considered "youth"; not just middle-class students or professionals, but the urban poor, rural youth, women, and émigrés. Those groups that could best mediate the political socialization of the majority of these categories, most notably the Progressive Socialist Party, Kataʾib, and

---

[7] Anderson, *The American University of Beirut* (2011), 219.

[8] Chamma, *Jumʿiyyat al-ʿUrwa al-Wuthqa* (2002), 183. As early as 1935, however, a woman served as the art director for the monthly *al-ʿUrwa* journal. Ibid., 102.

[9] Talaʾiʿ Organization Collection, Map.   [10] *Al-ʿUrwa*, May 1949.

Figure 3.1 Members and supporters of the Syrian Social Nationalist
Party in the late 1940s. Courtesy of Wikimedia Commons.

Syrian Social Nationalist Party (Figure 3.1), became the most successful,
powerful, and largest popular organizations during the 1940s to 1950s.

Even as popular organizations served as agents for inclusion, they
reinforced class, gender, and socioreligious differences – that is, sect-
based differences – that were already built into Lebanon. Hence,
popular organizations were cosmopolitan, exclusionary, and sectarian,
all at the same time. To understand this conundrum, I find it helpful
to again return to the theories of Pierre Bourdieu. Bourdieu starts
from the basis that social actors are both the product of structures and
fashion their own structures through discourse and practice.[11] For the
purposes of this chapter, Bourdieu's theories show that where and
how popular organizations expanded was, at the very least, contingent
on the demographic, migratory, and systemic political conditions set
in place in mid-twentieth-century Lebanon. These conditions were
based on one's sect, class, gender, and upbringing. At the same time,
with their populist and modernist performativities, both of which
existed within the global grammar of youth, popular organizations
were agents in the production of a particular social structure. At least
in the 1940s and early 1950s, this structure was based on a collective

[11] Bourdieu, *Outline of a Theory of Practice* (1977), 72–73.

identity that sought to cater to multiple types of youth and mobilize their energies.

All of this culminated in structural changes to Lebanon. One more so empowering trend would be the expanding political activism of young people beyond the zu'ama' and earlier forms of association. Popular organizations were also the engineers of an equally disruptive trend. These groups would explain their growing diversity through distinction making. Within the group, popular organizations created hierarchies along class, gender, and regional lines. Beyond the group, popular organizations would distinguish between who was, or who was not, considered sectarian in a pejorative sense. In short, Bourdieu then allows for the recognition of popular organizations, with their "structured agency," as integral to these inclusionary and discriminatory transformations. Tracing both are essential to understand the ways in which these groups not only broadened the base, but eventually could help produce sectarian violence in the mid-twentieth century.

Neighborhood Canvassing: Cross-class Unity and Distinction

It has already been established that interactions between popular organizations and state officials were particularly contentious, especially as it relates to physical and legal battles over space. Equally important, and connected, was the relationship between popular organizations and the "politics of the notables." This game centered around landed elites, the zu'ama', and their ability to provide goods and services to the populations they served.[12] Predominantly middle-class popular organizations were not let into this transaction when they emerged in the mandate period. Instead, through populist language, they defined their existence in contradistinction to these politics, or less frequently, served as muscle for certain zu'ama'.[13] But as they grew in size and capacity, they were able to provide similar levels of patronage to individuals living in areas that supported them, including the urban poor. Recall, for instance, the Kata'ib's providing affordable access to medicine during World War II or the Najjadeh hosting Ramadan lectures at a local orphanage in the

---

[12] For more information on the term, see Albert Hourani, "Ottoman Reform and the Politics of Notables," in *Beginnings of Modernization in the Middle East: The Nineteenth Century*, ed. William R. Polk and Richard L. Chambers (Chicago, IL: University of Chicago Press, 1969), 41–68.

[13] For examples of the latter, an attempt to co-opt popular organizations, see Zamir, *Lebanon's Quest* (1997), 233–235; Raghid el Solh, *Lebanon and Arabism: National Identity and State Formation* (New York: I.B. Tauris Publishers, 2004), 80; and Dueck, *The Claims of Culture at Empire's End* (2010), 212.

1940s. Therefore, popular organizations began to beat the *zu'ama'* at their own game, opening up new spaces for affiliation and contributing to their growing membership. This expansion did not change the reality that popular organizations were, at their essence, middle-class, intellectual, and professional-led movements. In the context of similar groups in mandate Syria, Watenpaugh argues that the modernity these groups attempted to project came "in conflict with the terms of participation with non-elite city people."[14] Put differently in our case, distinction and segregation within popular organizations was present, even as groups broadened their base into the urban poor. This is more obvious in some groups, less in others, and depends on ideology, approach, and where a particular group operated.

For the Progressive Socialist Party and Lebanese Communist Party, non-elite recruitment, and the dissipation of class conflict, was built into their ethos. For the latter, it is important to note the endurance of the slogan of the Lebanese People's Party: "long live the workers and peasants."[15] It was plastered on banners in the 1920s, and in the 1950s it was echoed in the Communist Party's cultural production. The inaugural issue of the party's 1954 newspaper, *al-Waqt* ("the Time"), read "this is your newspaper, laborers and employees, unions and unionists."[16] The Lebanese Communist Party not only talked at the working class, but celebrated individual members within it. For example, a 1944 edition of *Sawt al-Sha'b* ("Voice of the People") included the names of those who had recently joined the party. Sixteen were from Beirut and all from poorer Beirut neighborhoods, including Tariq al-Jdideh and Mousaytbeh.[17] The latter was actually the neighborhood where the party center was located.

The Progressive Socialist Party also operated in Mousaytbeh and sought to empower the working poor. Like the Lebanese People's Party, its slogans, "bread, labor, and social justice" and "pen and pick" were a nod to the party's populist, socialist foundations.[18] In newspaper cartoons of the 1950s, the group showed working-class factory workers, shop owners, and farmers – all male – standing side-by-side under the banner of the party.[19] Furthermore, its attempt to create new zones of support in Beirut was a part of its approach to working-class populations. Recall the 1953 speech party in the neighborhood of Manara, detailed in Chapter 2.

---

[14] Watenpaugh, *Being Modern in the Middle East* (2006), 257.
[15] *Al-Insaniyya*, May 15, 1925. Cited in Lebanese Communist Party, *Sawt al-Sha'b Aqwa* (1974).
[16] *Al-Waqt*, February 20,1954. Cited in Lebanese Communist Party, *Sawt al-Sha'b Aqwa*.
[17] *Sawt al-Sha'b*, October 1, 1944.   [18] *Al-Anba'*, April 6, 1951.
[19] Ibid., March 20, 1954.

The coastal neighborhood was a place that included both affluent and less affluent populations. This coming out party was not merely a way into Beirut, but a way into certain subsectors of the city.[20] This cross-class support still exists today in Manara, where one can see Jumblatt's face plastered on walls, and the flag of the Progressive Socialist Party, with the pen and pick symbol, flying high on telephone poles.[21]

Other popular organizations had more jaded relationships with Beirut's working class. This was the case even for groups that were populist and anti-elite, such as the Arab Nationalist Youth, Syrian Social Nationalist Party, and Kata'ib, or those that catered primarily to poorer populations, like the Najjadeh or Tala'i'. For the latter, recall that the goal of Baydun's 'Amiliyya Society and affiliated schools was to solve the Shi'i literacy problem. Yet in practice, Atiyyah argues, the school targeted a "selected group of Shi'ite young men," a Tala'i', or elite vanguard, not exactly all Shia in Beirut or elsewhere.[22] The middle-class foundations for the Najjadeh and Kata'ib are even more obvious, bleeding off the pages of their recruitment materials. In their application forms of the 1940s, they called their joining members "students," and as indicated in the specific lines of the applications, they assumed that recruits had jobs, education, and, at least in the case of the Najjadeh, the means to pay a membership fee.[23]

In the face of the middle-class modernity that many of these groups cultivated, and could not easily escape, they engaged in performances of inclusion. This is perhaps most clear in the Syrian Social Nationalist Party and Kata'ib. In 1940, the Kata'ib donated 200 bags of flour, 10 bags of rice, 5 bags of sugar, and oranges, sweets, soap, and clothing to poor Beirut residents; 1,986 families and 9,542 individuals in Beirut were provided care, which, in the words of an *al-'Amal* report, brought "a slight raise to their daily misery."[24] In the case of the Syrian Social Nationalist Party, Antoun Saadeh visited an orphanage of the Islamic Makassed Charity in June 1948. According to an internal publication for party members, Saadeh toured the orphanage, watched the children do "a short test in reading and counting," and reviewed artwork they made. Coupled with a performance by the children's choir, Saadeh experienced how education "raises the mind of the children." He left the

---

[20] Ibid., May 8, 1953.
[21] Notes from field-based research in Beirut, Lebanon, June 2, 2018.
[22] Atiyyah, "Development of Shi'ite Education in Lebanon" (1972), 153.
[23] Najjadeh Party, Fillable Application Form (?). Najjadeh Party Files; and Kata'ib Party, Party Fillable Application Form (?). Lebanese Kata'ib Party Files, Linda Sadaqah Collection, American University of Beirut.
[24] *Al-'Amal*, January 14, 1940.

orphanage with high hopes and a message: "children are the secret of able nations."[25]

Both cases show how these organizations provided for the non-elites of Beirut in need, incorporating them into their youth. Their donations and institutional support could, in theory, translate to wider support for these groups, and in turn, the participation of new people in popular politics under the wing of these groups. However, it is questionable if either group really wanted to make members out of any of these destitute children and families. Their ethos in the 1940s, unlike the Progressive Socialist Party and Lebanese Communist Party of the same decade, was a more exclusive modernity with middle-class foundations. Therefore, even as they reached out to those beyond this modernity, they saw them as victims, not agents of change for their organizations.

In the broader field of popular organizations, however, individuals from different classes in Beirut were brought into the fold. When this occurred contradictions could, of course, arise. For example, reviewing the leadership of the Arab Nationalist Youth demonstrates that beside George Habash, who came from a "modest social background," all the leaders of the group hailed from less than ideal financial backgrounds.[26] A clear example of this was Muhsin Ibrahim, a leader of the Lebanese branch in the 1950s. Ibrahim attended a government school in Sidon because his family could not provide a private education like that offered by AUB. But as the movement expanded, it did not forge networks with the urban poor masses of Beirut, nor open branches in poorer areas of the city. Instead, it fashioned an alliance with an intellectual cultural club, the Arab Cultural Club, and set up cells at private, elite universities, such as the University of Saint Joseph.[27]

In some groups, even as poor young people of the city were encouraged to join the organization, roles within the group were based on class background.[28] For the Tala'i', the most coveted position was on the organizational music team. Sixty-six of some 8,000 members were provided extensive musical training and a special badge indicating their affiliation to the music team.[29] It would hold that to be able to read and perform music in the band, members must also be literate. This elite

[25] *Al-Nashra al-Rasmiyya*, June 1948.
[26] Kazziha, *Revolutionary Transformation in the Arab World* (1975), 24.   [27] Ibid., 30.
[28] For an example of this in mandate Syria, see Watenpaugh, *Being Modern in the Middle East*, 260–262.
[29] FO 1018/29, "Activities of Parties and Organizations," August 28, 1947. *Records at the British National Archives*, London, United Kingdom; and 'Issa, *Munazzamat al-Tala'i'*, 159.

training for an elite group was perhaps the best money could buy, as the music instructor of the Tala'i' in the early days, Mustafa Kamal, was paid a monthly salary of 75 lira or roughly 1.25 USD a day.[30] And given this exclusivity, the music team was revered as of national caliber. One sympathizer later went so far as to say the Tala'i' band was "so outstanding that the government used to borrow it."[31] In contrast, Tala'i' guards did not wear special badges nor hold advanced literacy. Members of this team must only show mastery in sports, loyalty in their service, and be taller than 175 cm. This difference – brains vs. brawn – did not render the guards any less significant to the organization. They followed the president around everywhere he went, wore police uniforms, and had "the same power as the police force."[32] Nevertheless, different sections in this popular organization performed different duties based on a certain set of skills. These skills, whether reading music or keeping a watchful eye, speak to the different class foundations that worked to condition those abilities.

While class distinctions were present for all popular organization (for example, working-class members vs. middle-class leaders in the Lebanese Communist Party and Progressive Socialist Party), that does not necessarily mean multiple classes could not coexist within the group. This was clear when attending a Kata'ib celebration during a research visit in 2013. There were security guards, volunteers handing out flags, party members passing out water, performers singing songs, and leaders giving speeches. Some young rank-and-file members wore the new Kata'ib military uniform, including beige shirts, camouflage pants, and tan combat boots, while others wore suits. But in the end, they all played a part in producing the event I witnessed: the seventy-seventh anniversary of the founding of the Kata'ib.[33] And they all celebrated the organization that gave them the opportunity to participate in this moment of togetherness.

Penetrating the Periphery: Developments outside of Beirut

Overarching classism and tokenism in the capital was juxtaposed to the widespread and sustained outreach beyond Beirut. A snapshot of each

---

[30] Ibid.; and *La Commerce du Levant*, December 19, 1944.
[31] Early, "The Amiliyya Society of Beirut" (1971), 102.
[32] 'Issa, *Munazzamat al-Tala'i'*, 159–160.
[33] Notes from field-based research in Beirut, Lebanon, November 24, 2013.

group's earliest expansion activities shows the relative ease in which almost all popular organizations expanded:

- **Lebanese People Party** (f. 1924): In 1925, branches ranged from Bikfaya in the west to Zahle in the east[34]
- **Syrian Social Nationalist Party** (f. 1932): By 1934, had over fifteen branches from Akkar in the north to Qaraoun in the south[35]
- **Najjadeh Organization** (f. 1937): As of 1944, held branches in cities from Tripoli in the north to Sidon in the south[36]
- **Kata'ib Organization** (f. 1936): In 1937, had at least ten branches across northern coastal and Mount Lebanon[37]
- **Tala'i' Organization** (f. 1944): Immediately after its founding, had seven branches across Lebanon[38]
- **Progressive Socialist Party** (f. 1949): In 1950 alone, opened thirteen branches from towns as large as Baalbek to villages as small as Kfar Him[39]
- **Arab Nationalist Youth** (f. 1951): Made inroads in the Palestinian refugee camps; in Sidon's Ain al-Hilweh, some forty UNRWA teachers in the camp were affiliated with the group by 1957[40]

One interpretation for why these groups so swiftly mobilized resources for expansion is realist in thrust. Like the spatial battle in Beirut, surviving in a political arena dominated by the state and notables necessitated developing affiliations, wherever those affiliations may be. These affiliations could translate to support. Recall how in the late 1930s, Kata'ib youth from newly founded branches wrote in to *al-Bashir* newspaper to criticize French treatment of the group.[41] Eventually vocal support could turn into donations or votes, when many of these groups become recognized, national political parties in the late 1940s.

At the same, and from the perspective of the groups themselves, popular organizations were more than service providers, like the state and *zu'ama'*; they were true drivers of political socialization. In 1946, the Lebanese Communist Party spoke of one branch in the south as a place to "spread the slogans of struggle and independence."[42] And by

---

[34] Jazmati, *Musahama fi Naqd al-Harakat al-Siyasiyya fi Suriya wa-Lubnan* (1990), 11–12.

[35] Jibran Jiraj, *Min al-Ja'aba: Marawiyat, Mustanadat, wa-Adabiyyat 'an al-Hizb al-Suri al-Qawmi al-Ijtma'i* [From the Bag: Stories, Documents, and Literature on the Syrian Social Nationalist Party], vol. 1, November 16, 1932 – November 16 1935 (Lebanon: 1985), 169.

[36] *Ansar al-Sada*, May 30, 1944.   [37] *Al-Bashir*, November 21, 1937.

[38] Tala'i' Organization Collection, Map.

[39] Progressive Socialist Party, *Rub' Qarn min al-Nidal* (1974), 137.

[40] Sayigh, *Armed Struggle and the Search for State* (1997), 74.

[41] *Al-Bashir*, November 21, 1937.   [42] *Sawt al-Sha'b*, February 17, 1946.

the 1950s, the Progressive Socialist Party stated in its *nizam* that the purpose of a branch office was to employ members in "various urban [read renewal] and social activities," a means of training the local population.[43] Embedded in both statements is a dedication to cultivating all areas of Lebanon, whether toward social or political engagement. Also implicit in these statements is that the organizational base in Beirut would be the starting point for realizing this socialization.

Not unlike a centralized state, then, popular organizations monitored their branches. In August 1947, for instance, the Syrian Social Nationalist Party announced in its official publication that it recently dispatched the local broadcasting, or propaganda, committee (*al-lajna al-idha'iyya*) of the town of Baalbek to visit small villages in the outlying area. The committee's agenda was to "investigate their affairs and spiritual undertakings" for a ten-day period. "[F]riction in general opinion," the center understood, may occur.[44] Disputes like this were common, as only a month earlier the party's larger broadcasting agency was sent to the Mount Lebanon village of Bayt Shabab and "remedied an internal party situation."[45] In the case of the Baalbek dispatch, the party reported back that "[t]here is no doubt that . . . this trip is a benefit to the area." Accordingly, other small villages should consider themselves "warned," as an official visit to their branch was always a possibility.[46]

The Kata'ib monitored its branches in a slightly different way, as evinced in a particular form to be filled out by branches. In Circular #52, likely from the 1940s, the Department of the Regions (Maslahat al-Aqalim) established that it would begin "monitoring the circumstances of the economy" in the branches, "no matter how small" a branch was.[47] To facilitate this, the Department of Economic Affairs would send out a questionnaire to branches on the economic capacities of the region. It asks the following questions about agriculture:

- What are the types of crops in the town and the region?
- How many planting areas are there approximately?
- Is there arable land for agriculture that is not used for agriculture? What is the reason?
- How is the condition of agriculture today?[48]

[43] Progressive Socialist Party, *al-Nizam al-Dakhili* (1972), 12.
[44] *Al-Nashra al-Rasmiyya*, August 31, 1947.   [45] Ibid., July 31, 1947.
[46] Ibid., Aug 31, 1947.
[47] Lebanese Kata'ib Party, *Li-Taka Hayatana Hayat 'Amal wa-Qumma wa-Nishat* (?) Kata'ib Party Files, Linda Sadaqah Collection, American University of Beirut.
[48] Lebanese Kata'ib Party, Fillable Questionnaire on Agricultural and Industrial Capacities of the Regions (?). Kata'ib Party Files, Linda Sadaqah Collection, American University of Beirut.

After a few similar questions on industry, the last line of the form read, "Please return this leaflet, after responding to its questions, to our department by way of the Department of the Regions."[49] As many of these types of sources are blank, it is unclear whether the questionnaire was ever sent or if the branch office filled it out. One would think they were, given that returning it confirmed the discipline and dedication of a branch office. Nevertheless, the existence of the form confirms the Kata'ib's attempts to accrue economic knowledge of places outside Beirut toward capacity building. Indeed, if the Kata'ib was to gain ground over traditional landowners in rural areas of the country, it must know the state of affairs in these areas.

The reality at the local level, however, was perhaps not as exploitative as it first appears. While bottom-up documentation from periphery to center rarely exists, reading reports on specific rural branches renders a more autonomous picture. Take, for example, a set of 1946 Lebanese Communist Party festivals. These were organized at the local level to commemorate the 1944 National Pact for the party that separated the Lebanese and Syrian branches. Celebrations were held across at least fourteen villages, towns, and cities between January and February 1946. One such location was "Machghara" in southeast Lebanon; a village so small that the editor-(s) of *Sawt al-Sha'b* put its name in quotations. The "Communist Organization" there was led by Hashim al-Amin, who spoke to a crowd on the challenges facing not only the village but the country, such as the continued presence of foreign armies, "high prices," and "other economic pests."[50] In a later, connected festival in the nearby town of Jezzine, honoring the Communist Party pact unfolded a little differently. Of course, the party had its speech, here from branch representative Elias Markhal. Similar to Amin in Machghara, Markhal spoke of "the works which are carried out by the communist team," all of which secured independence for the country and party. However, the event was more festive, as "in the presence of different popular classes" attendees heard "popular songs" from the Jezzine music group.[51]

Why these 1946 celebrations were dissimilar, or for that matter reported differently, highlights some nuances about organizational life at the level of the branch. First, whether an event showcased the town band, or merely a grandiose speech about struggling against foreigners, the choice was not only up to party heads. This points to a diversity of experiences at the branch, as local representatives called the shots. In

[49] Ibid.   [50] *Sawt al-Sha'b*, January 30, 1946.   [51] Ibid., February 17, 1946.

turn, residences of the towns and villages either had the chance to dictate the agenda of an event or at least experience an event with a distinct flavor. Of course, the center may want the event to go a certain way, confirming the strength or expansion of the party. Nonetheless, it relied on these branches not only for support, but the diversity of information produced at the local level, including the reports of the celebration that would be included in the pages of *Sawt al-Sha'b*.

The terms of the relationship were similar in the realm of bureaucracy, where the center may push a standard on the branch, but the branch held autonomy for decision-making. Unique sources confirm this, as a very small branch of the Kata'ib in the Mount Lebanon village of Bdadoun has preserved letters and forms from the 1930s to 1940s. The branch was formed quickly after the youth organization was established and Kata'ib monitoring efforts of the branch date back to 1937.[52] The Department of the Regions sent circulars, informing the branch to implement certain standards and report procedures, much like the fillable form on agricultural and industrial capacities mentioned above. One such form was from the Department of Finance, which asked the Bdadoun branch to notate "intake" (member dues, donations, income) and branch "expenses."[53] Following an April 1940 visit to Bdadoun, an organizational official from the center in Beirut sent a handwritten letter to the president of the local chapter. It "congratulates" the branch, presumably for playing by the rules, adding that "we were pleased to unite God among you."[54]

Like with the Lebanese Communist Party reports on its 1946 celebrations, that a branch felt compelled to report its affairs, or even more fascinating, maintain documentation decades later, demonstrates the buy-in from populations outside Beirut. For reasons ranging from economic to political, these mostly young men wanted to be part of the fold and celebrated their incorporation. Furthermore, these documents from Bdadoun can be interpreted as symbols of empowerment over monitoring. The Bdadoun branch was allowed to spend money on its populations, whether for uniforms, cultural programming, or infrastructure, as long as it was "approved by the president of the branch."[55] The branch leader, of course, likely had Beirut's interests in mind. Nonetheless, that these choices were made locally, as a section of a largely decentralized

---

[52] *Daftar al-Waq'i' al-Kata'ib al-Lubnaniyya fi Bdadoun, 1937–1940* [Factbook for the Lebanese Kata'ib in Bdadoun, 1937–1940]. Kata'ib Museum Collection, Haret Sakher, Lebanon.

[53] Kata'ib Party, Fillable Expense Form (194?). Kata'ib Museum Collection, Haret Sakher, Lebanon.

[54] Kata'ib Party, Letter from the Center to the Bdadoun branch, April 16, 1940. Kata'ib Museum Collection, Haret Sakher, Lebanon.

[55] Kata'ib Party, Fillable Expense Form (194?).

organization, were part and parcel of the socialization that these groups were trying to drive. In order for the youth of an area to feel as if they were part of a whole, they had to have some space to make decisions that affected their own communities.

At the same time, different popular organizations with different ideologies often operated in the same very small villages. In Machghara, a village with a population never exceeding a few thousand, the Lebanese Communist Party was not the only player. In 1947, the Syrian Social Nationalist Party hosted a lecture on "The Way of Life," Syrian Social Nationalist life, at their Machghara branch office.[56] A rivalry likely had been in place between the two groups in this village, linked to national, political battles that they had been embroiled in since at least 1945.[57] Disputes between organizations in towns or villages, of course, varied from place to place, some more hostile, some more conciliatory. Yet, just as the branches had room in decision-making, they also could shape the course of these national events, entrenching certain rivalries that would hold importance in the development of popular organizations.

The Women's Question: Feminizing the Masculine?

In terms of the next category of expansion, young women, it must be remembered that all popular organizations first conceived of themselves as masculine, deploying masculine coding to talk about their group and its members. This started with the Lebanese People's Party. When the group addressed "the comrades of peasants and workers," it only used masculine nouns – *ila al-rifaq al-fallahin wa-l-'ummal*.[58] And recall how the Syrian Social Nationalist Party reached out to women in its earliest *al-Nahda* newspaper, targeting male readers to buy female products (pantyhose, for example) for their wives.[59] Masculine symbolism was even more obvious with the Kata'ib; its slogan since the 1930s was "God, Family, and Country," stressing the importance of the former two – faith in God

---

[56] *Al-Nashra al-Rasmiyya*, July 31, 1947.

[57] In the spring of 1945, the Syrian Social Nationalist Party and Lebanese Communist Party clashed in the streets of Beirut frequently. This was due to the government's recognition of the Syrian Social Nationalist Party, and not the Communist Party. For the back and forth between the two parties, see Syrian Social Nationalist Party, *al-Hizb al-Qawmi Yarad 'ala al-Hizb al-Shiyu'i* [The Nationalist Party Responds to the Communist Party] (Beirut: Syrian Social Nationalist Party, 1945).

[58] *Al-Insaniyya*, May 24, 1925. In the early days of the Lebanese People's Party and *al-Insaniyya*, writer(s) did not use feminine nouns like *rafiqat, fallahat*, or *'amilat*, nor address female readers.

[59] *Al-Nahda*, November 21, 1937.

and the patriarchal structure – in developing the third: the masculine nation (*al-watan*).[60] Leaders from different backgrounds and ideologies, ranging from Baydun to Jumblatt, referred to their followers in public as *ikhwati*, "my brothers," or *shabab*, the masculine noun for youth. This was reflected in the membership of the Tala'i', as no young woman ever joined its ranks.[61] Even groups like the Progressive Socialist Party, which fashioned themselves in distinction to early masculine, nationalist socio-political formations, pictorialized the party and its followers as all male in the first few years of its founding. This was the case in the earliest cartoons commemorating Yawm al-Barouk, which showed only men struggling to propel the party.[62]

Given these masculine foundations, it is notable that most groups spent considerable time debating the women's question starting in the 1940s. In a 1943 *Bayrut* article, titled "Lebanese Women: Their Merit in the Success of Our Cause," Nasuli, the founder and former president of the Najjadeh, asked "Do we run with the [women's] movement" of Europe or the "heritage of our ancestors?" To Nasuli, putting the two in contra-distinction did not necessarily mean women's empowerment was a pure import. He mentioned Qasim Amin, the nineteenth-century Egyptian supporter of women's rights, and quoted the much earlier Ibn 'Asakir, a twelfth-century Damascene historian, who preached "Nothing but kindness to women."[63] Following these great men, Nasuli supported emancipation – as long as Arab heritage was not forgotten – and cele-brated women's involvement in politics, whether during contemporary demonstrations in Egypt or Lebanon.

A later 1949 *al-'Urwa* journal article carried a similar message. In his "Women and National Life," author Hafez al-Hamali discussed how many men "see nothing more in women than an annoying parasitic organism." Hamali took issue with this characterization – what he saw as the product of "miserable thinking." But he did not "want to discuss these reactionaries for long" as he was "one who prefers to live instead of dying." With a touch of dark humor, these words are significant for their placement in an AUB student journal read by students that would even-tually be linked to the Arab Nationalist Youth. It points to Hamali's belief that these misogynistic opinions were not merely a problem within the

---

[60] *Al-'Amal*, December 3, 1939.

[61] Today, young girls make up a sizable portion of the 'Amiliyya school system, but girls' education – or literacy for that matter – did not appear to be an issue that concerned Baydun in the early years.

[62] *Al-Anba'*, March 30, 1951, and ibid., March 20, 1954.

[63] Muhyi al-Din al-Nasuli, "*al-Mar'a al-Lubnaniyya: Fadlaha fi Nijah Qadiyatuna*" [Lebanese Women: Their Merit in the Success of Our Cause], *Bayrut*, December 21, 1943. Cited in *Min Qalb Bayrut* (1992), 216.

religious establishment or among simple men. They were also rife in institutions of higher learning. In the face of such discrimination, Hamali advocated not for "effort of women appointed by men, but all effort possible," even that inspired by women.[64]

Key in both articles is a distinction, "between backwardness and progress (*bayn al-raj'iyya wa-l-taqaddum*)" as Hamali puts it, or traditional, often religious views, and modern, emancipatory power.[65] As the articles suggest, in theory, leaders and members of popular organizations leaned toward the latter or at least looked to square progress and tradition. Article titles across the press of popular organizations during the mid-twentieth century confirm this sentiment, including the Progressive Socialist Party's "Women and National Education," the Kata'ib's "The Revolution of Women on Tradition and Men and Its Effects," and the 'Urwa's "Islam and the Rights of Women."[66] Another theme in Nasuli's and Hamali's articles is equal effort, equal opportunity, as women "proved their rights equal to men."[67] With this belief, popular organizations began to recruit young, educated women into *their* youth. In the late 1940s to 1950s, the Kata'ib, Syrian Social Nationalist Party, and Progressive Socialist Party all included weekly columns in their newspapers with titles like "The World of Women," or "The New Woman."

Despite this incorporation, both in readership and authorship, popular organizations had relegated new female members into feminized cultural spaces. As the name of a Kata'ib column in 1948 signals, titled "In the World of the Arts, Women, and Cinema," these sections of the newspaper were baked with preconceived notions of women's activities and the necessity of women's character building.[68] A particular instance in the case of the Syrian Social Nationalist Party is instructive. In a May 14, 1953, edition of *al-Nahda*, the cover stories followed party appeals for the government to recognize it as an actual political party. The women's column for that issue, called "The New Woman," did not include a parallel call. In its place was an article, written by Samiya Jumblatt, titled "Some habits which hinder your progress and how to avoid them." For Jumblatt, the big questions of the day were not will the government heed "the [party] demand for legal license," as party officials wondered. Rather she asked her female readers, "Do you take things personal and react quickly" and "Are you under a ton of anxiety?"[69] Handling female emotions and masculine politics were to be separate spheres of

---

[64] *Al-'Urwa*, June 3, 1949.   [65] Ibid.
[66] *Al-Anba'*, December 14, 1951; *al-'Amal*, March 20, 1947; and *al-'Urwa*, February 1950.
[67] Al-Nasuli, "*al-Mar'a al-Lubnaniyya*."   [68] *Al-'Amal*, May 16, 1948.
[69] *Al-Nahda*, May 14, 1953.

knowledge, even if both were covered by the party, and the party served both women's and men's affairs.

This compartmentalization in text was not absolute. Sometimes stories in the women's column were about women's right to vote, which was won in 1952.[70] Moreover, the paradox of female wants – art, film, beauty – and male duties – nation building – was not reflected in physical practice. Put differently, women had been active in street politics throughout the mandate and early independence periods, and popular organizations were keen to harness youth female energies and forge networks with existing movements.[71] A 1944 edition of the Lebanese Communist Party's *Sawt al-Sha'b* included a story on the Lebanese Women's Association, one of the first female empowerment groups in the country. Like many other *Sawt al-Sha'b* articles, this one focused on protest, as the association made a "call for the women of Lebanon resisting high prices."[72] Similarly a year earlier, the Kata'ib sought to make connections with this women's social movement.[73] According to one Lebanese Women's Association member in the midst of 1943 independence demonstrations, the Kata'ib protected them, as "every three women marched abreast, with the men of the Kata'ib on both sides of the procession. It was very impressive!"[74]

Popular organizations did more than link with women's groups; almost all built their own women's branches. In the late 1940s, both the Kata'ib and Syrian Social Nationalist Party dedicated time and space to discussing the contributions of these sections of their organization. In *al-'Amal*, the Kata'ib celebrated the "rising activities of the women's branch."[75] This included the creation of a series of conversations and lectures, convened by May Joseph Fayyad Mendoza, on and for women, held every Saturday at Bayt al-Kata'ib.[76] Pierre Gemayel was invited to one of these meetings in 1949. He told the group, "We have recognized Lebanese women and the necessity of their help in national action alongside men" and that "they [women] work energetically in the cause of realizing Lebanon as a just and free country."[77] To encourage these

---

[70] For examples, see *al-'Amal*, June 20, 1947; and *al-Anba'*, August 24, 1951.
[71] For more information on women's activism in mandate Lebanon and Syria, see Thompson, *Colonial Citizens* (2000).
[72] *Sawt al-Sha'b*, February 19, 1944. For more information on the complex relationship between the Lebanese Communist Party, women, and unions in the 1940s, see Malek Hassan Abisaab, *Militant Women of a Fragile Nation* (Syracuse, NY: Syracuse University Press, 2010), 72–77.
[73] Thompson, *Colonial Citizens*, 239.
[74] Eugenie Elie Abouchdid, *Thirty Years of Lebanon & Syria* (Beirut: The Sader-Rihani Printing Company, 1948), 143.
[75] *Al-'Amal*, June 26, 1949.   [76] Ibid., April 18, 1948.   [77] Ibid., June 26, 1949.

efforts, Fayyad and Gemayel would travel to regions outside Beirut to "organize Kata'ib women's organizational sections."[78]

And in honor of a 1949 international women's conference in Beirut, the women's branch of the Syrian Social Nationalist Party produced a pamphlet, in English, presumably for conference goers. The writer(s) claimed this was the party for women, as it was the only one where women could "hold offices, perform duties, and carry responsibilities," similar to that of men.[79] And women were activists in the party, apparently heading protests in Kora, North Lebanon, in 1936, the first to be "organised totally by women in this country."[80] It appears that separating female and male spaces in print, as was evident in the party's *al-Nahda*, did not mean women were any less active than men. They certainly were not encouraged to be less active, as the pamphlet read the party had created a "new personality, a new home, and a new generation of Syrian men and women."[81]

These examples demonstrate how popular organizations' discourse of women's empowerment, dating back to the early 1940s, had come to fruition by the end of the decade. While rejecting a simple, teleological path – especially given *al-Nahda*'s distinction between female questions and male duties in 1953 – by the late 1950s, young women were a part of the organizational consciousness of popular organizations. A 1957 Progressive Socialist Party's women's branch meeting signals more changes to come. In the presence of members of the all-male administrative council, the meeting of the "women of the Progressive Socialist Party," or what was called the "branch of vigilance" (*far'at al-yaqaza*), was part of a "social renaissance" that women of the party had engineered. Through their service wherever women may be, including "in the house, the factory, the field of education, and in the office," these women were knowledge producers, connecting the male "popular circles" and "informed elite."[82]

As detailed in the *al-Anba'* article reviewing this meeting in Beirut, these women contributed out of their own volition, not because the party was "imposing them to leave the domain of the house or the family and melting them in the pure party crucible." At the same time, a female member, Ratiba al-Rifai, was aware of the positives of women's political socialization under the party. Its principles had allowed women to rise above social stigma. Al-Rifai declared that "We the progressive socialist

---

[78] Ibid., April 18, 1948.
[79] Syrian Social Nationalist Party, *A Note Concerning the Work and Achievement of the Women's Branch in the Syrian Social Nationalist Party: For the Political and Social Emancipation and Progress of the Syrian Woman* (Beirut: March 21, 1949), 5.
[80] Ibid., 8.   [81] Ibid., 9.   [82] *Al-Anba'*, March 22, 1957.

women are not distracted by hatred," but driven "by the progressive socialist ideology." It opened their world, believed al-Rifai, to "the duty to know women, which stems from women not from outside[,] and stems if fed by the principles [of the party] and the sense of women's duty to society."[83]

Fayyad of the Kata'ib, al-Rifai of the Progressive Socialist Party, and the writer(s) of the Syrian Social Nationalist Party's women's branch were not the only women to speak for themselves about themselves as it related to their life in the party. As alluded to in the case of Samiya Jumblatt of the Syrian Social Nationalist Party, young women penned articles for the newspapers and popular organizations that provided them a platform to speak. Sonya Latif of the Kata'ib wrote "An Appeal to Lebanese Women" in 1948, insisting women to "wake up," be more than a "superficial wife," fight for "your rights of freedom in labor, education" and "build the society of tomorrow."[84] And Janet Nasif wrote a letter to Kamal Jumblatt, published in al-Anba' in 1951, which celebrated the recent election victories for the Progressive Socialist Party. Nasif cautioned "I will not congratulate you [Kamal Jumblatt] ... because this victory does not depend on you personally as an individual ..." What may look like a criticism to some was a woman voicing something much bigger, as this moment "is a victory for Lebanon and a victory for the conscious youth (al-shabab al-wa'i)."[85]

But in the end, female empowerment in the world of popular organizations was not without contradiction. Women were still constricted by the society in which they lived. In this context, youth politics, parties, and the nation were conceived of as masculine, and the opponents of these male forces as sectarian. Regarding the former, alongside women's movements, popular organizations were some of the first to bring women into the male political sphere. But in this realm, women were to either exist in a separate space, as evinced in the women's column, or act like men. This may seem an unfair assessment when considering that the Progressive Socialist Party, for example, told women in the 1957 al-Anba' article that they could be women, and did not have to leave the home or family. This sentiment, however, was contradicted by other progressive socialist ideals, presented in the very same article: "No difference in our lives, but in party study and activity" and "no distinction between men and women but distinction in knowledge and activity."[86]

However, could women study as much as men if they had to maintain the home? Was knowledge in raising the family deemed as important as

---

[83] Ibid., March 22, 1957.   [84] Al-'Amal, January 1, 1948.   [85] Al-Anba', May 4, 1951.
[86] Ibid., March 22, 1957.

knowledge in the party field? Not unlike other iterations of patriarchal nationalism across the world, popular organizations were exploiting women's energies, labor or otherwise, for the sake of organizational goals, followed by a disregard – or control – of issues that afflict women.[87] This is typified by the fact that Lebanese women have never possessed the right to pass on their Lebanese citizenship, and popular organizations rarely spoke against this.[88] In the masculine nation, women could play a role, but never one that superseded that of men. As it relates to women embedded in a sectarian political culture, it is illustrative to return to the words of the women's branch of the Syrian Social Nationalist Party in 1949. These women celebrated their party's efforts to incorporate women in "this decisive stage of our national [secular] history," while disparaging those other women's movements that operated "within the narrow limits of local, sectarian, or other specific ends."[89] These groups were also backward, as they "profess sectarianism under the guise of nationalism" and contribute to a "religious barrier" between Christians and Muslims.[90] While not naming names, the women of the Syrian Social Nationalist Party were likely targeting the Kata'ib and Najjadeh, groups that men in the party had accused of sectarianism since the 1930s.

Like in those earlier cases, whether or not these groups are sectarian is only part of the equation. Yes, women of the Kata'ib were mostly Christian, as Najjadeh women, when they were present in the group, were mostly Sunni Muslim. Beyond demographic realities and the meanings that are assigned to them, the other critical part of distinction making and sectarianism in this case is that these young women were calling other groups sectarian. Their group, the Syrian Social Nationalist Party, is doing the "right" thing, and they were defining the "wrong" of their enemy in specific terms: "the cancer of sectarianism."[91] In this case, a hostile type of distinction making was being performed by, in theory, the most forward-thinking sectors of popular politics, women. But as popular organizations became more cosmopolitan, expanding their youth in the realms of class, region, and gender, exclusion also grew.

---

[87] For two examples, see Joan B. Landis, *Women and the Public Sphere in the Age of the French Revolution* (Ithaca, NY: Cornell University Press, 1988); and Laura Bier, *Revolutionary Womanhood: Feminisms, Modernity and the State in Egypt* (Stanford, CA: Stanford University Press, 2011).

[88] For information on the question of women's citizenship, see Mikdashi, "Sextarianism: Notes on Studying the Lebanese State" (2018).

[89] Syrian Social Nationalist Party, *A Note Concerning the Work and Achievement of the Women's Branch in the Syrian Social Nationalist Party*, 7 and 5.

[90] Ibid., 5 and 9.   [91] Ibid., 9.

Transnational Awareness: Across Borders and Peoples

Like popular organizations' considerations regarding the urban poor, rural populations or women, how to foster transnational solidarity played out differently from group to group, depending on approach, ideology, and what communities each group served. Nevertheless, the majority of groups strove first to develop bonds of support with like-minded populations in surrounding Arab countries. For instance, the Lebanese Communist Party reported on issues that afflicted Arab workers in the 1940s, including "[i]ncreasing the wages of textile workers in Damascus after a three-day bloody strike."[92] The party's support for Arab workers in particular was reciprocated by workers themselves. In 1944, following the Lebanese Communist Party's historic charter, a "team of youth in al-Qassaa neighborhood and communist Bab Touma," both in northeast Damascus, wrote letters of support that were published in *Sawt al-Sha'b*. They sent "cheers for the convening of your conference." This was alongside "the communist team of Bab al-Nasir" in Aleppo, which praised "your leadership and your treaty."[93] Regional buy-in for local political initiatives was also central to the Najjadeh's capacity building, albeit at the state level. In 1943, the Najjadeh sent a delegation to Syria to meet President Shukri al-Quwwatli. The team included Anis al-Saghir and Hussein al-Saja'an, current and past presidents of the Najjadeh. The delegation, in the words of Nasuli's *Bayrut*, was meant to promote "proximity between Arab countries and the two brotherly countries" of Lebanon and Syria with the Najjadeh in the middle.[94]

Official visits figured into the Progressive Socialist Party's transnational expansion efforts as well. In March 1951, against the orders of the government, the Progressive Socialist Party held a "secret meeting" in Beirut to convene regional parties with similar interests. This included the Egyptian Socialist Party (three delegates), the Arab Socialist Party (Syria, one delegate), the Democratic National Party (Iraq, could not attend but in support of summit), and the Progressive Socialist Party (two delegates). At the meeting, they put down a "statement of Arab socialist parties," which was then included in *al-Anba'*. Some aspects of this declaration were fairly typical for parties with socialist leanings, including that the groups agreed to "guarantee rights of the masses in life, labor, science, and freedom." Yet, item thirteen in the statement was quite unique. Following a note of gratitude to the "Iranian parliament and Iranian people for nationalizing petrol," and a declaration of support for countries who had "core interests in independence and freedom" from

---

[92] *Sawt al-Sha'b*, October 5, 1945.   [93] Ibid., January 22, 1944.
[94] *Bayrut*, October 2, 1943.

colonial powers, the statement included a "commemoration of the martyrs of the Progressive Socialist Party," presumably those members who died at the standoff with security forces in Barouk weeks earlier.[95] In this regional document, at a meeting organized by the Progressive Socialist Party, local party issues were put front and center and supported by their brothers in arms.

Other groups went further, founding branches in the field of regional politics. For Saadeh's vision of a Greater Syria to be realized, bases had to be set up beyond Lebanon. Accordingly, in the first few years, the party founded branches in Damascus, Homs, Hama, Aleppo, Jaffa, Jerusalem, and Haifa.[96] But like the battle with the Lebanese Communist Party in the small Lebanese town of Machghara, the Syrian Social Nationalist Party was not alone in the city of Haifa. As of 1946, the Tala'i' expanded beyond Lebanon and into mandate Palestine. With the emigration of many residents of South Lebanon to Haifa during World War II, the Tala'i' sought to establish official connections with this community.[97] The outcome was "a scouting team in Haifa" under the name of the "Lebanese Vanguard Club."[98] Unlike the Syrian Social Nationalist Party, which operated in secret in Haifa, the Tala'i' had received a permit from the British to recognize its some 150 scouts.[99] Thereafter, Tala'i' members donated some 1,500 Palestinian pounds to buy a "house for the club" and to fill it with furniture. Beyond building the headquarters, the group won third prize at a competition, and, according to one sympathetic newspaper, became the largest scouting group in Haifa.[100]

The only group that could claim it was more regionally focused than these five was the Arab Nationalist Youth. This was a product of their approach, founded in Beirut, but more invested in issues that afflict all Arab youth, and fighting the repression they faced at the hands of their own governments. In its first few years, it moved its base of operations from Lebanon to Jordan, then Jordan to Syria, and set up offices in Egypt, Kuwait, and elsewhere.[101] There was a strong connection between these branches, particularly as related to cross-branch activism. This was evident in January 1955, following a Western-backed defense alliance between Turkey and Iraq. This would set up the foundations for the February 1955 Baghdad Pact, something opposed by almost all popular

---

[95] *Al-Anba'*, March 31, 1951.   [96] Jiraj, *Min al-Ja'aba*, vol .1, 399–400.
[97] For more information on the trends, see 'Issa, *Munazzamat al-Tala'i'*, 163–164.
[98] *Al-Hayat*, March 19, 1946.
[99] Jibran Jiraj, *Min al-Ja'aba: Marawiyat, Mustanadat, wa-Adabiyyat 'an al-Hizb al-Suri al-Qawmi al-Ijtma'i*, vol. 2, November 16, 1935 – November 16, 1936 (Lebanon: 1986), 221–222.
[100] *Al-Hayat*, March 19, 1946.
[101] Kazziha, *Revolutionary Transformation in the Arab World*, 33.

organizations, but perhaps most vehemently by the Arab Nationalist Youth.[102]

As protests unfolded in streets and college campuses across the Arab world, including AUB, the Jordanian branch of the Arab Nationalist Youth chided those Arab heads of state who conspired "with imperialism and [made] possible the presence of Jews in our homeland."[103] In Cairo, the Egyptian branch of the movement voiced that "[i]t is imperative that every Arab participate in foiling these colonial conspiracies for [the sake of] preserving the Arab entity."[104] These two statements were published in *al-Rai* ("the Opinion"), the first official organ of the Arab Nationalist Youth outside Lebanon. The paper was based in Damascus, where since 1954 the movement had a branch led by founding member Hani al-Hindi.[105] Damascus, Amman, and Cairo were also connected to Beirut in the paper, as *al-Rai* published statements from the 'Urwa, and reports from *al-Tha'ir*, the first paper of the Arab Nationalist Youth in Beirut.[106]

The group that felt least comfortable in regional environs was the Kata'ib. This is because their ideology, vision for Lebanon, and view of the region ran counter to all other popular organizations. The Kata'ib's Lebanese nationalism put separate Lebanon first. Correspondingly, any Kata'ib overtures to Arab countries were not meant to gain rank-and-file support, but rather to ensure that other countries respected this agenda. The Kata'ib instead focused its expansion efforts across the Atlantic and Mediterranean, "laying the foundation for wide-ranging Kata'ib-*mahjar* [émigré] balance."[107] To build this base, it located Lebanese émigrés that were sympathetic to their platform, most if not all of which were Christians. In 1947, the Kata'ib founded a "Friends of the Kata'ib Club" in Mexico, and a year later, a similar association was established in Colombia.[108] Like the Syrian Social Nationalist Party, the Kata'ib was active in South America, but could not legally found branches. Still these affiliated cultural associations were sites for Kata'ib indoctrination.

And like Baydun and the Tala'i', the Kata'ib was also active in Africa. This is because many Christians, like the Shia discussed in Chapter 1, had emigrated to West Africa, either due to economic incentive or French colonial policy during the 1920s to 1940s.[109] In 1956, Elias Rababi, the

---

[102] For more information on the Baghdad Pact, see Salim Yaqub, *Containing Arab Nationalism: The Eisenhower Doctrine and the Middle East* (Chapel Hill, NC: University of North Carolina Press, 2004), 37–45.

[103] *Al-Rai*, January 24, 1955.   [104] Ibid., January 31, 1955.

[105] Kazziha, *Revolutionary Transformation in the Arab World*, 27.

[106] *Al-Rai*, January 24, 1955   [107] *Al-'Amal*, January 8, 1956.

[108] Ibid., October 1947 and April 1, 1948.

[109] For more information on Christian emigration to West Africa, see Mara A. Leichtman, "From the Cross (and Crescent) to the Cedar and Back Again: Transnational Religion

Kata'ib Director of the Regions, led a delegation to West Africa. This was the fourth of five delegations led by the Kata'ib between 1948 and 1956 that visited countries in the Americas and Africa in order to build "the natural ties between the Lebanese residing in Lebanon and those living abroad."[110] On this mission, Rababi visited countries where supporters resided, including Nigeria, Liberia, Sierra Leone, and Senegal.[111] Even in smaller towns, like Kaolack, almost 200 kilometers east of Dakar, Rababi "met a large number of [Lebanese] sons of the community," attended a reception at the house of a Kata'ib affiliate, and gave a speech in front of a big crowd.[112] Al-ʿAmal reported on the entire trip, confirming that everywhere Rababi and his team went, they were welcomed with "excessive hospitality and enthusiastic support for the Lebanese Kata'ib, its struggle, and principles."[113]

Rababi was presumably in Africa for two reasons. First, it was his job. The duties of the Director of the Regions included seeking out new youth supporters and directing local efforts in the *mahjar*. This continues to this day, where the Kata'ib have affiliates from Africa to Australia. His second reason for visiting Africa was in search of funds. Although al-ʿAmal did not report on donations, it is clear that popular organizations expanded abroad for more than words of support. Whereas the Syrian Social Nationalist Party in Lebanon depended on money coming from Argentina, funds from Africa were crucial for Rababi, as well as Baydun.[114] Regarding the latter, money sent by the *mughtaribun*, or "expatriates," in the 1940s helped fund the activities of the Tala'i', and Baydun's trip to Africa in 1953–1954 helped finance a girls' primary school at ʿAmiliyya.[115] This is similar in the case of the Kata'ib, as indicated in a 1958 pamphlet. It reads that these delegations were not only a means to "exchange information," but also future "commercial and economic services."[116]

Sometimes the *mughtaribun* came to the popular organization. In February 1947, for instance, the Najjadeh held a gathering at Bayt al-Najjadeh for "Lebanese expatriates present here currently." The president of the Najjadeh, Anis al-Saghir, gave a speech on the "expatriate

and Politics among Lebanese Christians in Senegal," *Anthropological Quarterly* 86, no. 1 (Winter 2013): 35–75.

[110] AG-056, United Nations Observation Group in Lebanon (UNOGIL) (1958), S-0666-0004, Al-Kateb al-Lubnaniah [The Lebanese Kata'ib], Beirut 1958 (English), 24. *Records at the United Nations Archives and Record Management*, New York.

[111] *Al-ʿAmal*, January 15, January 17, and February 24, 1956.

[112] Ibid., January 8, 1956.   [113] Ibid., January 17, 1956.

[114] Sharabi, *al-Jamr wa-l-Ramad* (1998), 200–201.

[115] ʿIssa, *Munazzamat al-Tala'i'*, 209; and Early, "The Amiliyya Society of Beirut," 74.

[116] S-0666-0004, Al-Kateb al-Lubnaniah, 26.

crisis."[117] The heart of the issue was that expatriates from the Sunni community, which the Najjadeh represented, were not counted as frequently as their Christian counterparts.[118] If they were, they would presumably vote for those with similar background and ideology to speak for them, like the Najjadeh and its allies. This speech, met by a round of applause, was followed by tea in the Najjadeh's cafeteria. The Najjadeh's hospitality and Saghir's "praise of the expatriates" point to a potential, additional level of support from expatriates beyond words and money: future votes.[119]

One popular organization had an exceptional relationship with the *mahjar* in the 1940s to 1950s: the Syrian Social Nationalist Party. This is because the main basis of the group since 1938, when Saadeh left Lebanon, was in the *mahjar*. While Saghir spoke to the *mughtaribun* in Beirut on the occasion of a crisis or Rababi visited Africa a few times, Saadeh led multiple gatherings across Argentina, his place of residence in the 1940s, from Buenos Aires in the east, Córdoba in the center, and Jujuy in the west. An examination of the party's affiliated newspapers in South America provides insight into a different trajectory for youth political socialization, starting in the *mahjar* and flowing through to Lebanon.

Since the early 1900s, Syro-Lebanese cultural elites ran newspapers in Argentina, many of which included Arabic alongside Spanish.[120] The paper most closely affiliated to the Syrian Social Nationalist Party was *al-Zauba'a*. This linkage was embedded in the title of the paper, a reference to "the Hurricane" symbol of the party, and the paper's slogan, "Freedom, Duty, Organization, and Strength," which dates back to editions of *al-Nahda* in the 1930s.[121] Based in Buenos Aires from 1940 to 1947, *al-Zauba'a* covered issues ranging from Saadeh's speech parties across the country to local efforts to celebrate him and the party. Since Saadeh had resettled in Buenos Aires in the late 1930s, he encouraged the formation of a Syrian Social Nationalist Party affiliate, called the Syrian Cultural Association.[122] With at least two branches in Argentina – one in Buenos Aires and one in Tucumán, a northwestern province – they operated more as a social club than a political wing, exploring the Syrian nation from

[117] *Al-Iyman*, February 10, 1947. Najjadeh Party Files, Linda Sadaqah Collection, American University of Beirut.

[118] For more information on the politics and policy of counting Muslim and Christian expatriates differently, see Rania Maktabi, "The Lebanese Census of 1932 Revisited. Who are the Lebanese?," *British Journal of Middle Eastern Studies* 26, no. 2 (Nov. 1999): 219–41.

[119] *Al-Iyman*, February 10, 1947.

[120] For more information on this phenomenon, see Steven Hyland, *More Argentine Than You: Arabic Speaking Immigrants in Argentina* (Albuquerque, NM: University of New Mexico Press, 2017), 7–9.

[121] For comparison, see *al-Zauba'a*, August 1, 1940; and *al-Nahda*, November 12, 1937.

[122] *Al-Zauba'a*, September 1, 1940.

ideology to literature.[123] As early as 1940, Syro-Lebanese in Buenos Aires had even created a "committee for celebrating Saadeh holiday," made up of both young men and women.[124] Alongside planning, supporters would teach the story of Yawm al-Bikfaya to their brethren and report on celebrations from North Africa to Brazil in the pages of al-Zauba'a.[125]

The paper also educated its readers on party affairs and developments unfolding in Lebanon. Providing a historical basis, one 1941 al-Zauba'a article, titled "Historic Days," detailed events from the founding of the party in 1932 to Saadeh's forced exile in 1938.[126] Other reports included news items as large as the Lebanese government's consideration to reinstate the party or as small as a routine party meeting at the Choueifat branch just south of Beirut.[127] In this way, notwithstanding the Arab Nationalist Youth, the Syrian Social Nationalist Party is the only popular organization that engaged in making a movement of youth supporters – not just a branch – abroad. This is juxtaposed to the Najjadeh, which claimed in 1947 that the Sunni Lebanese community living in Detroit, Michigan, "do not know anything about Lebanon."[128] The Najjadeh may have wanted to change this ignorance, but cultivating Najjadeh supporters in the United States was not essential to their existence. Instead, with their leader in the mahjar, Syrian Social Nationalists on both sides of the Atlantic were forced to imagine a national community that spanned from Buenos Aires to Beirut. But in 1947, al-Zauba'a closed down its office and ceased printing operations in Buenos Aires. After the leader Saadeh returned to Lebanon that year, editors in Buenos Aires either went with him or at least must have hoped that the Syrian Social Nationalist press in Lebanon would return the favor and report back to the mahjar and on the mughtaribun. They surely did, as al-Nashra al-Rasmiyya ("the Official Gazette") followed Syrian Social Nationalist Party youth camps in Lebanon and the affairs of the mahjar in a frequent column called 'Abr al-Hudud, or "Beyond the Borders."[129]

In sum, whether in nearby Syria or Senegal, popular organizations were building a transnational youth membership as well. Being modern and cosmopolitan knew no bounds, so these groups dispensed massive cultural and monetary capital to bring expatriates into the fold of Lebanese youth politics. At the same time, and much like the women's question, transnationality in the life of these groups was circumscribed by a critical question: Where does the group look to for support beyond Lebanon and

---

[123] Ibid., September 1, 1940, and December 1, 1943.   [124] Ibid., August 20, 1940.
[125] Ibid., March 1, 1941, March 1, 1942, and August 10, 1945.
[126] Ibid., February 1, 1941.   [127] Ibid., August 10, 1945.
[128] Al-Iyman, February 10, 1947. Najjadeh Party Files, Linda Sadaqah Collection, American University of Beirut.
[129] Al-Nashra al-Rasmiyya, August 21, 1947, and July 15, 1947.

why? A few examples suffice to answer this question. The Kata'ib visited Christians in West Africa to promote the indivisible sovereignty of Lebanon. The Tala'i' opened up to Shia in Haifa to promote its brand of Lebanese nationalism. The Najjadeh wrote on Muslims in Michigan to open up a Sunni base in North America. And the Lebanese Communist Party covered the plight of the Arab workforce in Damascus to foster transnational, Arab solidarity. Quite paradoxically, popular organizations promoted popular, transnational politics while entrenching both sect-based memberships and contending visions for Lebanon.

Conclusion: A Slice of Mass, Youth Politics and the Paradoxes of Mass, Sectarian Politics

While the previous analysis of constructing a culture for youth politics, building an organization, and producing space demonstrated the similarities in performativity of these groups, this investigation on expansion leans slightly more toward difference. Yes, all popular organizations sought to grow their membership and strategized accordingly. But if, where, and how a group reached out to the urban poor, Lebanese beyond Beirut, women, and émigrés depended on the demographics, vision, and locale of each group. This does not change the fact that popular organizations successfully broadened their base and encouraged the political socialization of a generation of young men and women, whichever way they chose. Of course, they were not the only agents in this expansion. Labor organizations, women's associations, school groups, cultural clubs, and expatriate community organizers played equally important roles in youth-centric popular politics during the twentieth century. However, the contributions of these types of groups have been outlined elsewhere, even as their youth foundations remain under-conceptualized.[130] What often lies at the margins, relegated to conventional political history and ideological analysis, is the "political party," or what I call the popular organization.

By way of investigating their cultural production, I find that they incorporated new groups of youth into politics, ranging from poor men to expat women, all in the name of capacity building and forging a new Lebanon with young people at the center. In this way, they first expanded conceptions of who could be considered youth – even if there were still hierarchies along class, gender, or regional lines – and who had access to *futuwwa* under the group. Accordingly, popular organizations played a significant role in ushering in an era of mass youth politics in Lebanon

---

[130] For examples, see Khuri-Makdisi, *The Eastern Mediterranean and the Making of Global Radicalism, 1860–1914* (2013); Khater, *Inventing Home* (2001); and Anderson, *The American University of Beirut* (2011).

Table 3.1 *Membership and growth of popular organizations: From local club to national political party*

Group (year founded)	Membership near founding (year of reported number)	Membership (ca. 1947)[131]	1951 elections (seats won, ran)[132]	Membership (ca. 1958)[133]
Lebanese People's/ Communist Party (1924)	10,000 (1944)[134]	20,000	0 for 1	40,000
Syrian Social Nationalist Party (1932)	5,000 (1935)[135]	15,000	1 for 1[136]	20,000
Kata'ib Organization (1936)	8,000 (1937)[137]	12,000	1 for 4	39,200
Najjadeh Organization (1937)	2,000 (1937)[138]	5,000	0 for 2	10,000
Tala'i' Organization (1944)	1,300 (1944)[139]	15,000	1 for 1[140]	N/A
Progressive Socialist Party (1949)	3,327[141]	N/A	1 for 1	10,497

[131] Membership numbers for all five groups existing in 1947 are found in FO 1018/29, "Political Parties," 1947.

[132] These results are found in Khalil Majid Majid, *al-Intikhabat al-Lubnaniyya, 1861–1992: al-Quwaniyyin-al-Nita'ij* [Lebanese Elections, 1861–1992: Laws to Results] (Beirut: al-Mu'assasa al-Jam'iyya al-Darasat wa-l-Nashra wa-l-Tawaza', 1992), 93–105.

[133] Non-cited numbers in this column found in Toufiq al-Makdisi, *al-Ahzab al-Siyasiyya fi Lubnan 'Am 1959* [Political Parties in Lebanon in 1959] (Beirut: Manshurat al-Jarida wa-l-Orienan, 1959).

[134] Membership numbers for the Communist Party (in 1944 and 1958) are found in Suleiman, *Political Parties in Lebanon* (1967), 73–74. Official numbers do not exist before 1944 as the party was not recognized by the government and the party did not keep detailed records (likely no more than 100 members in 1924).

[135] Patrick Seale, *The Struggle for Arab Independence: Riad El-Solh and the Makers of the Modern Middle East* (Cambridge: Cambridge University Press, 2010), 378.

[136] Ghassan Tuwayni was a party affiliate that won a parliamentary seat in Mount Lebanon.

[137] Thompson, *Colonial Citizens*, 194.

[138] Juha, *Ma'rakat Masir Lubnan*, vol. 2 (1995), 658.

[139] Based on smallest number reported close to founding. FO 1018/29, "Political Parties," 1947.

[140] While the Tala'i' was no longer a functioning organization by 1951, Baydun won a parliamentary seat in Beirut.

[141] Richani, *Dilemmas of Democracy and Political Parties in Sectarian Societies* (1998), 68.

Table 3.1 *(cont.)*

Group (year founded)	Membership near founding (year of reported number)	Membership (ca. 1947)	1951 elections (seats won, ran)	Membership (ca. 1958)
Arab Nationalist Youth/ Movement (1951)	N/A	N/A	N/A	N/A[142]
Totals	29,627	67,000	4 for 10	119,697 (9% population)[143]

and the Middle East. They were also the benefactors of this, as reflected in their rising membership numbers and roles in official politics by the 1950s (Table 3.1).

But as they empowered, they also entrenched the demographic and ideological patterns that were central to a group's identity. Stated differently, by way of their discourses, visions, cultures, and distinction making, all embedded within Lebanese political culture, they not only contributed to cosmopolitanism, but sectarianism. How these trends work in tandem may be most clear when investigating how popular organizations acted during a particular event: the 1956 earthquake. Following one of the worst natural disasters in the history of the Eastern Mediterranean, popular organizations were at the forefront of relief efforts, just like they were at the forefront of popular politics.[144]

The Kata'ib was on the ground almost immediately after the "disaster" that hit the Chouf District the hardest (Figure 3.2).[145] The male and female *shabab* of the Kata'ib, some from nearby branches like Bdadoun, surveyed at least ten affected villages across this district.[146] As they took notes and conducted interviews with "disturbed people on the road," they heard from these villagers that the "responsibly parties," or local and state

---

[142] No numbers are known for the Arab Nationalist Youth/Movement, because, in the words of Suleiman, "the Arab Nationalists refuse to divulge any information regarding their numbers, membership, or organization." Suleiman, *Political Parties in Lebanon*, 158.

[143] The closest official census data was recorded at 1.3 million in late 1951. AG-056, United Nations Observation Group in Lebanon (UNOGIL) (1958), S-0666-0005, Census of the Lebanese People (1958).

[144] For more information on the 1956 earthquake, in relation to others, see Martin R. Degg, "A Database of Historical Earthquake Activity in the Middle East," *Transactions of the Institute of British Geographers* 15, no. 3 (1990): 294–307.

[145] *Al-'Amal*, March 20, 1956.   [146] Ibid., and March 28, 1956.

Figure 3.2 Kata'ib male and female youth surveying a destroyed building after the 1956 earthquake. Antoun Jarji Jamhuri is third from the right. Courtesy of Kata'ib Museum Collection. Haret Sakher, Lebanon.

officials, were to blame for the destruction in their villages.[147] These same villagers, who received money, clothes, food, and youthful energy from the Kata'ib, praised the group for their "service of the affected."[148]

Najjadeh affiliates, like the Muslim Scouts in Tripoli, perhaps were not physically mobilized in the Chouf like the Kata'ib, but they were there in spirit. In a regionally focused column titled "News on Tripoli and the North," *Bayrut* reported on how the scouts collected donations, money, clothing, food, and ensured that all of the aid reached those in need.[149] Lastly, members and leaders of the Progressive Socialist Party organized donations. Twenty-three members of the Hasan family in the village of Ain al-Tineh, for example, donated 65,400 lira (or almost 20,000 USD) to those affected in the sister village of Sharton, some 80 kilometers away.[150] Since the "first hour," Jumblatt and the People's Committee

---

[147] Ibid., March 20, 1956.   [148] Ibid., March 20, 28, 30, and 31, 1956.
[149] *Bayrut*, March 22, 1956.
[150] Progressive Socialist Party, Donations from Ain al-Tineh (1956?). Progressive Socialist Party Collection, Dar al-Taqaddumiyya, Moukhtara, Lebanon, and Central Directorate of Statistics, *Al-Nashra al-Ihsa'iyya Rub' al-Sanawiyya, 1958* [Quarterly Statistical Bulletin, 1958] (Beirut: Ministry of Planning, 1958), 42.

of the party mediated these donations, as the former submitted a plan to parliament on how to rebuild from this disaster.[151] In the meantime, donations would go straight to Jumblatt, who would then use organizational infrastructure to disseminate aid relief.

This response was in part the culmination of these groups' expansion efforts since the 1930s. In this moment, young men, women, and branches united to help those from rural backgrounds affected by the earthquake. Although not mentioned in these reports, it is more than likely that donations poured in from abroad too. Due to the effective mobilization of these new categories of people by 1956, popular organizations were gaining ground at the expense of traditional power sources. They were filling the gaps that the state and notables could not, positioning themselves as integral to both elite and grassroots politics. Lastly, they set their sights on gaining more advocates and changing hearts and minds. According to the memoir of Antoun Jarji Jamhuri, a Kata'ib member central to the relief effort (pictured in Figure 3.2), doctors and charity organizations were reluctant to coordinate with the Kata'ib at first. But after seeing their strength and effort, even a Sunni Muslim doctor could not resist. She said the following to Jamhuri and his team: "I am Muslim and all the Islamic youth organizations [the Muslim Scouts and Najjadeh] have kept [you] away from me and for now [you, Jamhuri] will be responsible for all teams of the Red Cross."[152]

At its surface, this response is quite inspiring; a Christian youth had convinced a superior Sunni Muslim that they would benefit from working together. Nevertheless, this moment of cross-sect coordination, like all other categories of incorporation investigated in this chapter, did not unfold without contradiction. For one, the first picture of destruction that the Kata'ib's al-'Amal printed was not a Muslim's home, but a church.[153] Moreover, the Kata'ib worked closest with a French Christian charity in its surveying and providing of aid.[154] Finally, in all Kata'ib reporting, the affected peoples are framed as victims, not active Kata'ib members. Beyond the politics of humanitarian aid, it is worth asking why Jamhuri felt the need to mention this story on the Sunni Muslim doctor and that she preferred them over the "Islamic youth organizations." It was the same reason the Muslim Scouts in Tripoli felt the need to mention that even if their people in the north were neglected

---

[151] Al-Anba', March 23 and 30, 1956.
[152] Antoun Jarji Jamhuri, Thikrayat. Thikrayat al-Majud fi al-Quwwa al-Nithamiyya al-Kata'ibiyya, Ahdath 1958 [Memoirs: Memoirs of Commissionership in the Kata'ib Organizational Force, Events of 1958] (Beirut: Manshurat Dar al-'Amal, 201?), 8.
[153] Al-'Amal, March 18, 1956.   [154] Ibid., March 31, 1956.

by the nation in the past, including during a 1955 flood, "Today we are called to help *our* brothers."[155]

Indeed, these groups were playing the game of winning Lebanon, and this game was played in, beyond, and for Lebanon. Popular organizations, and the individuals who told and retold their stories, could not fully escape the classism, misogyny, regionalism, and sectarian discourse that prevailed across the country. Rather, they leveraged this context and expanded it. This is the case in both sect-based action, such as the Tala'i' working exclusively with Shi'i communities abroad, or in anti-sectarian discourse, like the case of the Syrian Social Nationalist Party's women's branches chastising other groups. This is not to dismiss the contributions of these groups to mass, youth politics and mobilization or to criticize pluralist measures as in bad faith. At the same time, sect affiliation, sect system, and anti-sect discourse all play a role in what we call sectarianism. These fields of language and practice are critical to understanding how the same groups that were central to cosmopolitanism through the 1950s were at the center of the production of sectarian violence in 1958.

---

[155] *Bayrut*, March 22, 1956 (emphasis added).

4   In Defense of Lebanon
The Nonsectarian Causes of the 1958 War

As the country is in the midst of political, social, economic, and moral crises that are worsening by the day, since progressive tendencies can only make their way through serious cooperation between parties ... in the eyes of both parties, constitutes the basis for joint action.[1]

In 1955, the Kata'ib Party and Progressive Socialist Party signed the above "charter of coordination" (*sighat mithaq al-ta'awun*). Four years earlier, the two popular organizations almost agreed to a merger.[2] They turned down this union, as well as backed out of a 1952 agreement to combine forces during the protests against President Bishara al-Khuri.[3] But given the crises endemic to the Cold War Middle East later in the 1950s, the two stressed now, more than ever, that there was no way forward except "earnest balance" between their movements. This call for parity did not merely reflect acquiesce to the other's role in youth, popular, and official politics, secured through a mixture of populist platforms, heroic struggles against the government, and sustained expansion efforts. Rather, the charter confirmed that the two popular organizations were working to implement a "reform program" based on full cooperation. Although the charter was vague on particularities, the foundations were clear: "The two parties [above all accept] Lebanon as a sovereign, parliamentary democracy."[4]

Three years later, this charter was shattered. It was October, five months into the 1958 War, and at least 4,000 individuals had perished.[5]

---

[1] *Sighat Mithaq al-Ta'awun bayn al-Kata'ib wa-l-Hizb al-Taqaddumi al-Ishtiraki* [The Formula of the Charter of Balance between the Kata'ib and the Progressive Socialist Party] (1955). Cited in Jean Charaf, *Tarikh Hizb al-Kata'ib al-Lubnaniyya* [The History of the Lebanese Kata'ib], vol. 4, 1953–1967 (Beirut: Dar al-'Amal li-l-Nashr, 2009), 335.

[2] Suleiman, *Political Parties in Lebanon* (1967), 214.

[3] For more information on this union in 1952, and why it fell apart, see Progressive Socialist Party, *Rub' Qarn min al-Nidal* (1974), 169–70; and Lebanese Kata'ib Party, *al-Kata'ib al-Lubnaniyya: Hizb Dimuqrati Ijtima'i* [The Lebanese Kata'ib; A Social Democratic Party] (Beirut: Maslahat al-Da'ayya fi al-Kata'ib al-Lubnaniyya, 1958), 62.

[4] *Sighat Mithaq al-Ta'awun*, 335.

[5] Hudson, *The Precarious Republic* (1968), 108. Hudson provides a range from 2,000 to 4,000 deaths, based on multiple sources. Ibid., 118.

At this juncture of the conflict, Kata'ib fighters waited behind barricades in east and central Beirut to fire at oppositional forces allied with the Progressive Socialist Party. Moreover, Kata'ib women and younger members came out in large numbers across the country to protest against a cabinet formation that favored Kamal Jumblatt's revolutionary forces. On the other side, the Progressive Socialist Party was embroiled in a battle in central and east Lebanon against a new ally of the Kata'ib: the Syrian Social Nationalist Party. In the words of one UN report, as Progressive Socialist Party men prepared for battle, "local women [affiliated with the party] embroidered armbands for issue to personnel."[6]

In the course of the 1950s, the two most powerful popular organizations in Lebanon went from almost merging their groups to fighting on opposite sides of a war. These two had already, by 1958, made strides toward winning Lebanon. Demographically, they had added many new members to their respective organizations, ranging from young men in the city to women in the countryside. Symbolically, they had entrenched their own specific visions of Lebanon, both democratic in theory, but one more limited and nationalist – the Kata'ib – the other more expansive and socialist – the Progressive Socialist Party. Lastly, they had won Lebanon politically, as both had several members in parliament and mass support on the streets. With this expansion at their backs and a war at their front, they could now mobilize all of these energies for the fate of Lebanon.

This chapter is the first of two to focus on the 1958 War, a conflict where popular organizations and their young members were front and center. In particular, the chapter takes up the causes for the war and positions of popular organizations vis-à-vis the war. As popular organizations had successfully built their credentials through non-elite populism, youthful activities, and expanding conceptions of who could be youth, now they were ready to shift the conversation toward adult political socialization and duty. Indeed, popular organizations of all shades mobilized young people to fight, at least ideologically, by focusing on official politics, the constitution, and Lebanon's place in the region and the world. For these reasons, I find it necessary to first assess their official positions in this chapter before moving, in Chapter 5, to the place of youth culture and rituals in the violence, and the courses by which young people would become known as signs of reckless *futuwwa*.

To reconstruct, as best as possible, their stances before the production of sectarian violence, I turn again to the cultural production of these popular organizations, ranging from pamphlets to press conferences.

---

[6] S-0166, United Nations Observation Group in Lebanon (UNOGIL), Summary Liberation Army (October 8, 1958), 3.

Sometimes these sources were published in their newspapers and sometimes they were reprinted in US and UK diplomatic records. From this
vantage point, it is found that all popular organizations believed their
position was in defense of Lebanon as a sovereign democracy. However,
this position depended on their vision for Lebanon. On one side were the
oppositional parties. They included the Progressive Socialist Party, the
Najjadeh Party, the Lebanese Communist Party, and the Arab
Nationalist Youth. These popular organizations and their allies were in
opposition to the Lebanese government and its head, President Camille
Chamoun (1952–1958). Leading up to the crisis in May 1958, they
communicated and understood their plights on constitutional grounds,
arguing that Chamoun's recent authoritarian actions, whether election
fraud or pro-Western alignments, represented a challenge to Lebanon's
sovereignty, and necessitated revolt.

As these groups made a case for corruption and violations to Lebanese
sovereignty, the groups on the other side made a similar claim. They were
the Kata'ib Party and the Syrian Social Nationalist Party, which also
stood in defense of Lebanon's absolute sovereignty. While they took
issue with Chamoun, they accused outside forces of trying to destroy
that independence and criticized oppositional parties for their complicity
in this treachery. Therefore, I argue that support for and against the
Lebanese government cut in many different ways that cannot be reduced
to a simple sectarianism, even for groups with sect majorities, such as the
Kata'ib or Najjadeh. While scholars have accounted for this complexity at
the level of the *zu'ama'*, charting their diverse perspectives on the crisis,
not exclusively linked to sect, a similar attempt has not been made for
popular organizations.[7] This chapter represents a call to rethink sectarianism and its transformative features for youth-centric organizations in
the 1950s. More specifically, I find that mostly nonsectarian inputs made
up the sectarian violence that these groups helped produce.

To chart these multiple perspectives, the chapter moves chronologically up to 1958, first detailing the positions of oppositional parties and
then moving to those who defended, even tenuously, the status quo. The
major plot points range from the oppositional losses during 1957 parliamentary elections and the Progressive Socialist Party's plans for an armed
revolt thereafter, to the earliest stages of the war in 1958 and the Kata'ib's
decision to stay out of the conflict. In between, there are discussions of

---

[7] For three works that highlight differences within and among the *zu'ama'*, see
Michael Johnson, *Class and Client in Beirut: The Sunni Muslim Community and the
Lebanese State, 1840–1985* (London: Ithaca Press, 1986), 127–135; Nir, "The Shi'ites
during the 1958 Lebanese Crisis" (2004); and Baroudi, "Divergent Perspectives among
Lebanon's Maronites during the 1958 Crisis" (2006).

each popular organization in relation to the field, whether the Najjadeh's reemergence in 1958, or the Syrian Social Nationalist Party's historic transformations that brought it and the Kata'ib together. The chapter concludes with an analysis of a particular group in between opposition and government: the Shia of Lebanon, and in particular, the founder of the Tala'i', Rashid Baydun. While Shi'i politicians and Shi'i-majority groups would be central to the left during later junctures in Lebanese history, they were absent in this conflict. Indeed, the alliances in this war predated the sectarianism that became so pervasive in later wars for Lebanon.

Justifying Revolution: The Progressive Socialist Party against Chamoun and the West

Since at least 1949, several popular organizations had become official political parties.[8] In addition to moving their discourses toward adult politics, they replaced their more abstract populist stances – against everything that is not for *al-shabab* and *al-sha'b* under their vision – with ones on specific domestic and regional policies. In this realm, they framed their populism in relation to the Lebanese constitution and the executive's adherence to it. For the majority of popular organizations, President al-Khuri was the violator in 1952, and President Chamoun was the violator in 1958. Ironically, Chamoun was one of the heroes of the 1952 White Revolution. He stood hand in hand with other oppositional politicians across sect lines, including Jumblatt and the Progressive Socialist Party. Armed with a populist, anti-old guard, and inclusive agenda, Chamoun won the presidency based on a promise that he would protect the constitution, not overstep his bounds as the executive, and find balance and cooperation between Lebanon and its Arab neighbors.[9] To the Progressive Socialist Party and their allies, what unfolded was exactly the opposite.

In domestic politics, Chamoun dismantled the system of distributive powers enshrined in the Lebanese constitution. For example, he proposed and passed an electoral law in 1953 that "sectarianized" districts, making them homogenous. In turn, gone were the days of ensuring electoral victory through campaigns across large districts and cross-confessional support;

---

[8] This followed the government's banning of the Syrian Social Nationalist Party after the execution of Antoun Saadeh in 1949, and the officialization of some former associations (the Kata'ib, for instance). The Progressive Socialist Party was an exception as it was always considered a political party since its founding earlier in 1949. For an analysis of this transformation, see Baun, "The Gemmayzeh Incident" (2017), 113–114.

[9] Traboulsi, *A History of Modern Lebanon* (2007), 128–129.

politicians, whether of the *zu'ama'* or not, were now constrained to a confessional cliental.[10] Chamoun then pushed through another law in 1957 that further entrenched the gerrymandered, electoral system.[11] In short, these actions appeared to signal Chamoun's true intentions: he was attempting to pack parliament with supporters, who would then stand behind his desire to change the constitution so he could sit for a second term. Chamoun did little to assuage these fears before May 1958, never publicly affirming or denying the claim.[12]

In regional affairs, Chamoun made a number of remarkable decisions without consulting parliament, reversing the precedent of collaboration on foreign policy issues. They included the following:

• Rejecting the Egyptian-sponsored Arab Defense Pact and nearly joining the pro-Western Baghdad Pact in 1955 – the latter of which the Arab Nationalist Youth referred to as part of broader "colonial conspiracies."[13]

• Refusing to break diplomatic ties with Britain and France after the 1956 Suez Canal Crisis – what Egyptian President Gamal Abdel Nasser considered Chamoun "stab[ing] us ... in the back."[14]

• Approving the Eisenhower Doctrine (a pro-US economic and defense treaty targeting Nasser and his regional allies) in 1957 before it was even approved by US Congress.[15]

These decisions at home and abroad symbolized Chamoun's co-option of the state apparatus and abandonment of Lebanon's neighbors. Concurrently, they were an attempt to constrict what social movement theorist Doug McAdam terms the "political opportunities" for other actors under a pluralistic system.[16] These developments jumpstarted a new oppositional assemblage to Chamoun and his policies. At its center was Jumblatt and the Progressive Socialist Party.

While the two were once close, it appears as if Chamoun had played Jumblatt. Chamoun catered to Jumblatt's anti-Khuri sentiments (recall

---

[10] For more information on the implications of the law, see Hottinger, "Zu'ama' and Parties in the Lebanese Crisis of 1958" (1961), 131; Theodor Hanf, *Coexistence in Wartime Lebanon: Decline of a State and Rise of a Nation* (London: The Centre for Lebanese Studies, 1993), 82; and Elizabeth Picard, *Lebanon, A Shattered Country: Myths and Realities of the Wars in Lebanon*, trans. Franklin Phillip (New York: Holmes & Meier, 1996), 72–73.

[11] Qubain, *Crisis in Lebanon* (1961), 53.

[12] Gerges, "The Lebanese Crisis of 1958" (1993), 3.

[13] Traboulsi, *A History of Modern Lebanon*, 130–133; and *al-Rai*, January 31, 1955.

[14] *President Gamal Abdel-Nasser's Speeches and Press Interviews*. Cited in Gerges, "The Lebanese Crisis of 1958," 4

[15] Attié, *Struggle in the Levant* (2004), 111–119.

[16] Doug McAdam, *Political Process and the Development of the Black Insurgency* (Chicago, IL: University of Chicago Press, 1982).

the Khuri-Jumblatt row that culminated with Yawm al-Barouk, discussed in Chapter 2) and got him to support his presidency in 1952, only to accuse him a year later of receiving money from communists in India.[17] In 1954, tensions between Jumblatt and Chamoun hit an all-time high. Following the Western-backed defense pact between Turkey and Pakistan, which set the framework for the Baghdad Pact, students demonstrated at AUB on March 27 and the police fired shots on them.[18] Several students were injured and one was killed. That student was Hassan Abu Ismail, a young man enrolled at Makassed College who was also a member of the Progressive Socialist Party.[19] Following these "student events," the government defended their police action, and in the words of a contemporary British diplomat, Jumblatt was "now openly bent not so much on a change of Government as a change of regime."[20] Moreover, as one of their young comrades was killed at the hands of a government that seemed to not care, members of the Progressive Socialist Party supported Jumblatt's position and used yearly memorials around Ismail's death to voice their disdain.[21] Only a year later, as reported in *al-Anba'*, "students, parties, associations, and youth [came to] the tomb of the martyr" Hassan to remember him, as well as what he represented: "against the military pacts and in the cause of freedom and happiness of the people."[22]

To turn this anger into official action, Jumblatt and others in parliament formed the United National Front (Jabhat al-Ittihad al-Watani). While it started off rocky – Jumblatt did not sign its first manifesto in April 1957, arguing it had no teeth – the front eventually united around clear and decisive opposition to Chamoun.[23] In a letter sent to the president himself on April 1, 1957, the front claimed that he and his allies were "ignoring the wishes of the people expressed many times and through different means." They included a list of five demands, ranging from ending press censorship to rejecting defense pacts chosen exclusively by the president, followed by this ultimatum: "We must notify you that in case all these demands should not be given effect to, we shall have

---

[17] FO 1018/94, July 30, 1953.

[18] For more on these protests in 1954, see Anderson, *The American University of Beirut* (2011), 142–143.

[19] FO 371/110958, "Student Demonstrations in Beirut," March 30, 1954. *Records at the British National Archives*, London, United Kingdom.

[20] *Al-Anba'*, April 24, 1954; FO 371/110958, "Student Demonstrations in Beirut."

[21] This practice continued into 1958. *Al-Anba'*, March 29 and April 5, 1958.

[22] *Al-Anba'*, April 1, 1955.

[23] Al-Jabburi, *Nasha'a al-Hizb al-Taqaddumi al-Ishtiraki* (2009), 121. For the first manifesto, see Manifesto of the United National Front issued on 1 April 1957. Cited in M. S. Agwani, *The Lebanese Crisis, 1958: A Documentary Study* (New Delhi: Asia Publishing House, 1965), 31–32.

apprehensions regarding the basis of the [upcoming elections] and we shall be compelled to take such practical measures as required in the interests of the country."[24]

In the eyes of the United National Front, none of these demands were fulfilled, especially regarding "an atmosphere of true freedom and honesty" for the parliamentary election of 1957.[25] According to multiple oppositional figures, backed in their assessments by Western diplomats, Chamoun rigged the election to make sure that leaders linked to the United National Front or other anti-Chamoun politicians were not reelected. Instead, younger, Chamoun loyalists took their seats.[26] Perhaps the biggest blow was dealt to the Progressive Socialist Party. For all its strength across the country, and victories in past parliamentary elections, the party failed to win one of its eight attempted campaigns. Jumblatt, who had held his seat since 1943, lost by around 2,000 votes to Kahtan Hamadeh, a political newcomer who supported Chamoun.[27] In a few words, this loss was, according to one al-Anba' headline, "the great conspiracy on Lebanon (mu'amarat al-kubra 'ala Lubnan)."[28]

To Jumblatt, it was Chamoun's corruption that conditioned his party's movement toward armed revolt. In his book, *The Truth of the Lebanese Revolution: The True Motives for the Recent Lebanese Uprising* (1959), he writes: "From that time [the election loss] ... we began to think that revolution had become inescapable (al-thawra idhat la mafhar minha)."[29] Moukhtara, the village of the Jumblatt family estate, became the seat for preparing an armed campaign. As Qubain notes, "Junblatt established the rudiments of a government including armed forces, supply, police, justice and various administrative units."[30] The armed forces, mostly

---

[24] *United National Front's Memorandum to the President of Lebanon*, April 1, 1957. Cited in Agwani, *The Lebanese Crisis*, 33–34.

[25] Agwani, *The Lebanese Crisis*, 34. Just weeks before the election, an oppositional demonstration ended with tear gas fire from the police, over 300 arrests, and the death of at least 15. Qubain, *Crisis in Lebanon*, 54.

[26] Chamoun's election interference, sponsored by the US, was outlined by CIA operative Wilbur Crane Eveland. He describes how "before each area election, he [Chamoun] and I could review the slate of candidates in order to discuss those deserving of support and the amount needed to ensure their election." Wilbur Crane Eveland, *Ropes of Sand: America's Failure in the Middle East* (Toronto: W.W. Norton & Company, Inc, 1980), 251.

[27] Richani, *Dilemmas of Democracy and Political Parties in Sectarian Societies* (1998), 35; and Majid, *al-Intikhabat al-Lubnaniyya* (1992), 121.

[28] *Al-Anba'*, June 21, 1957.

[29] Kamal Jumblatt, *Haqiqat al-Thawra al-Lubnaniyya: al-Dawaf'a al-Haqiqa li-l-Intifada al-Lubnaniyya al-Akhira, 1959* [The Truth of the Lebanese Revolution: The True Motives for the Recent Lebanese Uprising, 1959] (Beirut: Lajnat Turath al-Qa'id al-Shahid, 1978), 52. Also cited in Qubain, *Crisis in Lebanon*, 87.

[30] Qubain, *Crisis in Lebanon*, 75.

young men associated with the Progressive Socialist Party, were trained in the fields and mountains in and around the Chouf, wearing the traditional headdress synonymous with a number of Arab nationalist revolts, including the 1925 Great Syrian revolt and the Arab revolt in Palestine of 1936–1939 (Figure 4.1).[31] Thereafter, training, shooting, and organizing marked the lives of the young rank and file of the Progressive Socialist Party. Dressing the part and holding a gun replaced, for the meantime, waving a party flag.

The parliamentary election loss itself, however, was not the only reason for the Progressive Socialist Party's preparations toward revolution. A July 5, 1957, al-Anba' cartoon indicates as much. It shows a chicken, dressed like Uncle Sam, giving birth to Chamoun. The caption refers to his US-backed coronation as the "egg of the Eisenhower Plan in the Lebanese elections!"[32] In short, Jumblatt and his party's attitudes on international politics and alignments had shifted drastically since its founding. For instance, earlier in the 1950s, Jumblatt contemplated a visit to the United States, part of the State Department's attempts to guide his policies.[33] But by late 1958, he decried Lebanon's "occidental alliance that the United States ... back[ed] up with all their strength."[34] With the West and Chamoun as the enemy of the people, Jumblatt and the Progressive Socialist Party then justified their local path toward insurgency as part of something much bigger. They were part of a constellation of leftist, progressive, and anti-colonial movements across the world. Al-Anba' gave credence to these movements. It provided coverage on "the popular right for the sake of independence," citing liberation struggles in Palestine, the Arab Gulf, South Africa, and Indonesia as inspiration for Lebanon.[35]

To celebrate a new hope for the region and the globe, Jumblatt traveled to Damascus with a large group in February 1958, commemorating the merger of Syria and Egypt, or the United Arab Republic (1958–1961). Young men and women were in tow, listening to speeches of Gamal Abdel Nasser alongside Jumblatt.[36] A British diplomat reported on this trip as follows:

---

[31] For a description of the similar garb associated with the Arab revolt, see Laila Parsons, *The Commander: Fawzi al-Qawuqji and the Fight for Arab Independence 1914–1948* (New York: Hill and Wang, 2016), 121.
[32] *Al-Anba'*, July 5, 1957.   [33] FO 1018/94, "US Invite Jumblat," November 5, 1953.
[34] Farid Assaf, "*al-Hizb al-Taqaddumi al-Ishtiraki*" [The Progressive Socialist Party], in *Ahzab Lubnan* (2003).
[35] *Al-Anba'*, April 5, 1958.   [36] Ibid., March 15, 1958.

Figure 4.1 Two different Progressive Socialist Party battalions, one training (a), the other posing (b), ca. 1957–1958. Progressive Socialist Party, *Rubʿ Qarn min al-Nidal* [A Quarter Century of the Struggle] (Beirut: Progressive Socialist Party, 1974). Courtesy of Dar al-Taqaddumiyya, Moukhtara, Lebanon.

It is being reported in the Opposition press that in the ten days that President Nasser has been in Damascus he has received congratulatory delegations from Lebanon amounting to 300,000 people, or one quarter of Lebanon's total population, an average of one per family. Even allowing for the obvious exaggeration of these figures, the stream of chartered buses and taxis which have been threading [*sic*] their way over the mountains in the past week, and the number of demonstrations which have been held in all the main towns, has given ample evidence of the appeal which the new Union exerts on the Moslem [*sic*] masses of this country. Both Nasser and the Opposition leaders have, on the whole, played their cards well.[37]

This account captures local support for Pan-Arabism and its manifestation: the United Arab Republic. What it fails to recognize, given its full investment in sectarianism as a fixed reality of life, is part of the logic behind this visit. Those who went to Damascus saw the violations in their country as the result of an overreaching executive and a Western-backed Lebanon. Hence, they sought out more progressive partners in their struggle to liberate Lebanon.

Riding the Revolutionary Wave: Claiming a Spot in the Opposition

The Progressive Socialist Party was at the crux of preparations for rebellion; not only organizationally, but geographically. As this popular organization planned a campaign from Mount Lebanon, it was joined by others to make a revolution. They included a host of *zu'ama'* across the country, who hoped to redeem their once coveted positions through a change to the status quo. Saeb Salam (1905–2000) was a *za'im* from Beirut who moved toward "extra-parliamentary and increasingly insurrectionary tactics" following the elections.[38] There was also Ahmad al-Assad (1902–1961), a *za'im* from South Lebanon who "controlled the South" during the 1958 uprising and used its momentum to regain a parliamentary seat in 1960.[39] The *zu'ama'* were not the only ones to join Jumblatt. Several popular organizations, including the Najjadeh Party, Lebanese Communist Party, and Arab Nationalist Youth, joined the opposition. While not in direct communication with Jumblatt, they all followed the Progressive Socialist Party's lead. They criticized Chamoun's authoritarianism, pro-West policy, and stressed that the Lebanese revolution was a case in point for decolonization in the Global South. Unlike the Progressive Socialist Party, their stability and popularity waned in the 1940s–1950s, given internal and external crises. Accordingly, they looked to leverage the revolution to claim a spot within the parliamentary and extra-institutional opposition.

They would need the youth, however, to succeed. At the center of the Najjadeh's reclaiming of the youth, at least *their* youth, was Adnan al-Hakim

---

[37] FO 371/134154, "Lebanon and the U. A. R.," March 6, 1958.
[38] Johnson, *Class and Client in Beirut*, 123.
[39] Rodger Shanahan, *The Shi'a of Lebanon: Clans, Parties and Circles* (London: I.B. Tauris, 2005), 69–70.

(1914–1990), a so-called "symbol for the Najjadeh youth."[40] Hakim joined the group as a young man in the 1930s during his days at the Makassed College, a key Najjadeh recruitment center in Beirut. He later became a troop leader in the 1940s, teaching the youth what it meant to be a *najjad*.[41] And when he became president in the 1950s, he was integral to the Najjadeh organization's reestablishment as a political party. After the organization was disbanded by government decree in 1949 – the same decree that banned the Tala'i' and Kata'ib – and did not reconstitute immediately (unlike the Kata'ib), the Najjadeh stood behind other, more powerful popular organizations.[42] For example, in 1952, the Najjadeh was a part of the oppositional alliance against President Khuri, but held no more than a token role in comparison to the Progressive Socialist Party or Kata'ib.[43] Nevertheless, a year later, Hakim helped resurrect the group through a more radical, anti-colonial platform. In this objective, he reached out to both regional and transnational stakeholders.[44] Bayt al-Najjadeh, where scout meetings were once held, ostensibly became a "resistance house," as Hakim hosted revolutionary leaders from Algeria to Eritrea.[45]

In addition to hosting them, the Najjadeh Party also lobbied on their behalf to the Lebanese government. In late 1957, Hakim sent a statement to the Lebanese Foreign Ministry, writing at length on the Dutch-Indonesian crisis, one in which former colonized Indonesia attempted to seize what it saw as its rightful territory in West Guinea. The document included a picture of Hakim next to a picture of the Indonesian independence leader, Sukarno, and maps of the disputed area. In the text, Hakim framed the crisis as a classic case of egregious "colonial retention" of the "Indonesian motherland." He also criticized other Western powers for supporting Dutch "aggression" and called for the Lebanese government to "hold responsibility in this important issue and to take initiative before others."[46]

As Hakim attempted to bring his group in line with anti-colonial leftist, populist politics, he also moved toward Nasserism. Ideologically

---

[40] Farid Assaf, "*al-Hizb al-Najjadeh*" [The Najjadeh Party] in *Ahzab Lubnan*.
[41] For biographical information on Adnan al-Hakim, see ibid.
[42] *Marsum 'Adad 10691, Hal al-Munazzamat wa-l-Jam'iyyat Shabu al-'Askariyya bi-Istathna' al-Jam'iyyat al-Riyadiyya al-Sarfa* (July 20, 1949).
[43] Traboulsi, *A History of Modern Lebanon*, 125.
[44] Najjadeh Party, *al-Qanun al-Asasi* [Basic Laws] (1953), 3. Najjadeh Party Files, Linda Sadaqah Collection, American University of Beirut.
[45] Assaf, "*al-Hizb al-Najjadeh*."
[46] Najjadeh Party, *Muthkara hawl Tatur al-'Alaqat bayn Indunisiyya wa-Hawlanda* [Notice on the Development of Relations between Indonesia and Holland] (December 11, 1957). Najjadeh Party Files, Linda Sadaqah Collection, American University of Beirut.

speaking, this was not a difficult move for Najjadeh youth. Since the 1930s, they had been taught to celebrate both the Arab and Sunni Muslim foundations for Lebanon, as well as Lebanon's brotherly relations with its Muslim, Arab neighbors. The 1952 Egyptian revolution, an anti-colonial struggle in the most populous Arab country with a Muslim majority, was the catalyst for an even closer unity between Lebanon and Egypt. Under Hakim's vision, the Najjadeh rebranded itself in 1953 as the "cooperative socialist democratic Arab nationalist Najjadeh Party" with the slogan "Arab countries for Arabs (*bilad al-'Arab li-l-'Arab*)."[47] Two years later, Hakim first met Gamal Abdel Nasser. According to one sympathizer, from that trip on Hakim was "treated like a minister" to the Egyptian president.[48]

While Hakim did not run for parliament in 1957, other pan-Arab candidates did and lost. One of them was Saeb Salam. Like Jumblatt, Salam had lost his seat by a margin of 2,000 votes to a political newcomer who supported Chamoun.[49] Salam and Hakim were by no means close friends, as both operated in Beirut, competed for young recruits, and, at least into the early 1940s, the Najjadeh posed a real threat to the Beirut Sunni *zu'ama'*. Yet, in the fallout from the election, it appears both Salam and Hakim realized they could benefit from each other. Salam used Hakim and his Najjadeh youth as a training ground for an insurgency in Beirut. The official name was the Popular Resistance (al-Muqawama al-Sha'biyya), which was led by Salam and commanded by Hakim. Once a scout leader, Hakim thrived in this capacity, organizing and disciplining youth. At the same time, Hakim gained from Salam's connections and influence, which were all disseminated through *Bayrut al-Masa'* ("Beirut by Night"), a new newspaper owned and ran by Salam. With this model, the Najjadeh Party then launched a radio station and newspaper in the midst of the conflict. Named *Sawt al-'Uruba*, "the Voice of Arabism," both presented the conflict to Najjadeh youth and worked to mobilize them.[50]

The story for the Lebanese Communist Party and Arab Nationalist Youth was slightly different. Unlike the Najjadeh, both groups operated underground during the first half of the 1950s. This was in part a result of the large-scale repression they faced, blocking their entrance into official politics.[51] Nevertheless, both groups still had sizable youth

[47] Najjadeh Party, *al-Qanun al-Asasi*, 4.   [48] Assaf, "*al-Hizb al-Najjadeh.*"
[49] Majid, *al-Intikhabat al-Lubnaniyya*, 118.
[50] Multiple popular organizations launched radio stations in 1958, including the Kata'ib and Syrian Social Nationalist Party. This author has been unable to locate any radio files from these groups.
[51] For two examples of repression, see Ismael and Ismael, *The Communist Movement in Syria and Lebanon* (1998), 44; and Kazziha, *Revolutionary Transformation in the Arab World* (1975), 29.

memberships – usually university students and workers – that believed in their social justice, transnational, and radical foundations. Given these credentials, and the momentum of the crisis itself, both reemerged in 1958 as stronger and more effective than ever. The rebuild did not start off well for the Lebanese Communist Party. In the 1957 elections, its preferred candidate in North Lebanon, 'Abdallah Hreiki, only garnered 276 votes, compared to Charles Malik (1906–1987), Lebanon's current foreign minister and supporter of the Eisenhower Doctrine, who received 10,000 more.[52] Moreover, the party did not receive backing from the United National Front, which considered it an "unwanted and embarrassing ally."[53] The reasons for the losses and lack of support stem from a simple fact: the party was communist.

With the backing of the US, UK, and the Eisenhower Doctrine, the "communist threat" became the rallying call for those who defended Lebanon's absolute sovereignty on anti-Nasserist grounds, such as the Kata'ib and the Syrian Social Nationalist Party. On the other side, pan-Arab zu'ama' and popular organizations like the Progressive Socialist Party, Arab Nationalist Youth, and Najjadeh Party never truly embraced communism due to its supposed anti-pluralist foundations. The Lebanese Communist Party's isolation on the domestic front was compounded by regional challenges. As communist powerhouses from China to the Soviet Union celebrated the creation of the United Arab Republic, Nasser purged communists in Egypt and Syria in his goal to create a one-party state.[54]

Primarily because it was on an island, the Lebanese Communist Party dug into its populist, domestic and regional platforms. Farajallah al-Helou (1906–1959), the Secretary General of the Lebanese Communist Party, came out against Chamoun's authoritarianism and actually welcomed the United Arab Republic.[55] More than pleasing regional and domestic leaders, it is likely Helou realized young leftists in Lebanon, whether of the Lebanese Communist Party or other left-leaning groups, would support Nasser's anti-colonial and anti-West platforms. The

---

[52] Qubain, *Crisis in Lebanon*, 57; and Majid, *al-Intikhabat al-Lubnaniyya*, 123.

[53] Qubain, *Crisis in Lebanon*, 56.

[54] For more information on Nasser's repression of communists, both before and after the creation of the United Arab Republic, see Joel Beinin, "The Communist Movement and Nationalist Political Discourse in Nasirist Egypt," *Middle East Journal* 41, no. 4 (1987): 568–584.

[55] Ismael and Ismael, *The Communist Movement in Syria and Lebanon*, 51. This was in contrast to Khalid Bakdash, the leader of the Syrian Communist Party, who rejected the merger and, according to British diplomats, fled to Czechoslovakia following the creation of the United Arab Republic. FO 371/134113, "Report on Communist Policy and Propaganda for King Hussein," March 13, 1958, 2–3.

Lebanese Communist Party's newspaper, *al-Akhbar* ("the News"), then found space for all of the following: articles criticizing the Eisenhower Doctrine and Baghdad Pact, reports on "the decomposition of French colonialism" in Algeria, and a confirmation of the party's support for "the Arab nationalist strugglers" and "demands of the Lebanese people."[56] Hence, even if the official opposition rejected the Lebanese Communist Party, on ideological grounds, the party stood by the opposition's choice to support armed revolt.[57] For this reason, in their time of need, the armed opposition could count on the Lebanese Communist Party. As George Hawi (1938–2008), young communist and eventual leader of the Lebanese Communist Party, fondly remembers, he and his party "participated [in the revolution] with all means available."[58]

It is perhaps hardest to track the Arab Nationalist Youth in the lead-up to 1958, because this popular organization was the only one that preferred to operate in secret – until moments of uprising, that is. In the mid-1950s, its cells across the region waited for the opportunity to become a thorn in the side of Arab heads of state. Recall the group's protest to the pro-West defense pacts, the pact supporters in the Arab world (Jordan and Iraq most notably), and reports that criticized the "clique of [Arab] tyrants" in its newspaper, *al-Rai*.[59] Once the crisis unfolded in Lebanon, the Arab Nationalist Youth began to raise its voice. In early May 1958, the Beirut cell released a statement decrying "Lebanon shackled by chains of colonialism and slavery," and declaring full support for the United Arab Republic and its "uprising to liberate the Arabs."[60]

Simultaneously, the group began to organize for revolt. According to Kazziha, Nayif Hawatmeh (b. 1935), a twenty-three-year-old Jordanian Arab Nationalist Youth leader based in Damascus at the time, organized the movement's armed preparations in Tripoli, while Muhammad al-Zayyat, a Lebanese Arab Nationalist Youth leader from South Lebanon, did the same in the southern city of Tyre.[61] That this group had supporters in cities outside Beirut, and functioning branches, was a product of its expansion efforts in the 1950s. Moreover, that this group could train its young members in shooting and fighting was a product of its militant populism and Habash's dedication to armed struggle.

---

[56] *Al-Akhbar*, May 15, 1958. Cited in Lebanese Communist Party, *Sawt al-Sha'b Aqwa* (1974).
[57] Suleiman, *Political Parties in Lebanon*, 70.
[58] George Hawi in Assaf, "*al-Hizb al-Shiyu'i al-Lubnani*" (2003).
[59] *Al-Rai*, January 24, 1955.
[60] Arab Nationalist Youth, *al-Sadis min Ayar Yawm al-'Aruba fi Lubnan* [The Sixth of May is the Day of Arabism in Lebanon] (May 6, 1958), 1951–1952 Political Crisis Files, Linda Sadaqah Collection, American University of Beirut.
[61] Kazziha, *Revolutionary Transformation in the Arab World*, 32.

In the midst of the growing revolution in Lebanon, and the summer 1958 coup in Iraq that toppled its autocrat, the Arab Nationalist Youth adopted the name the "Arab Nationalist Movement."[62] It appears that Habash believed that the organization's revolutionary agenda had caught on, now constituting an adult, regional movement. Then, side by side with other leftist forces in Lebanon, the Arab Nationalist Movement used its spheres of control to launch a revolution. Both Tripoli and Tyre were on the verge of secession before the army entered the cities to clamp down on demonstrations in early 1958.[63] This was at the very same time Hakim and the Najjadeh youth trained in Beirut, and Jumblatt and his forces readied for their campaign from the Chouf toward Beirut. The government was effectively under siege, but so were popular organizations that were threatened by the opposition's embrace of the United Arab Republic and regime change. This included the Kata'ib and Syrian Social Nationalist Party.

Between Ambition and Ambivalence: The Kata'ib's Take on the Crisis

Commenting on the Kata'ib's disdain for President Chamoun in 1956, the Maronite Patriarch Paul Peter Meouchi stated at a press conference that "I was myself the means of persuading the Phalangists [Kata'ib] to give up their violent campaign against him."[64] The Kata'ib's opposition in 1956 is juxtaposed to its actions by July 1958. Members fought pitched battles alongside Chamoun's security forces and Pierre Gemayel signed a statement indicating "We will continue our [armed] effort in the cause of our independence and freedom."[65] Something changed for the Kata'ib in two years, from their activism against Chamoun to their support in his defense. Equally plausible, as the statement alludes, is that the Kata'ib joined the war in 1958 to defend its vision of sovereign Lebanon, not merely Chamoun.

However, neither of these explanations are present in the majority of scholarship on the 1958 War. In 1961, Qubain contended that "The Phalanges were natural allies of the government" throughout the war, and in 2005 Kanaan claimed that the Kata'ib had "unwavering support for Chamoun and the American landings" to end the conflict in July 1958.[66] Similarly, Picard argues that the Kata'ib acted "in

---

[62] Barut, *Harakat al-Qawmiyyin al-'Arab* (1997), 70.
[63] FO 371/134116, "Riots in the Lebanon," April 3, 1958; and Report, May 11, 1958, Record Group 59, Records at the United States National Archives, College Park, MD.
[64] FO 371/134120, "Press Conference with Patriarch," May 31, 1958.
[65] *Al-'Amal*, July 9, 1958.
[66] Qubain, *Crisis in Lebanon*, 84; and Kanaan, *Lebanon 1860–1960* (2005), 279.

accordance with communal alignments"; that is, it physically supported its Maronite Christian president since the beginning of the crisis in May.[67] These scholars and others mobilize the analytical frame of sectarianism, which conveniently assumes that the Kata'ib was a steadfast supporter of Chamoun because he was Maronite.[68] In contrast, evidence suggests that Gemayel, as the spokesman for the non-elite wing of Christian youth politics, had larger ambitions himself. To be clear, by late 1958 the Kata'ib's actions were a product of the party's sectarian power claim, defending the Christian-led status quo. Nevertheless, this claim must be situated within its changing practices vis-à-vis Gemayel's conflicted position: in contention with Chamoun, but ultimately striving to uphold the system that Chamoun led.

At the same time President Chamoun supported Western defense pacts, challenged freedom of expression as libel, and blocked political activity outside his orbit, the Kata'ib inched closer to the Progressive Socialist Party. Recall their 1955 coordination charter, noted in the introduction of this chapter. It stressed their shared progressive ideologies, in defense of the people, as the reason they "agreed to achieve a better society whose political, economic, social, and education systems derive from the country's potential."[69] A set of al-'Amal articles in 1956 provide details on the renewed alliance, citing judicial reform and Lebanon's sovereign oil rights as key places of joint agreement.[70] None of this amounts to the anti-Chamoun protest that the Patriarch noted in the 1956 press conference.[71] Nonetheless, these public announcements of fraternity with the Progressive Socialist Party must be put in the context of Jumblatt and Chamoun's worsening relationship, especially after the 1954 student protests. Here, acknowledging points of unity between the parties pointed to Kata'ib disapproval with the current government.

The Kata'ib eventually distanced itself from the Progressive Socialist Party, in part due to its more radical calls for regime change in 1957. Instead, Gemayel contemplated entering another anti-Chamoun oppositional front. It styled itself the "non-aligned politicians" or "third force." Gemayel signed a document in late 1957 that characterized Chamoun's foreign and domestic policy as "alarming," and an affront to the

---

[67] Picard, Lebanon, A Shattered Country, 75.

[68] As the Kata'ib was a strong ally of Chamoun by 1975, it is also plausible that those scholars writing in a post-civil war context, like Picard and Kanaan, projected this alliance onto 1958.

[69] Sighat Mithaq al-Ta'awun, 335.   [70] Al-'Amal, January 22 and 29, 1956.

[71] This is not to argue that the Patriarch was exaggerating. He was likely referencing the Kata'ib criticism of government inaction after the 1956 earthquake. For examples of this criticism, see al-'Amal, March 20 and 27, 1956.

constitution, "against the very aims its framers laid down."[72] Gemayel quickly left this group, claiming its main signatory, Ghassan Tuwayni – editor in chief of *al-Nahar* ("the Day") newspaper and supporter of the Syrian Social Nationalist Party – had "known partisan considerations" that contradicted the name of the group.[73] In addition to the party's concerns regarding Chamoun's overreach, Gemayel considered joining this group as a reaction to the Kata'ib's recent rise in official politics. While Jumblatt and others decried the "physical forgery" of the 1957 parliamentary elections, the Kata'ib celebrated "the wonderful victory" that saw party members Joseph Shadir and Joseph Skaff win parliamentary seats.[74] This was the most political power the Kata'ib ever had, and according to the opposition, it was fraudulent and guaranteed by Chamoun himself.[75] However, rather than greet Chamoun with open arms in this moment, Gemayel considered allying with other politicians that were against him. Either Gemayel perceived an opening, one in which he could compete against Chamoun, or he just did not care that much about the president.

One event that illuminates this ambition or ambivalence, even closer to the 1958 War, was Gemayel's trip to the United States in March. Invited by Lebanese expats in the United States and authorized by the State Department, Gemayel spent two days in Rome, three in Paris, and one in London before boarding a steamboat to New York City.[76] While Chamoun was surely an ally of the US, signified by his support of the 1957 Eisenhower Doctrine, it is telling that he disapproved of Gemayel's trip. He informed CIA operative Wilbur Crane Eveland that Gemayel's trip must be postponed as the Kata'ib's "support of [the] govt might prove [a] major factor in time of crisis." Chamoun acknowledged he had not discussed this with Gemayel yet. Still, he needed a Kata'ib response soon to "ensure their previously questionable support" for him.[77]

Chamoun apparently felt the Kata'ib's coldness and looked to change it. Against the wishes of Chamoun, Gemayel went to the US and met with a "large number of US officials" and contacts within the New York and DC Lebanese expat community.[78] One conclusion is that Gemayel

---

[72] *Manifesto Issued by a Group of "Non-aligned" Politicians*, October 2, 1957. Cited in Agwani, *The Lebanese Crisis*, 37.

[73] *Al-'Amal*, October 3, 1957.

[74] *Al-Anba'*, June 21, 1957; and *al-'Amal*, June 9 and 11, 1957.

[75] The Katai'b won two seats in 1951, but lost one in 1953, Majid, *al-Intikhabat al Lubnaniyya*, 93 114.

[76] *Al-'Amal*, March 27, 1958.   [77] Report, March 19, 1958, RG 59.

[78] This trip to the United States is detailed in several *al-'Amal* reports. See *al-'Amal*, March 27, March 29, and April 29, 1958.

assessed that reaching out to diasporic supporters, part of Kata'ib transnational expansion efforts over the last decade, was more important than
being linked to Chamoun. Another is of direct defiance: that Gemayel
went on the trip to signal that the Kata'ib's actions were not determined
by Chamoun, even in his time of need. Either way, Gemayel represented
a challenge, as within the sectarian political system, he could also be the
leader of the country if and when Chamoun wavered. Accordingly, before
the conflict began, Gemayel seemed unconcerned with Chamoun's
defense. He did not return to Lebanon from the US until May 4:
a month after protests broke out against Chamoun across the country
and a week before the start of the 1958 War.[79]

While these dynamics demonstrate the complexity behind Gemayel's
official position regarding Chamoun before the war – simplified as intra-
sect, class-based power struggles – the Kata'ib and its rank and file in no
way aligned with oppositional parties. This was because members of the
Kata'ib were terrified by the creation of the United Arab Republic under
Gamal Abdel Nasser in February 1958 and oppositional interest in it. In
late 1956, Kata'ib youth watched party officials return from the first
general conference with consensus on the "Kata'ib principles" in defense
of the "national unity" of Lebanon.[80] In 1957, Kata'ib members themselves attended lectures on these very principles, with titles like "On the
Constancy of Lebanese Union."[81] The merger of Arab socialist Egypt
and the Ba'ath Party's Syria, right next door, then "directly challenged
[their] notions of [Lebanese, Christian-led] sovereignty."[82]

As the United Arab Republic took shape, members began to subscribe
to the logic that elements emanating from Syria and beyond were
attempting to infiltrate and destroy Lebanon. This was referred to collectively as "the conspiracy" (al-mu'amara), a word with populist rationale
that the Kata'ib had used in the past to describe not only attempts to
threaten Lebanon, but also the group's defense of it.[83] In this context,
even as the Kata'ib refused to come out in support of Chamoun, al-'Amal
ran articles on "the elements of conspiracy," particularly "destructive
communist methods" that were hoping to undermine Lebanon's independence as enshrined in its constitution.[84]

---

[79] From al-'Amal articles of the time, it appears that Gemayel's trip was indefinite, without
a clear return date. However, on April 29, 1958, Gemayel announced he would be
returning home, still a month since the start of anti-Chamoun protests. Al-'Amal,
April 29, 1958.

[80] Lebanese Kata'ib Party, Tawsiyat al-Hizb al-Kata'ib (1993), 5.

[81] Al-'Amal, March 14, 1957.   [82] Kanaan, Lebanon 1860–1960, 244.

[83] For more information on the Kata'ib's deployment of populist conspiracy theories, see
Baun, "The Gemmayzeh Incident of 1949."

[84] Al-'Amal, June 1, 1957.

Perhaps more threatening to the Kata'ib than the merger itself was mass support for it; recall that tens of thousands of Lebanese attended its official coronation in Damascus. Furthermore, multiple popular organizations defended it. That the Kata'ib's once ally, the Progressive Socialist Party, would celebrate this union, and its leader would publicly address crowds next to Nasser himself, was one of the many factors that brought long-time enemies, the Kata'ib and Syrian Social Nationalist Party, onto the same side of this eventual war.

Strange Bedfellows: The Syrian Social Nationalist Party Defends Lebanon?!

The Kata'ib and Syrian Social Nationalist Party had come a long way since a street brawl in 1949 that ended in the government-sanctioned execution of Antoun Saadeh.[85] Only three years later, the two groups stood side by side at an oppositional rally organized by Jumblatt against President Khuri.[86] This meeting alone likely did not smooth over what many Syrian Social Nationalist Party members saw as the Kata'ib-government conspiracy of 1949 to end Saadeh and the party. But in the midst of war in the summer of 1958, the Syrian Social Nationalist Party worked alongside the Kata'ib to defend Lebanon. This convergence was the product of a common enemy. As the Kata'ib ran articles on the conspiracy to end Lebanon, Syrian Social Nationalist Party headlines read "The president of the party exposes the Nasserist communist plan against Lebanon."[87] Regardless of the validity of these accusations, they demonstrate the shared ideological foundations of the Kata'ib and Syrian Social Nationalist Party at this moment in 1958. Of course, the two groups had different views on Lebanese sovereignty, one a staunch Lebanese nationalist, the other for Greater Syria. At the same time, they both perceived Nasserism as a major threat to their position within and outside Lebanon.

Given that the Syrian Social Nationalist Party had rarely supported the Lebanese state, let alone came to its physical defense, it is integral to understand how the party and its 20–25,000 members understood this transformation.[88] Its new position was most clearly outlined in an early

---

[85] For more information on the street brawl, see Baun, "The Gemmayzeh Incident of 1949," 106–112.

[86] This was part of a broader anti-Khuri coalition that included the Progressive Socialist Party, Najjadeh, and Lebanese Communist Party. Traboulsi, *A History of Modern Lebanon*, 125.

[87] *Al-'Amal*, June 1 and 9, 1957; and *al-Bina'*, May 27, 1958.

[88] Al-Makdisi, *al-Ahzab al-Siyasiyya fi Lubnan 'Am 1959* (1959), 105.

1958 pamphlet following the creation of the United Arab Republic, titled "The Recent Unions and Current Affairs." While the writer(s) stresses a belief in Lebanese constitutionalism, they reject the "national sectarian pact (*al-mithaq al-watani al-ta'ifi*)," arguing that it "carries the seeds of its demise."[89] These seeds not only affect Lebanon, they forbid true Syrian unity and allowed "Egyptian conquest for Syria." This subjugation of Syria to Egypt in the form of the United Arab Republic was an "arbitrary political union," not the "unity of social life" for Syria that Saadeh promoted since the party's founding in 1932.[90] Indeed, according to the pamphlet, Saadeh, who, recall, was sentenced to death by the Lebanese government in 1949, would want the transformation of Lebanon as a political religious entity to one that "preserved the general, popular, national wants."[91] Appropriating Saadeh, and the anti-sectarian, popular basis of the party likely resonated with young party members. For the last decade, they had attended yearly celebrations dedicated to Saadeh's martyrdom, as they listened to speeches from current members evoking his name and what he would want for the party.[92] Mobilizing the founder also legitimized the threat from the United Arab Republic and a merger with once-held enemies like the Kata'ib.

Another reason the Syrian Social Nationalist Party linked with the government and Kata'ib was based on the party's recent history. In 1955, a supposed member of the Syrian Social Nationalist Party in Syria killed a colonel named Adnan Malki. The Syrian government then used this murder, one it linked to the Syrian Social Nationalist Party, to justify a sweeping campaign against the party.[93] Back in Lebanon, in a move to gain an unlikely ally, the Chamoun government refused to hand over party officials to the Syrian government.[94] The anti-Chamoun United National Front that was taking shape criticized the president's decision, while others sought measures to neutralize the party. In 1957, for example, unknown assailants assassinated a Syrian Social Nationalist leader in west Beirut.[95] And as the rebellion against Chamoun began in 1958, protesters destroyed Syrian Social Nationalist Party property in Tripoli.[96] While this likely further drove the party into the hands of

---

[89] Syrian Social Nationalist Party, *al-Ittihadat al-Akhira wa-Shaw'an al-Sa'a* [The Recent Unions and Current Affairs] (February 20, 1958), 28–29. Syrian Social Nationalist Party Files, Linda Sadaqah Collection, American University of Beirut.
[90] Ibid., 16.   [91] Ibid., 31.   [92] For one example, see *al-Safa'*, March 3, 1953.
[93] For more information on what is referred to as the "Malki Affair," and its impacts for the Syrian Social Nationalist Party, see Martin, *Syria's Democratic Years* (2015).
[94] Qubain, *Crisis in Lebanon*, 48.
[95] FO 371/134114, Annual Report of Lebanon for 1957, March 3, 1958.
[96] Report, May 11, 1958, RG 59.

Chamoun, this is what many in the Syrian Social Nationalist Party wanted. This included Asad al-Ashqar (1908–1986), the current leader of the group, who realized the historic opportunity of government cover. He then looked to consolidate it, moving closer to Chamoun, and expelling those members who disagreed with the transformation.[97]

From another angle, the Syrian Social Nationalist Party not only sought government protection; it attempted to leverage the energy around the crisis to resurrect and distinguish itself. In multiple statements in 1958, the leadership of the party challenged the Lebanese government's decision to internationalize the crisis, calling it "the biggest blunder," the West's decision "to rely on the old school politics [which] hurled many of the young men of the Arab World into the folds of Communism," and the opposition for "open[ing] the door to the intervention of foreign forces."[98] These statements, highlighting their supposed non-aligned credentials, were often published in the party's new newspaper, al-Bina' ("the Building"), which only just started printing in 1958.

Therefore, threat and opportunity led the Syrian Social Nationalist Party to the Kata'ib and Chamoun, even at the same time that it criticized the president. Like the Kata'ib, it was not a blind supporter of Chamoun, but ironically, became dedicated to Lebanon's sovereignty under the status quo. In a statement only a few days after the war began, the Syrian Social Nationalist Party told the "noble Lebanese people" that given the worsening situation, the party had "mobilized ('aba') all its forces to defending the safety of the citizens, their lives, and livelihoods in every region of Lebanon against this sabotage."[99] In a historic shift, the Syrian Social Nationalist Party began to brand itself as the physical defender of Lebanon.

Not Quite Politicized . . . Yet: Shi'i Perspectives on the Rebellion

Between all of these movements, in support of Lebanon's sovereignty under Chamoun, or against Chamoun, were pillars of the Shi'i community. Indeed, one major generalization surrounding 1958 was that the Shia were largely absent in this war.[100] Individual biographies may

---

[97] For more information on the split within the party in 1957, see Suleiman, *Political Parties in Lebanon*, 98–99.
[98] S-0666–0004, "More about the Crisis: A Survey of the Middle East Tension as Viewed by the Syrian Social Nationalist Party" (August 1958), 4, 9, and 22.
[99] Statement from the Syrian Social Nationalist Party Leaders to the Noble Lebanese People (May 13, 1958). 1958 Crisis Files, Linda Sadaqah Collection, American University of Beirut.
[100] Nir clarifies this in his article, "The Shi'ites during the 1958 Lebanese Crisis," 109.

complicate this claim. There was Ahmad al-Assad, the Shi'i *za'im* who armed and led his supporters in South Lebanon.[101] Or the Speaker of the Parliament, Adel Osseiran (1905–1998), who took a more intermediary role, shuttling between Chamoun, foreign diplomats, the United Arab Republic (which he supported), and his community.[102] Yet, with the Tala'i' defunct since 1949, there was no one popular organization that mobilized based on the plight of the Shia in 1958.

It may appear, then, that non-elite Shia, or more specifically, Shi'i youth, in no way participated in contentious politics in this period of Lebanese history. But as Weiss has shown in the context of the 1930s, and I have established with the Tala'i' in the 1940s, young Shia were politically engaged and active during the early independence period.[103] Grounded in a nationalism that wrote the Shia into Lebanon, Tala'i' leaders advocated for a space in popular and official politics, with a youth vanguard doing its bidding. Thus, instead of assuming passivity, I find it useful to explore where the ancillaries of Shi'i youth politics, including Baydun and his first supporter, Kamel Mroueh, stood during the crisis.

Regarding the former, recall that Baydun was an ally and friend of Khuri since the founding of the Tala'i' in 1944. This placed him in opposition to the new executive and government following Khuri's ouster in 1952. In telling fashion, a year later Baydun lost his parliamentary seat to eventual United National Front member 'Abdullah al-Hajj.[104] But over the years, Baydun proved himself to be a reliable ally for Chamoun. Like Osseiran, Baydun was respected across the political spectrum, which was useful as Chamoun implemented pro-Western policies that received major pushback. Consequently, Baydun rebounded in the 1957 elections, regaining his seat in a landslide victory.[105] Baydun did not comment on allegations of electoral fraud, like Jumblatt and other opposition members. He did, however, make a call for "stability and friendly brotherly cooperation" in this tumultuous time.[106] Those who were a part of the United National Front likely saw this call as slightly disingenuous. This was because Baydun won his seat in this rigged election as part of the "National Unity List," alongside the Kata'ib's Joseph Shadir, Prime Minister Sami al-Solh, and other Chamoun allies.[107]

---

[101] Hottinger, "Zu'ama' and Parties in the Lebanese Crisis of 1958," 130.
[102] For an example of Osserian caught between US interests and the opposition, see *Foreign Relations of the United States, 1958–1960: Lebanon and Jordan*, Volume XI, ed. Louis J. Smith (Washington, DC: Government Printing Office, 1992), Document 192.
[103] Weiss, *In the Shadow of Sectarianism* (2010).
[104] Majid, *al-Intikhabat al-Lubnaniyya*, 108.   [105] Ibid., 108, 119.
[106] Maki, *Rashid Baydun* (1967), 127.   [107] *Al-'Amal*, June 13, 1957.

In early May, days before this war started, UK ambassador George Middleton referred to Baydun, longtime parliamentarian, founder of the prestigious ʿAmiliyya school, and leader of the Talaʾiʿ until its dissolution, as a "genial Moslem [sic] hack politician of no great significance."[108] This is contradicted by a contemporary news report that referred to Baydun as "one of the biggest personalities in Lebanon."[109] On balance, it appears that Chamoun valued Baydun very much. In March 1958, he appointed him to the post of Minister of Defense. The timing of this appointment was no coincidence, quickly after the announcement of the United Arab Republic and Jumblatt's subsequent visit to Damascus. Chamoun and his allies saw the journey and endorsement as a threat, and wanted a strong, reputable person to enter the position.

Baydun's first major duty as Defense Minister was a fact-finding mission in Tyre, ground zero for the revolt in the making. On April 4, he visited the southern coastal city, made a report of suggestions that ostensibly reflected the "position and demands" of the people in Tyre, and then sent it to the government.[110] He was tasked to do the same thing in Tripoli in May, but could not go because of the upheaval there led by the Arab Nationalist Movement and Lebanese Communist Party.[111] A few weeks later, Baydun gave a speech to his supporters. He said the following:

The security situation in the country is not stable, which spreads chaos and concern, of particular [concern] that some regions of Lebanon are devoid of security forces ... [.] The situation is deeply affecting me, it destroys my heart, and in my soul, I feel that I have to submit my resignation.[112]

Baydun's official reason for his resignation, then, was guilt. His post was to defend the country, and he had let his country down, which crushed his soul. Out of professional courtesy to the president, not opposition to his rule, he could no longer serve. Perhaps unsatisfying in its straightforwardness, it is confirmed by events that followed. Baydun did not immediately switch sides, nor criticize Chamoun for his handling of the war. In fact, he criticized Fuad Shihab (1902–1973), army general and president-elect (1958–1964), for his decision to remain neutral as the conflict began.[113] On the other hand, Middleton claims in reports back to London there was "strong Moslem [sic] pressure" for Baydun to resign.[114] Moreover, after the conflict, Baydun adopted more of a pan-Arab, Nasserist line,

---

[108] FO 371/134115, Annual report of leading personalities in Lebanon, May 2, 1958.
[109] Maki, *Rashid Baydun*, 126   [110] Ibid., 133–134.
[111] Report, May 11, 1958, RG 59.   [112] Maki, *Rashid Baydun*, 135.
[113] Nir, "The Shiʿites during the 1958 Lebanese Crisis," 120.
[114] FO 371/134119, Middleton, no. 593, May 23, 1958.

potentially discarding the Lebanese nationalism that built up the Tala'i''s platform and the youth that embodied it.[115] Regardless of whether he was honest about his rationale for resignation, Baydun was torn. On one side was the sectarian system that he had lobbied so hard within, and had given himself, his community, and his group a space. On the other side was the opposition that guaranteed total, democratic social revolution with a seat for him at the table.

Kamel Mroueh, the once 'Amiliyya teacher and the Tala'i''s first endorser (discussed in Chapter 1), also found himself in a precarious position in 1958. While concerned with Chamoun and the sectarian political system, in a similar vein to the Kata'ib and Syrian Social Nationalist Party, Mroueh also raised more issues with communism, Nasser, the United Arab Republic, and the opposition's move toward them. This may be why his newspaper, *al-Hayat*, and its offices in Beirut were the site of a bomb attack in September 1957.[116] He was also targeted because of his support of loyalist Shi'i politicians like Baydun. He never gave up his friendship with Baydun, and during the 1957 elections, supported his candidacy, reporting on him favorably in issues of *al-Hayat*.[117] None of these affiliations or criticism meant that Mroueh was not an Arab nationalist. Rather, like those on the left, he sought out solidarity with Arab countries and independence struggles, including Algeria. On April 1, 1958, *al-Hayat* publicized an event held in Beirut by the "the National Committee to Support Algeria." This benefit included a call for donations and speeches from Lebanese advocates of the cause. One speaker was Rashid Karami (1921–1987), future Lebanese prime minister who would support the rebellion in 1958.[118] While he gave a symbolic space for these anti-colonial, pan-Arab, nationalist ideals, he withheld praise for Nasser and the United Arab Republic.[119]

This was juxtaposed to Nizar al-Zein, the editor in chief of another Shi'i-led publication, *al-'Urfan* ("the Knowledge"). *Al-'Urfan* was printed out of Sidon in the south, which was known as an oppositional center. In comparison with *al-Hayat*, this journal was much more sympathetic to the United Arab Republic and regional alignment behind Nasser.[120] A June 1957 article aired support for the "democratic goals of the United Arab National Front" and promised to "fight any treacherous colonial aggression and expose all foreign conspiracies."[121] And later in July 1958, the journal printed a poem that took up the current armed

---

[115] Nir, "The Shi'ites during the 1958 Lebanese Crisis," 127.
[116] FO 371/134114, Middleton, no. 33, March 3, 1958.   [117] *Al-Hayat*, June 11, 1957.
[118] Ibid., April 1, 1958.   [119] Nir, "The Shi'ites during the 1958 Lebanese Crisis," 122.
[120] Ibid., 127.   [121] *Al-'Urfan*, June 1957.

struggle in Lebanon. It framed the revolution as one between "the people of revenge and the army [that] fears the owners of the house."[122] The latter is a reference to the Christian-led state and its surrogates, who did not care about Arab causes in general or Shi'i ones in particular. At the same time, Mroueh printed pictures of destruction to the house. While he did not chastise the opposition, nor make a strong case for a foreign conspiracy, al-Hayat provided evidence of the impacts of explosions outside government buildings.[123]

Mroueh and Zein reflect two, intellectual Shi'i responses to the war, one tepidly in support of the status quo, like Baydun, one riding the waves of revolution. While Zein and his writers mobilized his readership to act, Mroueh and Baydun stressed this to their communities: remain calm and trust in Lebanon's sovereignty. Baydun and Mroueh's views, those which gave the Shia a platform within the system in the 1930s, became more and more passé with time. By the 1960s, such status quo views were perceived as being supportive of colonial designs. That Mroueh held onto this stance for Lebanon, even if critical of its governing, would be of great consequence; he was assassinated in 1966 by an ardent Nasserist.[124]

Unfortunately, the available sources do not allow a retelling of what happened to those thousands of young men who came up through 'Amiliyya schools, the 'Amiliyya scouts, and the Tala'i', or what they thought of the conflict. Shanahan suggests that many joined the Arab Nationalist Movement. This was because Muhsin Ibrahim, the Lebanese leader of the movement, was Shi'i and those who shared his class background (poor, uneducated, from the south), were drawn to the group.[125] Other young Shia joined the Lebanese Communist Party or the Progressive Socialist Party, as scholars record that nearly 50 percent of their members were Shia by the mid-to-late twentieth century.[126]

The actions of young Shia, some thirty years later, appear to confirm this movement left. Shi'i social movements like Amal and Hezbollah transformed community politics, from being content with a space to mobilizing disenfranchisement through militant rhetoric and action.[127] Indeed, Baydun and Mroueh were some of the last of their kind. They either hid or subsumed Shiism as a means to be Lebanese. Thereafter,

---

[122] Ibid., July 1958.   [123] Al-Hayat, May 21, 1958.
[124] Nir, "The Shi'ites during the 1958 Lebanese Crisis," 122.
[125] Shanahan, The Shi'a of Lebanon, 98.
[126] Richani, Dilemmas of Democracy and Political Parties in Sectarian Societies, 70; and Majed Halawi, A Lebanon Defied: Musa al-Sadr and the Shi'a Community (Boulder, CO: Westview Press, 1992) 111.
[127] For more information on the foundation of Amal and Hezbollah, see Augustus Richard Norton, Amal and the Shi'a: Struggle for the Soul of Lebanon (Austin, TX: University of Texas Press, 1987).

individuals like Musa al-Sadr (1928–1978), Nabih Berri (b. 1938), Ragheb Harb (1952–1980), and Hassan Nasrallah (b. 1960) were the agents in the production of a new Shi'i contentious politics. It was Lebanese, like those before, but in violent opposition to the Christian-led Lebanese state and its allies.

Conclusion: Rethinking Sectarianism in the 1958 War

This chapter has meant to establish the causes for the 1958 War, and in turn, the diversity of perspectives among popular organizations leading up to the war. Indeed, there were two main camps: those against President Chamoun and his domestic and foreign policies, and those who assessed the status quo was better than a Nasserist alternative. But within these camps, some organizations led the charge while others followed their lead. Others stood with the government on principle, others based on opportunity. At the same time, all groups deployed an understanding of sovereign, constitutionally bound Lebanon, and its place within the world, as the backdrop for their claims. However, foreign diplomats did not often stress these nuances when discussing the roles of popular organizations in the war. For instance, in one 1958 profile of Hakim, all the UN noted was that he was forty years old, the "Leader of the Moslem [sic] Youth Organisation AL NAJJADH," that he "has money, is young fanatick [sic]," and he is "not very intelligent."[128] Also, across UN, US, and UK reports in 1958, one would be hard-pressed for any reference to the Progressive Socialist Party. Instead, in its place, like one UK report read, was reference to "the Druzes [sic], under command of Kamal Jumblatt."[129]

Apparently, the UN never investigated Hakim's 1957 call for Lebanon to support anti-colonial efforts in Indonesia. Otherwise, officials would have known he was at most, well-read, or at least, connected to those who were. Moreover, the UK must have forgotten that Jumblatt lost his parliamentary seat in the 1957 elections to Kahtan Hamadeh, a pro-Chamoun Druze Muslim who had support, however little, from the Druze community of Mount Lebanon. As the analysis of Baydun, Mroueh, and Zein demonstrated, even communities – Shi'i or Druze – were split on whether this was a revolution that must be realized or a crisis that must be stopped. As scholars have accounted for this fact within the zuʿamaʾ, including those Christians that were against Chamoun, or those Muslims who were for him, I find it necessary to rethink sectarianism for popular organizations in 1958.

[128] S-0666–0005, Intelligence on Adnan Hakim (1958).
[129] FO 371/134123, Middleton, no. 793, June 17, 1958.

With this approach, I argue that these groups were torn on the issue of how best to defend Lebanon, not merely the sect that their group represented. To be clear, any popular organization that stood closer to Chamoun defended the Christian-led, sectarian status quo. Nevertheless, their reasons and actions cannot be reduced to sect alone. They must be paired with other factors, including group ideology (sometimes irrespective of sect, like the Syrian Social Nationalist Party), ambition (the Kata'ib, as a group that could benefit from Chamoun's demise, as long as the system was intact), and intra-sect class disputes (Gemayel and the non-elite Kata'ib versus Chamoun). More broadly, all groups' perspectives in this specific moment of contentious politics were both shaped by the sectarian structure of politics, and worked to change or reinforce the structure. This reality for popular organizations illustrates their agency, even if that agency is structured by – or against – sectarian power claims.

That both sides of the war used Lebanon as the foundation, and that their disparate arguments worked in recruiting young members to fight, represents what was at stake in 1958: winning Lebanon. These groups were no longer just youth-centric though. As reflected in their name changes in the 1950s, such as the Najjadeh Organization to the Najjadeh Party, or the Arab Nationalist Youth to the Arab Nationalist Movement, popular organizations were now adult political parties and movements with adult concerns and causes. However, as they shed off their youth in theory, in practice, the culture of being young and active followed them into 1958. Whether it was their rituals or populist discourse, youthfulness was central to the production of sectarian violence.

5   Fighting the Punks
The Routine Practices and Sectarian Outcomes
of the 1958 War

Renée Bakhos and Amin Farid Fuleihan were desperate. It was the summer of 1958, they were in their twenties, they had recently finished college, and both needed a job. Bakhos, a graduate from Souers Franciscaines (a Franciscan women's college), was fluent in Arabic, French, and English, and applied for a typist position.[1] Fuleihan, an AUB alum, had just started his second year of medical school at the same institution and looked for "any job that is available."[2] They sought positions with the same employer: the United Nations Observation Group in Lebanon (UNOGIL). UNOGIL was tasked in late June to observe the war for Lebanon, and in particular, government accusations of widespread infiltration from Syria into Lebanon. Fuleihan had heard "the U.N. Observation Group is in need of some educated people" and was "interested in helping the U.N. Group in any kind of work that will help my country to overcome this crisis."[3]

At the same time, "the representatives of different young Lebanese communities" made a very different case to foreign actors. Following the US military intervention on July 15, these youth penned the following appeal, in English, addressed to American soldiers:

We represent all young people of the freedom-loving Lebanon and we have been always fighting in the past for friendly relations with the United States, because we believed that America respected the ideals of liberty and independence of the small peoples. However, the occupation of our country . . . gave us evidence that to-day's [sic] America of Eisenhower-Dulles is a worst enemy of all peoples in the world and you, the soldiers of that America should play the role of the bloody butchers and murderers . . . [.] We strongly demand: Yankee, Go Home! . . . If our just demand are not fulfilled . . . we, together with our fathers and brathers [sic] shall take our arms and fight against you till the full victory . . . [.] Let the ideals of the liberty bless us in this sacred struggle as they blessed the American

---

[1] AG-056, United Nations Observation Group in Lebanon (UNOGIL) (1958), S-0650–007, Application, Renée Bakhos to UNOGIL (Sept 30, 1958).
[2] S-0650–007, Application, Amin Farid Fuleihan to UNOGIL (July 9, 1958).   [3] Ibid.

people in 1776 in his struggle for the independence of America. Long Live Free Lebanon![4]

It is unclear if any popular organization coordinated this appeal, or if the signers were members of popular organizations that opposed the US landing on the shores of Beirut. However, given the call to arms, it is likely that these youth fought alongside groups within the opposition, whether the Najjadeh in Beirut, the Arab Nationalist Youth in South Lebanon, the Lebanese Communist Party in North Lebanon, or the Progressive Socialist Party in Mount Lebanon. And as the press of these popular organizations and their allies reported, young people, aged in their twenties like Bakhos and Fuleihan, scarified their *futuwwa*, died in the war, and became martyrs for Lebanon.

Bakhos, Fuleihan, and the Lebanese youth against the US represent the multiple reactions of young people in the midst of the 1958 War. Some flocked to the UN for jobs, hoping that their steps toward adulthood would pay off, even in the context of war. Others took this moment of upheaval to join a popular cause and war that they equated to the US Revolution of 1776, a revolution they had clearly studied. Having discussed in Chapter 4 the causes and ideological reasons by which popular organizations and their young members came to participate in this war, the present chapter turns to the practices of young people in the war, and those popular organizations that mobilized them. From this vantage point, we see reactions not addressed in the applications of Bakhos and Fuleihan or the calls of the Lebanese youth. First are the rituals of popular organizations, those that were observable in their earlier histories and became central to the daily life of young fighters during the war. Second is the process by which their youth culture became perceived not as a source of pride, but sectarian violence.

The chapter starts in May 1958 with the spark of the war: the assassination of oppositional journalist Nasib al-Matni on May 8. It sketches the Kata'ib's shift toward preparing for war in July and its full investment in the current sectarian order by August. This eventual defense was, in part, the product of UNOGIL's findings: there was no widespread intervention into Lebanon from the United Arab Republic. Once the Kata'ib's Lebanon appeared to be in jeopardy, they began to fight for it. The chapter then takes up two critical fronts from the perspective of oppositional and pro-government popular organizations. The first is the Chouf campaign and the Mount Lebanon front. This area was a battleground between the Progressive Socialist Party and Syrian Social Nationalist Party throughout the summer of 1958. A focus on the small town of Shemlan, with two branches of organizations fighting each other, allows

---

[4] S-0666–0004, Undated, unsigned appeal from Lebanese youth to American soldiers (? 1958).

for an exploration of logics of violence at the micro level. The sources that emerged from this war, whether individual reports or collective memories, help confirm the role of both ideology and ritual in the war.

The other front that this chapter analyzes was in the capital, largely fought over by the Kata'ib and Najjadeh. The focus on the Beirut front is broken into two. First, I investigate the place of rituals in the Kata'ib's acts of war during their so-called general strike (late September to mid-October). Whether a protest flanked by women and boys, or a funeral to a young martyr, I argue that what young people did during this war was not unlike the youthful activities they had engaged in for decades. This was similar for popular organizations within the opposition as well, which used holidays, activities, and martyrdom as tools to get young people to fight. Led by the youth themselves, these rituals, then, allowed young people to make sense of their violent practices. Second, I take up the production of sectarian violence in Beirut with the help of popular organizations. As the battle for the capital was along Christian-Muslim lines, in predominantly Christian-Muslim neighborhoods, scholars have aptly characterized the violence as sectarian. Yet, I find that more often than not, scholars have used this simple reality to project blatant, fixed, and explosive sectarianism onto this phase of the war.

A look at the sources of popular organizations, their elite allies, and reports from foreign diplomats, both before and during this last phase of the war, uncovers something more complex. When the opposition singled out popular organizations that supported the government, including the Kata'ib and Syrian Social Nationalist Party, they often described them using coded language. The terms included were "boys," "lads," "deviants," and "punks," which were then similarly used by the Kata'ib and Syrian Social Nationalist Party to describe their foes. All of these words turned youth empowerment and *futuwwa* on its head. Used by multiple groups, they were meant to link the youth culture these groups forged directly to sectarianism. This feature was one new aspect of the violence in 1958. Not only were the acts of violence committed by young people, but they were depicted as maddened – implicitly sectarian – youth. Second, the war took place across the country, for Lebanon as a nation-state, which was different from prior moments of collective violence, such as the 1860 War that created the phenomenon of sectarianism.[5] In a final difference to earlier episodes of violence in Lebanon, the war and its sectarian other was explained through a discourse of populism, one that had been mobilized by popular organizations since the 1920s. As will be described in the conclusion of this chapter, these trends, unfolding in

---

[5] For more information on this case, see Makdisi, *The Culture of Sectarianism* (2000).

1958, share striking similarities with later cases of sectarian violence in Lebanon and beyond.

From Study Sessions to Drilling: The Kata'ib Mobilizes for War

If the "spark" of the 1975–1990 Lebanese Civil War was the infamous Kata'ib shooting of twenty-eight Palestinian men, women, and children riding a bus from a rally, the 1958 War was set off by the death of another innocent bystander. Nasib al-Matni (b. ca. 1910) was editor in chief of a newspaper called *al-Tallaghraf* ("the Telegraph"), which in recent years had been quite critical of President Camille Chamoun's domestic and regional decision-making. On the early morning of May 8 while walking between his office and apartment in west Beirut, Matni was shot in the heart by unknown assailants. Some believed these assailants were linked to the Syrian Social Nationalist Party.[6] To add to the intrigue, anonymous letters were found on Matni's body, letters he presumably received, which threatened his life if he continued to criticize Chamoun.[7] Later that day, leaders and parties of the opposition called for a general strike across the country against the government, and president, that could let this happen.

The Kata'ib followed suit. It dedicated the May 9 edition of *al-'Amal* to Matni, "the father of jihad," and called on state authorities to find his murderers and hold them responsible. After a meeting to discuss these "acts of crime and terrorism," they also participated in the subsequent newspaper strike alongside oppositional papers like the Progressive Socialist Party's *al-Anba'* and Ghassan Tuwayni's *al-Nahar*.[8] However, following their initial respects to Matni, the Kata'ib continued to invest in a foreign infiltration narrative; that is, outside forces exploited the tragedy to sabotage Lebanon and opposition forces helped along the way. For instance, a May 18 headline in *al-'Amal* read "Syrian officer and soldier arrested in the Chouf."[9] Disclaimers like this were meant to implicate Kamal Jumblatt and the Progressive Socialist Party, based in the mountain, directly in the destruction of Lebanon under Syrian guidance. The Kata'ib's new ally, the Syrian Social Nationalist Party, took a similar approach, leading a May 24 edition of *al-Bina'* with the following: "2,000 Syrian infiltrators (*mutasaliyyun Shami*) attack 'Adbel in

---

[6] FO 371/134116, Lebanese Opposition Paper Chief Murdered, May 8, 1958.
[7] For the most detailed retelling of Matni's death, see Desmond Stewart, *Turmoil in Beirut: A Personal Account* (London: Allan Wingate, 1958), 23; and Qubain, *Crisis in Lebanon* (1961), 68–70.
[8] *Al-'Amal*, May 9, 1958.   [9] Ibid., May 18, 1958.

Akkar."[10] In these examples and others, these groups acted like a legal team, compiling a case file for infiltration.

This compilation of evidence served more than a warning to their reading publics; it was meant to get world powers involved in the fate of Lebanon. This coincided with the Lebanese government's official complaint to the United Nations on May 22. Apparently after trying to make contact with both the United Arab Republic and the Arab League, Karim Azkhoul, Lebanon's representative to the UN, argued in front of the Security Council that "the intervention of the United Arab Republic in the internal affairs of Lebanon . . . is likely to endanger the maintenance of international security and peace."[11] This complaint generated UNOGIL's mission, which was to "ensure that there is no illegal infiltration of personnel or supply of arms or other materials across the Lebanese borders."[12]

There were a number of individual cases of infiltration (including, according to US intelligence, the smuggling of arms from Syria to Lebanon by the former Belgian consul general to Syria), but UNOGIL's most damning finding regarded an incident that took place in Beirut on June 16.[13] Two Syrian youth from Jableh – some 95 kilometers north of the Syria-Lebanon border – working as fishermen in Lebanon were charged with throwing bombs near Rivoli cinema in the center of downtown. While one of the accused pleaded innocent in front of a Lebanese military court, the other, Ibrahim Muhammad Moussa Sulayman Haydar (seventeen years old), admitted he threw a bomb. According to the initial interrogation reports and first UNOGIL report, Haydar stated that while back in Jableh in March 1958, the other accused, Mahmoud Abboud Ibrahim (twenty-one years old), led Haydar to a "recruiting place." Thereafter, "he [Haydar] was brought under pressure to Beirut and kept under surveillance at the house of a local opposition leader," and "they [the Lebanese handlers] told me that if I did not come back [without detonating the bomb], they would denounce me to the Lebanese army."[14]

---

[10] *Al-Bina'*, May 24, 1958.

[11] *Lebanese Complaint to the Security Council*, May 22, 1958. Cited in in Agwani, *The Lebanese Crisis* (1965), 120.

[12] AG-056, United Nations Observation Group in Lebanon (UNOGIL) (1958), S-0650–0001, Resolution adopted by the Security Council at its 835th meeting (June 1958).

[13] McClintock to Secretary of State, May 12, 1958, RG 59, no. 3787.

[14] AG-056, United Nations Observation Group in Lebanon (UNOGIL) (1958), S-0650–0008, First Report of the United Nations Observation Group in Lebanon (July 4, 1958), 9; and S-0666–004, Interrogations – 23rd and 24th June 1958 (June 25, 1958), 5–6.

In between Syrian youth such as Haydar and the United Arab Republic were oppositional popular organizations like the Arab Nationalist Youth. While I already discussed their preparations for revolution in Chapter 4, it is important to consider who was funding this group. As al-Kubaisi notes, "the late 1950s can be considered the climax of the Arab Nationalist reliance on the UAR in their fight against the Chamoun government." More specifically, he claims that when the group fought against Chamoun's private security in the north of the county, they were doing so with arms provided through a Syrian United Arab Republic army officer.[15] Collectively, examples like this worked to fuel the Kata'ib and Syrian Social Nationalist Party's infiltration narrative and their perception of threats, whether these threats came from external forces or local actors.

While both were threatened by the United Arab Republic-oppositional alliance, only Syrian Social Nationalist Party youth were active in the first phase of the war. From May 8 to July 4, the Kata'ib, at least in any organized sense, did not prepare for war. Pierre Gemayel admitted in late June that although "some comrades armed for self-defense," the party was not yet buying and supplying weapons for its members.[16] A few weeks later, al-'Amal carried this "newsworthy" information: student study sessions would be held throughout the summer to prepare for the upcoming year of classes. It also noted the "summer schedule" of the central political office. This body, the basis of organizational coordination, was only holding public meetings once a week, as far as two months into the war.[17] Juxtaposed to this apparent aloofness was a July 5 al-'Amal call, included below in its entirety:

Due to the extraordinary conditions that inflict the nation we plead to the Kata'ib inhabitants in Beirut and the nearby areas which are able to come to the party center (bayt al-hizb al-markazi) for the sake of formal training (al-tadrib al-nizami) and to register your name among the officials in the party office for a census (ihsa'hum) and practice deliberation exercises (mawlat al-tamrin) in the place [Bayt al-Kata'ib] before the general regulatory body and this [will take place] every day starting at 5 p.m.[18]

This ad ran for three more days, where ostensibly the party was gathering new recruits in Kata'ib-linked neighborhoods each day. Then on

---

[15] Basil al-Kubaisi, Harakat al-Qawmiyyin al-'Arab [The Arab Nationalist Movement] (Beirut: al-Ittihad al-'Am li-l-Kitab wa-l-Sahafahiyyin al-Filastiniyyin, 1974), 77–78.

[16] McClintock to Dulles, June 25, 1958, RG 59, no. 5100.

[17] Al-'Amal, July 4, 1958. Also, these updates were the first of their kind throughout the summer of 1958 (i.e., not daily reminders), indicating they were considered newsworthy events from the Kata'ib perspective in July.

[18] Al-'Amal, July 5, 1958.

July 8, there was an "oathing ritual," or party (*hilf al-yamin*), celebrating these newly trained members in the company of hundreds of supporters.

From preparing for school to practicing military drills, something changed in early July. In part, this can be attributed to increased fighting over the last month near Kata'ib headquarters in Beirut. Bombs were placed near the shops of Bab Idriss in downtown Beirut and the east Beirut neighborhood of Gemmayzeh, and pitched street fighting continued into early July along the Bishara al-Khuri highway that divided Basta (and the headquarters of Saeb Salam's campaign and the Najjadeh) from the neighborhoods near downtown, which the Kata'ib, Syrian Social Nationalist Party, and gendarmerie forces occupied.[19] These occurrences were punctuated by the death of the first Kata'ib member in the 1958 War. This reality worked to transform the Kata'ib policy from rhetorically to physically armed.

On July 7, 1958, two days after the initial Kata'ib mobilization announcement, Nadim Baddur was a "victim of gunshots" while working at the Air France headquarters in downtown Beirut. Baddur, a young man who hailed from the village of Hammana in Mount Lebanon and served as a member of the party in the Department of Expatriates, was shot in the neck while trying to close the main window of the office to prevent the barrage of fire from entering the building. The obituary in *al-'Amal* laments the loss of Baddur first and foremost, but also points to Air France's office location in the middle of other civilian destinations, including hotels, other office buildings, and the Capital cinema. That the "traitorous criminals" (*al-mujrimun al-khawana*) would attack such an area demonstrated a new, immediate threat.[20] This distinct framing around death marks the beginning of the Kata'ib's use of individual youth martyrs to mobilize living young people to fight.[21] Accordingly, they gave Baddur an honorific, "the strength of the youth," *al-'aziz al-shabab*. They also sponsored multiple remembrance gatherings for him, ranging from Bayt al-Kata'ib in Beirut to the youth organization in Hammana.[22] In other words, common frames and routine Kata'ib rituals were now being deployed to get other Kata'ib *shabab* to defend Lebanon in new ways.

---

[19] Examples of Beirut violence the Kata'ib found worth mentioning included, *al-'Amal*, June 4 and 5, 1958.
[20] *Al-'Amal*, July 8, 1958.
[21] For more information on how parties to Lebanon's later civil war mobilized martyrs, see Zeina Maasri, *Off the Wall: Political Posters of the Lebanese Civil War* (London: I.B. Tauris, 2009).
[22] *Al-'Amal*, July 8 and 9, 1958.

Another immediate reason for the Kata'ib shift was UNOGIL's findings, detailed in its first report, released on July 4, one day before the Kata'ib mobilization announcement. UNOGIL found that this was a domestic crisis; there was no conclusive evidence for a sustained United Arab Republic intervention in Lebanon. As noted in the report, "there is little doubt ... that the vast majority [of 'armed men'] was in any case composed of Lebanese."[23] In the bluntest of terms, no foreign interference meant that Lebanon's complaint to the UN would not trigger a Security Council vote for UN intervention. The connection between the release of this report on July 4 and the Kata'ib's public reaction and mobilization of members on July 5 is more than coincidental. Even if not a Chamoun loyalist, Gemayel had for some time supported the government in its attempts to "marshall all their resources to get help available" from the international community to protect Lebanon's sovereignty.[24] The UN decision then dashed Gemayel's hopes of an outside solution, and from the party's perspective, meant that no one was coming to rescue Lebanon. Instead, the Kata'ib had to save its vision for Lebanon.

This moment of action, however, could not just begin. In line with membership rituals of popular organizations since their early days, the moment needed to be made official. The July 8 Kata'ib oathing ceremony incorporated and trained new members and authenticated youth rank-and-file participation in the war. Moreover, the event speaker declared to the youth members, in the midst of the ordinary pageantry of these events, "stand up to the fire while it engulfed the enemies." Here, this ceremony placed violent practices within routine group life: dressing up in uniforms, flag waving, and singing.[25] This shift was surprisingly seamless, also clear in the Hammana ceremony to remember Baddur, the first Kata'ib martyr of 1958. Interestingly enough, the same band that played anthems months before the war to celebrate new members were now drumming and marching in practices related to death and those that signified future, physical action.[26]

At least for the Kata'ib, this move toward fighting was short lived. This was due to the US intervention of July 15. The quick shift in US and UK policy, due to revolution in Iraq and potential overthrow in Jordan, fulfilled Gemayel's wishes and provided security around Kata'ib downtown locations.[27] For the meantime, there was no reason for Kata'ib

---

[23] First Report of the United Nations Observation Group in Lebanon (July 4, 1958), 7.
[24] McClintock to Dulles, July 9, 1958, RG 59, nn, 335.   [25] Al-'Amal, July 13, 1958.
[26] Recall the Hammana member festival described in Chapter 1. Al-'Amal, April 7, 1958.
[27] For more on the US policy shift toward intervention in Lebanon, see Gendzier, Notes from the Minefield (1997).

fighters to lift a finger. Thus, this history not only demonstrates under what conditions the routine practices of the Kata'ib were transforming. It also shows that their ad hoc attempts to recruit new young fighters in July, not May, were determined by unfolding events, not an immutable sectarian affiliation to Chamoun.

The Chouf-Beirut Campaign: Logics of Violence on Both Sides of the Conflict

By midsummer, war had become a reality of life in many parts of Lebanon (Figure 5.1). What started as mere rhetoric transformed to routines of violence. One of the key sites for these practices of war was the Chouf and Mount Lebanon front in June to July. Neighborhoods, villages, and their linked highways and streets became boundaries for different fighting forces. On the south and east side of the Mount Lebanon region was the Progressive Socialist Party, and on the north and western boundary, the Syrian Social Nationalist Party. A British diplomat saw the two as "the most effective armed supporters of President Chamoun and the Opposition respectively" in the area.[28] The Progressive Socialist Party considered the Syrian Social Nationalist Party to be the embodiment of treachery and treason. Jumblatt himself believed that the group was doing Jordan and Iraq's bidding to realize the Western-supported "fertile crescent project." In a June 1958 interview, he stated that in return, "the government in Baghdad had been feeding the Nationalists . . . money and arms for some time."[29] In return, the Syrian Social Nationalist Party saw Jumblatt, the Progressive Socialist Party, and their "failed revolution" as the stooges of the United Arab Republic and the saboteurs of Lebanon.[30]

Beyond this war of words, we have the privilege of seeing the physical conflict through various, competing vantage points, including those of foreign diplomats, fighters, and later memorials for fighters. The town of Shemlan was of particular importance to both groups.[31] Thirty-one kilometers northwest of Moukhtara, and twenty from Beirut, Jumblatt's

---

[28] FO 371/134134, Scott, no. 1358, September 18, 1958.
[29] *Al-Siyasa*, June 4, 1958. For more information on the fertile crescent project, realized later in the Iraqi-Jordanian Hashemite union in 1958, see Malcom H. Kerr, *The Arab Cold War: Gamal 'Abd al-Nasir and His Rivals, 1958–1970*, 3rd ed. (New York: Oxford University Press, 1971); and Elizabeth Bishop, "Steadfast and Rejectionist Front of Arab States: Iraq's 14 July 1958 Coup and the Unraveling of the Arab Union," conference paper, American Historical Association annual meeting (Chicago, US, 2019).
[30] *Al-Bina'*, May 22, 1958.
[31] For more on this battlefront, see Nadiya Karami and Nawwaf Karami, *Waqi'at al-Thawra al-Lubnaniyya 1958* [The Reality of the 1958 Lebanese Revolution], 2nd ed. (Moukhtara, Lebanon: Dar al-Taqaddumiyya, 2010), 204–214.

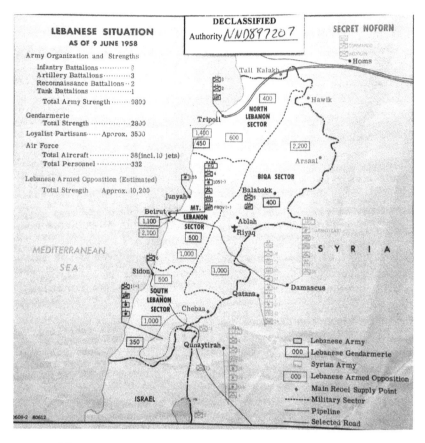

Figure 5.1 Map compiled by US State Department intelligence one month into the 1958 War. Shemlan is not labeled on this map, but is located right under the "Mt. Lebanon Sector." "Current Intelligence Weekly Summary," June 12, 1958, RG 59. Courtesy of United States National Archives, College Park, MD.

campaign saw the town as a command post on the way to Beirut and Beirut International Airport. However, the Progressive Socialist Party did not have a base of operations in Shemlan. While its closest branch to the town was likely in Moukhtara, the Syrian Social Nationalist Party had offices nearby, including in two villages connected to Shemlan due west.[32] The Syrian Social Nationalist Party and the Progressive Socialist Party then met for battle in the town, as the former received help from the

---

[32] Jiraj, *Min al-Ja'aba*, vol. 1 (1985), 169.

gendarmerie forces and even an occasional air strike from the armed forces.[33]

As of June 11, the Progressive Socialist Party had captured twenty-eight Syrian Social Nationalist fighters in nearby towns.[34] Although the Progressive Socialist Party never detailed the fate of those caught behind enemy lines, it was later reported that members of the Syrian Social Nationalist Party were beheaded.[35] There were claims of brutality on the other side of the conflict as well. One contemporary book, written by authors sympathetic to the opposition, states that Syrian Social Nationalist Party fighters would enter the houses of innocent bystanders in Shemlan who were singled out as Jumblatt supporters. One such man was Sheikh Farid al-Sha'r, who "was killed alongside his son who was no older than fifteen years old."[36] Casualties on both sides of this battle ranged in the hundreds. And even when this front was neutralized by the army, the fighting continued into early October.[37]

A particular report from Shemlan allows for a level of detail into the logic of violence, unmatched elsewhere. It comes from Kamel Abu Kamel, a mid-ranking, middle-aged Syrian Social Nationalist Party officer. Abu Kamel grew up in Baaqline in the Chouf to a Druze family, was exposed to the principles of the party by a friend in the 1930s, and thereafter, alongside twenty-eight other youth, helped establish a branch of the party in Baaqline.[38] By 1958, Abu Kamel was a "Chief of Staff" in the Mount Lebanon front as he led some 150 Syrian Social Nationalist Party fighters in Shemlan. A US Foreign Service Officer, Robert Chase, interviewed Abu Kamel in July as a part of a State Department campaign to assess the situation in interior Lebanon.[39]

The first detail provided about Abu Kamel, besides that he owned a pharmacy in the nearby Souq al-Gharb before the war, is that he and other Druze members of the party are "anti-Jumblatt rather than pro-Chamoun." In his capacity as a Druze representative for the Syrian Social Nationalist Party, Abu Kamel saw himself as "protect[ing] the country from a return to feudalism or from becoming part of Nasser's empire."

---

[33] While the army often remained neutral in the war, Jumblatt's campaign was an exception. For more information on the role of the army in 1958, see Oren Barak, *The Lebanese Army: A National Institution in a Divided Society* (Albany, NY: State University of New York Press, 2009).

[34] Qubain, *Crisis in Lebanon*, 77.

[35] FO 371/134133, Jordan Still Worried about Lebanese Situation, 1261, August 11, 1958. That these claims come from Jordanian supporters of the Syrian Social Nationalist Party, in particular Queen Zein, make them suspect.

[36] Karami and Karami, *Waqi'at al-Thawra al-Lubnaniyya 1958*, 211.

[37] FO 371/134127, Middleton, no. 936, July 5; *Bayrut al-Masa'*, October 9, 1958.

[38] For more information on Abu Kamel, see Jiraj, *Min al-Ja'aba*, vol. 1, 237–242.

[39] Conversations detailed in Robert Chase and Adil Yacoub, July 11, 1958, no. 39.

While the latter reflects the party's stance on Nasser's Pan-Arabism, the former is a shot at Jumblatt, questioning whether his populism is just a cover for sect-based rule. In contrast to the reports of Syrian Social Nationalist Party murders in Shemlan, Abu Kamel explains to Chase how his teams retrieved loot stolen by Progressive Socialist Party fighters and returned it to local residents. In the end, Chase got the following impression: Abu Kamel's "support of the Government was based on a desire to protect his home and property in the absence of regular military forces and an opposition to the assumption of power in the district by Jumblatt and his socialist followers."[40] While Abu Kamel does not explicitly mention his party's ideology, he is like those nationalists reading the party paper, *al-Nahda*, in the 1930s. He is aware of the party's nonsectarian basis and the validity of its universal claim over the people.

This foray into the Mount Lebanon front during the 1958 War helps, even if by a small margin, reconstruct the back and forth, campaigns and counter-campaigns, and justifications for violence (or at least defense) in 1958. More broadly, micro-analysis like this and the Kata'ib's shift toward war can begin to unravel how practices of violence were produced – in short, through a mix of ideology and routine. What remains unanswered, however, is the legacy of these practices. Unlike other conflicts in Lebanon, including the 1860 War or the Lebanese Civil War of 1975–1990, there is not much awareness around remembering, or forgetting, the 1958 War. Still, there is at least one site in the country that memorializes those who died in 1958. In the Chouf town of Baqata, 30 kilometers south of Shemlan, there is a memorial to the fighters of the Progressive Socialist Party.

The site was inaugurated in 1960 and is detailed in length in Lucia Volk's *Memorials and Martyrs in Modern Lebanon* (2010). While Volk and this author were granted access to the memorial at different times, it is not open to the public. One must call municipal authorities to unlock the door to the memorial.[41] Once in the site, the visitor first sees a stone on the right with a picture of Nasser alongside four fighters in garb associated with the Arab revolt.[42] On the left, there is a stone with pictures of fighters alongside two flags: one for Lebanon, the other for the United Arab Republic. Then, looking up, one sees some sixty grave sites, lined in two rows. Each stone includes an insignia that reads "the martyr," followed by the name of the martyred, where they were from, and the "battle" in which they were killed.[43]

[40] Ibid.   [41] Notes from field-based research in Baqata, Lebanon, June 1, 2018.
[42] For a picture of this stone, see Lucia Volk, *Memorials and Martyrs in Modern Lebanon* (Bloomington, IN: Indiana University Press, 2010), 87.
[43] Notes from field-based research in Baqata, Lebanon, June 1, 2018.

To Volk, the mural to Nasser represents both "unison" behind him and "cross-generational unity," as two of the four fighters are old, the rest young.[44] As for the actual gravestones, Volk argues they "marked the fate of regular civilians, who had taken up arms against forces loyal to the Chamoun government – also civilians – and they were given burial as comrades-in-arms, lying side by side."[45] What I would like to add to Volk's thorough analysis is who did not mark their comrades in arms. While the Progressive Socialist Party celebrates its martyrs, and even has a veterans group, called the Qudama Mujahidi Thawra 1958, or the "Veteran Mujahidin of the 1958 Revolution," no such commemoration stands for the Syrian Social Nationalist Party.[46] In fact, given the party's movement toward the left by the 1970s and beyond, Syrian Social Nationalist Party members feel uncomfortable talking about 1958, or see it as an aberration.[47] Hence, some young lives are remembered, mobilized, while others are forgotten. But as Abu Kamel reminded a US diplomat in the middle of the fighting, the reality was more complex, as people were torn between town, country, and ideology. This nuance becomes hard to resuscitate given the ensuing battle of Beirut, the first moment of so-called sectarian violence of 1958.

The Kata'ib General Strike: Subaltern Constitutionalism, Rituals, and Martyrdom

After the US intervention in July, and the cessation of most hostilities by September, no one party or bloc could claim they truly "won" the war. The stalemate was symbolized by the slogan of "no victor, no vanquished" (*la ghalib wa-la maghlub*), used by new prime minister Rashid Karami and new president Fuad Shihab, who appointed Karami to form a cabinet.[48] The Kata'ib and Syrian Social Nationalist Party interpreted this phrase to mean that no popular force would be left out of the postwar cabinet. At the same time, Karami also stated that the new cabinet would "reap the fruits of the rebellion," one against Chamoun and his allies.[49] Karami then blocked these so-called loyalists from joining the cabinet. Upon this news, the Syrian Social Nationalist Party expressed its displeasure in the headlines of *al-Bina*': "All of the cabinet does not

---

[44] Volk, *Memorials and Martyrs in Modern Lebanon*, 86.   [45] Ibid., 88.
[46] Conversations with Wassim Mroueh, email correspondence, June 24, 2018.
[47] This is confirmed by personal interviews I have conducted with members since 2013, who skirt questions about the role of 1958 in the history of the party.
[48] Entelis, *Pluralism and Party Transformation in Lebanon* (1974), 178.
[49] Traboulsi, *A History of Modern Lebanon* (2007), 137.

represent the people."[50] The Kata'ib also deployed populist discourse in their response, arguing that the "formation of the present government" posed a "challenge to the will of the Lebanese people."[51]

The Kata'ib, however, did more with their anger than the Syrian Social Nationalist Party. They launched a general strike, or counter-revolution, which began on September 22, 1958, and continued until Gemayel was given four of a possible fourteen cabinet portfolios on October 14, 1958.[52] Amin Gemayel (b. 1942), the son of Pierre, aged sixteen during the 1958 War, later explained, "we declared three weeks strike and we hit the streets to send a clear message to Fuad Shihab that the revolution ended without any winners and that we refused that there would be winners and losers in the fight."[53] While this strike had elite overtones, it was flanked by young people, women, and children, some of whom died for the party and Lebanon.

What began in May as a fight over sovereignty and/or infiltration transformed to one about local politics by September. Ordinary young members in support of the Kata'ib strike used constitutional logic to justify their actions, while opposition actors claimed it was a sectarian power grab flanked by Kata'ib punks. While the opposition was not wrong about the Kata'ib's sectarian defense of the status quo, the Kata'ib argument was somewhat different; their party was represented in the constitutionally bound parliament, was a popular political actor, and hence, should have a seat, or seats, in the cabinet. This was a loose interpretation of the constitution, unsupported by any demographic reality. In fact, as the Kata'ib only won two seats in the highly controversial elections of 1957, it was not even guaranteed a seat in the cabinet. Regardless of the strength of its claims, constitutionalism was the frame that the Kata'ib mobilized. This is shown through the pages of the party paper, al-'Amal, during the general strike, whereby writers, editors, and words from members and supporters worked to portray the strike and its supporters as diverse. The lines of diversity included class, gender, region, and country, demonstrating the culmination of the Kata'ib's cosmopolitanism and expansion efforts. One UNOGIL

---

[50] Al-Bina', September 21, 1958.
[51] FO 371/134134, No Change in General Situation, Scott, 1395, September 26, 1958.
[52] The new cabinet, announced on October 14, 1958, included four individuals: Rashid Karami, Hussein al-'Uwayni, Raymond Eddé, and Pierre Gemayel. Geyamel was awarded the Minister of Public Works, Education, Agriculture, and Health. McClintock to Dulles, October 15, 1958, no. 1966, In Foreign Relations of the United States, 1958–1960: Lebanon and Jordan, Volume XI, 613.
[53] Amin Gemayel. Interviewed in Assaf, "al-Kata'ib al-Lubnaniyya," in Ahzab Lubnan (2003).

observer was quite impressed with the results, noting in a report that Kata'ib "strikers [are] under a rather good centralized control."[54]

In regards to class and region, rank-and-file members protested on the streets of urban Beirut, the rural Metn district, and towns as far east as Zahle, while business owners in central Beirut closed down their shops in defense of the Kata'ib. Editors of *al-'Amal* depicted this diversity. In multiple issues, they included both pictures of protesters in the lower-income suburbs of Beirut and empty storefronts in the upper-income area of Bab Idriss, providing visual evidence that the show could not go on without the Kata'ib.[55] On another level, women were often those protesters found out on the streets. Take, for example, "a letter from the women of Furn al-Shubak to High President Shihab" on October 8. The women of this east Beirut neighborhood first proclaim that they are "in solidarity with the Kata'ib Party," and accordingly, they "do not accept the cabinet" created by Karami. In fact, they find that the state of affairs represented "[a]ll derogation for our rights as citizens . . . [which] rot the heart of social justice."[56] Their protests were not seen by all as rational. Multiple diplomatic sources refer to Kata'ib women protesters as "excited" "young girls" who "behave hysterically."[57] Yet, the letter to Shihab was the product of the political socialization that popular organizations had sought to engineer since the 1940s. These Kata'ib women were active, vocal, and, in their own words, against all "elements hostile to Lebanon."[58]

This letter also hints to how physical protest was coupled with words of support. Like earlier moments of activism and violence, including the 1937 blood baptism discussed in Chapter 2, the Kata'ib included "letters of encouragement" for its strike in its paper. On October 5, a Yousef Salilati of Qub Elias, a village near Zahle, called out the government for violating its own "no victor, no vanquished" slogan, "reveal[ing] the intentions of the conspirators."[59] On October 6, Edward Barbar of Haret Sakher, a village north of Beirut, wrote that the "old and youth salute the [Kata'ib] struggle (*tahiyi nidalkum*)."[60] On October 8, a family from 'Ajiltun, another village near Beirut, praised Gemayel and the Kata'ib, writing that these men were

---

[54] S-0666-0005, Summary of Events and Preliminary Evaluation from 2 to 8 October, Beirut HQ area.

[55] Pictures of protesters are found in *al-'Amal*, October 5 (from Beirut), October 10 (from al-Metn), and October 12 (from Zahle). Two examples of empty storefronts are found in *al-'Amal*, September 30 and October 2, 1958.

[56] *Al-'Amal*, October 8, 1958.

[57] S-0666-0005, Summary of Events and Preliminary Evaluation from 2 to 8 October, Beirut HQ area, S-0666-0004, Perinterp no. 17. Events 2–5 October 1958.

[58] *Al-'Amal*, October 8, 1958.   [59] Ibid., October 5, 1958.   [60] Ibid., October 6, 1958.

"a symbol of sacrifice, dedication, and heroism for the cause of saving Lebanon and we know that this battle is a battle [for Lebanon]."[61]

On October 9, a letter was sent from Mexico, reading that the six signing members of the "Managing Council of Mexican-Lebanese Union" "approve absolutely your fight against the traitors and . . . [we] are ready to undertake with you the defense of Lebanon."[62] Equally significant as this Kata'ib support across the Atlantic was the words of a female Kata'ib member, Sumya Younis. She describes her rationale for wanting to join the fight in an October 4 letter of encouragement:

O heroic comrades,
    Our slogan is the preservation of the independence of Lebanon and this is your slogan too . . . I am a woman from the Bkassine [in the Chouf Mountains] branch, ready to stand by [heroic comrades] and carry arms with you, if necessary, and we will give a lesson to the treacherous and defend the people of Lebanon and its strength and dignity.[63]

In this one letter, Younis combines nation, village, party, populism, enemy imagery, and the necessity to carry and use a weapon. The Kata'ib's claim to diversity is also on display here, spanning lines of class, gender, and region. Nevertheless, it must be remembered that this diversity was circumscribed by the sectarian political system in which the Kata'ib existed and sought to perpetuate. In the context of the 1958 general strike, there was no way getting around the fact that it was only observed in Christian majority cities and neighborhoods. Moreover, one could not ignore that strike participants were almost exclusively Christian and their position, even if muted, was that a populist, Christian party should be represented in the cabinet. In turn, al-'Amal and its supporters could only sell the strike as diverse, not cross-confessional.

As protesters barricaded certain areas, shop owners closed down their stores, and Kata'ib youth marched throughout the country, discourses of constitutionalism, undergirded by sectarian claims to power, were in the air. Loss and death were also conditioning striking practices. One of the key martyrs was Fuad Haddad, the editor in chief of al-'Amal, who was kidnapped on September 19, 1958, never found, and presumed dead. In the initial Kata'ib call for strike, published in al-'Amal and other newspapers across Beirut, the cabinet formation issue was not mentioned. The focus was on Haddad and how his abduction symbolized "acts of aggression" terrorizing Lebanon. This statement posed if

---

[61] Ibid., October 8, 1958.
[62] AG-056, United Nations Observation Group in Lebanon (UNOGIL) (1958), S-0666–0009, October 9–10 1958.
[63] Al-'Amal, October 4, 1958.

"barbaric actions ... [were] to prevail over all Lebanese individuals in the future," what would become of Lebanon? This question, not those regarding the constitution, was what led the Kata'ib's "appeals to you all to participate with [the Kata'ib] in its peaceful strike in the capital."[64] But to label the Kata'ib general strike as peaceful is misplaced, as street fighting around Beirut and retributive kidnappings only increased after Haddad's death.[65]

One such battle saw the death of "Kata'ib youth" Cesar (or Qaysar) al-Bustani (Figure 5.2). On September 20, a day before the Kata'ib announced their general strike, Bustani was rushed to Hospital Hotel Dieu after receiving fatal gunshots in the Furn al-Shubak neighborhood.[66] The nature of the battle is unknown and the assailants who killed Bustani were never identified, although it is likely that fighters of the Popular Resistance, Najjadeh members or otherwise, were responsible. Furthermore, little is known about Bustani himself. He had been active in the party since at least 1952, participating with other Kata'ib members in the popular uprising against Bishara al-Khuri.[67] Kata'ib primary sources and secondary sources alike are silent on his age, rank, education, or family background.[68] In his obituary, only vague qualities are mentioned, such as he was "loving, exuberant, and enthusiastic," and died repeating "God and Lebanon."[69] Haddad, not Bustani, became the symbol for the general strike, as he was memorialized well after the 1958 War.[70] Nonetheless, and in a more intimate way than material relating to Haddad, the words on and events after Bustani's death provide insight to the precise ways in which the rituals and youth cultures of popular organizations were embedded in practices of violence in 1958.

"In protection of God and homeland: O good comrade and dearest friend" read the headline of an article, on page four of four, dedicated to "the strong comrade Cesar al-Bustani" in the party newspaper. He is celebrated as a "martyr who sacrificed his life on the altar of jihad, honor, and Lebanon" and represented how "youth die to protect Lebanon's youth." Commenting on his strength, the writer(s) notes that Bustani

[64] Ibid., September 21, 1958.
[65] FO 371/134134, Belief That Fuad Haddad Is Dead, Beirut to FO, no. 1375, September, 22, 1958.
[66] Al-Nahar, September 21, 1958.
[67] Bustani is pictured in a 1952 issue of al-'Amal alongside other Kata'ib Party members during the White Revolution. Al-'Amal, September 15, 1952.
[68] Kata'ib officials I interviewed, none of whom were alive during 1958, did not know who Bustani was when I showed them a picture.
[69] Al-'Amal, September 21, 1958.
[70] In 1979, the Kata'ib monthly magazine included a dedication to Fuad Haddad, on the twenty-first anniversary of his death. Lebanese Kata'ib Party, al-'Amal Monthly Magazine, vol. 14 (Beirut: Dar al-'Amal, 1979), 53–59.

Figure 5.2 Cesar al-Bustani in 1952 (a) and ca. 1958 (b). (A), *al-'Amal*, September 15, 1952, and (b), *al-'Amal*, September 21, 1958. Courtesy of Jafet Library, American University of Beirut, and the Kata'ib Party.

was the embodiment of "true manhood and pride."[71] Youth struggle for the sake of the nation was not a new concept for the Kata'ib; neither were the words God and homeland, which in addition to family – *Allah, al-Watan, al-'A'ila* – constituted the party slogan since the 1930s. They were now being appropriated in an extreme instance, one where the youth died

[71] *Al-'Amal*, September 21, 1958.

in the just war. Masculine strength for the sake of the party and Lebanon were virtues instilled in Kata'ib youth since the beginning, whether they were performed through marching or fighting.

On September 24, the Kata'ib organized a funeral procession for Bustani, the "martyr of duty and the nation," attended by the High Bishop of the Maronite church in Beirut, clergy, Gemayel, party comrades, and the family of the martyr.[72] It started at Hospital Hotel Dieu where Bustani died under treatment. "Kata'ib guards wearing official uniform (al-haras al-Kata'ibi bilbasu al-rasmi)" gave a "salute to his body (al-tahiya li-l-juthman)" and carried his coffin – draped with a Kata'ib flag – over two miles to a church in the neighborhood of Rmeil. There the bishop gave the eulogy, mentioning "a number of qualities of the late strength [of Bustani] and his duty of generous sacrifice for the sake of Lebanon." Then, the Kata'ib keepers carried the coffin an additional mile to a cemetery in the neighborhood of Mar Mikhael. Once his body was in its grave, party members close to Bustani, named Joseph Abu Sharaf and Tayinus al-Hamalawy, "lamented over the grave ... in the name of the party." Thereafter, Kata'ib youth fired "gunshots in the air" in his honor.[73] After the final gun salute, members and funeral attendees could return to Bayt al-Kata'ib to give their condolences to the family and party.[74]

Not unlike the oathing ceremony of early July 1958 at Bayt al-Kata'ib, which authenticated new youths in the fight against the enemy, this procession made sense under the basic facets of Kata'ib youth culture and party rituals. Members wore their uniforms, they performed their salute, and they marched from place to place. Moreover, the report in al-'Amal, which is quoted at length above, emphasized all of these things about the procession. And while Bustani was the symbol and reason for this event, his death gave Kata'ib leadership an opportunity to focus on the cause ahead. This phenomenon became more prevalent in the later Lebanese Civil War. As mentioned above, young martyrs were used to recruit new youth fighters. But, and perhaps more intriguing, Baddur, Bustani, and others who died in 1958 were rarely the focus in commemorations; the group and duty they died for were instead placed front and center.

Nevertheless, this was not just a routine event; someone had just died. The details of the funeral, then, illuminate that practices inside and outside conflict are not opposites. Youth members, who would have been drilling for sports training months and years ago, were now drilling for the

---

[72] Ibid., September 24, 1958.   [73] Ibid., September 25, 1958.
[74] Ibid., September 24, 1958.

fight. Trekking was replaced by weapons training, music festivals by funerals. Kata'ib member Antoun Jarji Jamhuri, the darling of the 1956 earthquake relief effort, explains this new existence in his memoir on 1958 as follows: "We were hundreds of youth going to the middle of Kisrawan for its openness, with rifles and machine guns. We carry them secretly to the training fields. And we practice the militia."[75] These grounds, and others in Mount Lebanon, had long severed as Kata'ib summer retreat camping sites. Similarly, sites for "Social Nationalist Camp[s]" in the summer of 1949 had by the summer of 1958 become, according to a US Naval intelligence report, places for Syrian Social Nationalist Party members to "hold target practice on the hilltop."[76] The same structures and spaces that had served the community of young members for decades were now meant for new actions and to show a new level of commitment.

This holds for other popular organizations on the other side of the war, which made use of routine youth culture and populism to make sense of the conflict. Take the Progressive Socialist Party, for example. Beyond posing for pictures (Figure 4.1), training, and arming, the group also prepared its supporters rhetorically and visually. On June 7, before the party's campaign toward Beirut began, the party's newspaper included a cartoon depicting President Chamoun and Uncle Sam running toward the sea. The despot and his conspiring allies were being chased by a fist, inscribed with the words "of the people," which arose over the cedars of Mount Lebanon. The caption below was suggestive to say the least: "The fist which will expel the intruders."[77] In earlier days, cartoons also communicated messages to readers, including the Progressive Socialist Party's dedication to Yawm al-Barouk in 1952. The medium for dissemination was similar, as well as a depiction of *al-sha'b* against the status quo. However, the intention was quite different by 1958. While the cartoon at once had been a place for commemoration or contentious politics was now a visualized justification for assault on the capital.

And at the height of the war in 1958, the Najjadeh also dedicated time for photo shoots and celebrations. On September 1, members posed in military formations for an in-depth report "with the youth of the resistance." In one particular posed picture, included in the group's *Sawt al-'Uruba* newspaper, a dozen or so members wore berets, held guns, and were all smiles alongside a headline that read "The revolution on their shoulders."[78] They were not the only ones posing. "One of the girls in the

---

[75] Jamhuri, *Thikrayat* (201?), 6.
[76] *Al-Nashra al-Rasmiyya*, January 1949, and "Information Report – Office of Naval Intelligence," June 30, 1958, RG 59.
[77] *Al-Anba'*, June 7, 1958.   [78] *Sawt al-'Uruba*, September 1, 1958.

Najjadeh practice[d] using a rifle" in another staged picture.[79] And later in September, as the battle of Beirut raged between their forces and that of the Kata'ib, the Najjadeh sponsored a public celebration for the birthday of the Prophet Muhammad.[80] It did not matter that the enemy was creating chaos. Like the Progressive Socialist Party, which celebrated Yawm al-Barouk in the lead-up to the war, the Najjadeh prioritized the commemoration of religious figures and events central to their collective identity.[81] In sum, regardless of the popular organization that mobilized ritual or routine for violence, the way in which the violence was carried out was not entirely unrecognizable. Indeed, I find it important to ask, how could violent practices make sense to the young members of these groups otherwise? In short, the answer is that everyday and mundane rituals of youth and organizational culture also lay at the center of practices of violence.

The Final Battle for Beirut: The Young Punks as Sites of Violence

Contemporaneous with the Kata'ib strike was the most brutal violence Beirut had witnessed since the war began. While casualties are not recorded for what can be thought of as the final battle for Beirut, the first day was quite tumultuous. On September 22, 1958, 40 people were killed and 100 were injured.[82] Thereafter, and for three weeks from late September into mid-October, this battle was fought in the southeastern neighborhoods of Furn al-Shubak and Tariq al-Jdideh. In prior decades, most residents of these two neighborhoods were either aware of, or held membership in, the Kata'ib or Najjadeh. In the context of the war, the peoples in these neighborhoods were either fighting for, or at least commandeered by, the Kata'ib, Syrian Social Nationalist Party, and gendarmerie, or forces of the Popular Resistance, led by Saeb Salam, and filled out by the Najjadeh.

According to Fahim Qubain, by late September the war "took an exclusively religious coloration."[83] Entelis goes one step further referring to the battle in Beirut as an "open Christian-Muslim War."[84] And Goria argues that the battle, the "highest level of violence" during 1958, took on "an increasingly sectarian and ugly form."[85] Khalaf mirrors these other

---

[79] Ibid., September 22, 1958.   [80] Ibid., September 27, 1958.
[81] *Al-Anba'*, March 22, 1958.
[82] Entelis, *Pluralism and Party Transformation in Lebanon*, 179. This is the only statistical indication provided as to casualities in the battle.
[83] Qubain, *Crisis in Lebanon*, 158.
[84] Entelis, *Pluralism and Party Transformation in Lebanon*, 180.
[85] Wade R. Goria, *Sovereignty and Leadership in Lebanon 1943–1976* (London: Ithaca Press, 1985), 48.

scholars. To him, this phase was the peak of Christian-Muslim "uncivil and guilt free" sectarian violence.[86] He describes the shift from peaceful protest to violence as such:

Soon these activities degenerated into vicious, spiteful acts of sectarian violence: kidnapping, torture, and gangster-like operations became more recurrent and were committed with unprecedented savagery and display of religious bigotry. For the first time, and on both sides, religious symbols and edifices were desecrated. Tortured victims were often branded with religious insignia.[87]

Khalaf and others are correct that this phase was marked by an uptick in the most severe violence of the war, punctuated by retaliatory attacks and kidnappings. Both the pro-Chamoun and oppositional press documented young abductees, who were almost always returned with signs of torture. And on August 19, a UN observer was visited by a fifteen-year-old Muslim named Khalil Jawad Bahjat, who was "beaten up" by the Kata'ib. In the words of Captain Friis, "they made a cross on his chest with a dagger. The cross was only on the surface of the skin and approximately 12 x 15 cm. There were no other signs of cruelty."[88]

This evidence is the closest to a smoking gun, proving that Kata'ib members engaged in performing sect in the violence of 1958. Nevertheless, the Kata'ib, Najjadeh, or other popular organizations did not choose to document this or other instances of religious branding in their newspapers. By extension, scholarship of the last sixty years describes this phase of the war as pervasively and collectively sectarian without providing direct quotation or evidence from the actual conflict. In fact, none even cite the UN report mentioned above. This is not to ignore that Kata'ib youth engaged in this practice of branding, nor omit the instances when multiple popular organizations characterized their enemy as sectarian. Rather, I use this mismatch between evidence and explanation to show that sectarianism as an analytical frame has a certain momentum, irrespective of what sources are consulted or how they are consulted. In the case of 1958, scholars argue for sectarianism solely because Christian youth killed Muslim youth, or vice versa. In turn, they depict popular organizations as sectarian bloodletters with little investigation of the terms of that social interaction. Instead, the reality of how these groups helped produce sectarian violence is much more nuanced.

---

[86] Khalaf, *Civil and Uncivil Violence in Lebanon* (2002), 138.
[87] Ibid., 141. Qubain also notes "Muslim victims were branded with the sign of the cross." Qubain, *Crisis in Lebanon*, 159.
[88] S-0166, United Nations Observation Group in Lebanon (UNOGIL), Special investigation of maltreatment to people from Basta Quarters, Friis to Chief of Staff, August 19, 1958.

Tied to this complexity, scholars do not blame all levels of these organizations for the sectarian violence. For instance, Khalaf argues that the violence in Beirut toward the end of the war was "carried out mostly by followers without the consent or knowledge of leaders and often without their control."[89] US diplomats are more specific. They discuss how Gemayel "sought in fact to restrain his most fanatic followers," but to no avail.[90] UNOGIL confirms this scholarly and diplomatic sentiment as pertains to the opposition, reporting "a decrease in some areas in the ability of opposition leaders to control their followers and a noticeable increase in acts of lawlessness."[91] Oppositional popular organizations were no different in their explanations. They accused the Kata'ib young "punks," or *ghalman*, of perpetuating the violence. Decades apart, whether combatants, diplomats, or scholars, these accounts collectively blame the youth rank and file for the violence of late 1958. Characterizations about young participants in the war, including that they were unrestrainable, mad, and prone to primordial behaviors, then became core generalizations about sectarian violence, within and beyond 1958. Stated differently, what popular organizations attempted to harness, *futuwwa*, became central to explanations of the violence they performed. Thus, the story of the final battle for Beirut is also the story of how youth and youthfulness, terms with little link to sect before 1958, became cornerstones in popular and scholarly discussions of sectarian violence.

This shift unfolded months before September 1958, as oppositional popular organizations and their allies used populist distinction making to explain their enemy and their tactics. A particular word used throughout the conflict, which could substitute for accusations of sectarianism without mentioning the term, was *fitna* or "strife." A June 7 *al-Anba'* article took up this topic, titled "What is behind the *fitna*." *Al-Anba'* writer 'Amil Tarbiyeh claimed that the *fitna* dated back to the Crusades when "the West entered in the name of religion." Now in the 1950s, outside forces use the "cover of protecting [Arabic word for victory, *intisar*] of religious minorities" as grounds for their imperial and economic interests. The local "tyrants," who accepted foreign help under the banner of the "Lebanese cause," were as guilty as their overseers.[92] While Tarbiyeh does not mention the Kata'ib or Syrian Social Nationalist Party, the "Lebanese cause" serves as a replacement for

---

[89] Khalaf, *Civil and Uncivil Violence in Lebanon*, 137.
[90] *Foreign Relations of the United States*, 1958–1960: Lebanon and Jordan, Document 192.
[91] S-0650–0001, Third Report of the UNOGIL to the Security Council (August 16, 1958), 2.
[92] *Al-Anba'*, June 7, 1958.

these reactionary popular organizations and their justifications. The two, like Chamoun, were happy to invite the West into what is "an internal conflict only." At this early juncture of war, Tarbiyeh and his party did not go so far to label the enemy as a specific internal force. However, Tarbiyeh considers the anti-sectarian opposition as a panacea to pro-Chamounist sectarianism. It would end the *fitna* as the Progressive Socialist Party would continue to "seek liberation and emancipation."[93] To fight for democratic, populist ideals would deal a blow to imperialism, outside forces, and internal strife. Hence, without ever mentioning internal actors by name or their sectarian ways, articles like this worked to set the context for who was good and bad in the strife, and how good or pure elements could defeat evil.

Other oppositional forces, however, called out particular punks and their treachery well before the battle for Beirut. *Bayrut al-Masa'*, the newspaper of the Popular Resistance leader, Salam, ran an article in mid-May titled, "The Kata'ib house becoming a place of torturing Syrians and Palestinians." At the same time the Kata'ib was sharpening its infiltration narrative, some forces of the opposition were establishing the "Kata'ib gangs" as enemies of Arab brotherhood. *Bayrut al-Masa'* reported that members of the Kata'ib would abduct innocent men and "slap, hit, and kick them." Four individuals in particular, Michael Ayliya and Nawaf al-Darubi from Homs, and 'Abd al-Fitah al-Hajj Abu Dan, and Adam Rustum Dandash from Aleppo, had sustained injuries to their arms, sides, and legs. Perhaps worse was that the authorities knew about these Kata'ib detentions, as the group continued "wreaking havoc on the land."[94]

In this report, the writer(s) of *Bayrut al-Masa'* frames the Kata'ib as violating normal, civil standards, and rejecting unity between Arab brothers. The site of the violation was Bayt al-Kata'ib, which *Bayrut al-Masa'* referred to as "the caldron (*al-tamirjal*)."[95] As diplomatic actors were not yet reporting day-to-day violence at this point of the conflict, it is difficult to verify this claim. While it could be valid, the language and its intention itself is equally useful for our purposes. First, the writer(s) suggests to the readers, and broader residents of Beirut, that there is a stain in the capital and that stain is supported by the government. Second, without saying it, the story alludes to why the Popular Resistance is fighting in Beirut: to rid out or at least contain these forces. Third, and most importantly, that the Kata'ib home of youth belonging could be transformed to a house of torture is meant to be alarming to the reader. By using coded language, such as "gangs" taking cover in their "home" in the city, this actor in the

---

[93] Ibid.   [94] *Bayrut al-Masa'*, May 16, 1958.   [95] Ibid.

growing anti-Kata'ib front set the contours for what the people should look for in sectarian actors and actions.

Bayrut al-Masa' continued using this type of language when detailing the troubling behaviors of the Kata'ib as well as the Syrian Social Nationalist Party. The "gang," "lads," and "punks" were challenging democratic, plural Lebanon.[96] Other oppositional popular organizations adapted this discourse to describe youth on the other side. In July, the Lebanese Communist Party referred to the "turncoats of the Nationalist Socialist Party gangs." With the Kata'ib at its side, both "humiliated the people and made their blood flow like rivers, in order to make Lebanon a servant of imperialism and a base for conspiracy."[97] This language was not wholly invented; it built off of Yusuf Yazbak and Fuad al-Shamali's first distillations of populism in the 1920s. It also dovetailed with the populist discourse perfected by the Arab Nationalist Youth under George Habash in 1950s. It then went one step further: it linked a grand conspiracy against the people to local enemies. Those enemies were, in fact, young punks of the Kata'ib and Syrian Social Nationalist Party. Fighting them, as the Lebanese Communist Party urged its members to do, was to beat that darkness that fomented within these youth.

What did the young punks of the Kata'ib and Syrian Social Nationalist Party do with this characterization? They also weaponized it, playing up the conspiring acts and their young perpetrators on the other side. Both the Kata'ib and Syrian Social Nationalist Party newspapers discussed the "sectarian strife" and "sectarian formations" emanating from oppositional popular organizations and their allies in the new Karami government.[98] In July, the Kata'ib used the term "leaders of the Jumblatti gangs" in the pages of *al-'Amal*, when accusing the Progressive Socialist Party of smuggling weapons from Syria.[99] And a month later, the Syrian Social Nationalist Party's *al-Bina'* referred to its opponents as the "deviants," a term, like punks, meant to make readers question the enemy's youth.[100] Finally, it imbued these claims with a language of populism. In late September 1958, the Syrian Social Nationalist Party gave a speech titled "sectarian violence is in the service of colonialism."[101]

Like with the Lebanese Communist Party, anti-colonial rhetoric was a vestige of the populist foundations of these groups. Since the 1920s, they had claimed their enemy, whether the French, the Lebanese government, or another group, was on the wrong side of their utopian vision to

---

[96] Ibid., May 16 and July 12, 1958.
[97] *Summary of Statement by the Communist Party of Lebanon*, 21 July 1958. Cited in Agwani, The *Lebanese Crisis*, 297.
[98] *Al-Bina'*, June 14, 1958; and *al-'Amal*, October 4, 1958.   [99] *Al-'Amal*, July 8, 1958.
[100] *Al-Bina'*, August 22, 1958.   [101] *Sada al-Shamal*, September 29, 1958.

win Lebanon. Therefore, on balance, popular organizations and their allies on both sides of this war employed a familiar language of populism. Then, after reacting to the actions of others in real time, colored it with the new markers of sectarianism: our cause vs. the punks and their sabotage. But, and more importantly for understanding sectarian violence as a practice – not just a discourse – popular organizations were also acting based on this language. They placed barricades and checkpoints to control the national geography, handed young people guns, and defended their populist visions against the other's treachery.

In exploring practices of sectarian violence, emerging in 1958, we are benefited by accounts from the Najjadeh during the final battle for Beirut. Its newspaper, *Sawt al-'Uruba*, a daily that began printing on August 25, immediately reported on the "crimes," "injustices," and "provocative acts" of the "Chamounist gangs from the Kata'ib and Syrian Social Nationalist Party" and their "sectarian character."[102] They included two fires set by the Kata'ib during the first day of intense fighting in September. One was of an energy plant in al-Hadath, part of the "national factories" that fueled the country.[103] Another fire was of a family-owned garage in Furn al-Shubak, which destroyed over thirty cars.[104] When the owner, Mustapha Karakira, a Sunni Muslim, found these Kata'ib men, he was stunned by his "attackers." They had "glimmer of treachery in their eyes," what the report referred to as a "Kata'ib darkness (*al-Kata'ibiyyin al-thalam*)."[105]

This instance of Christian youth damaging Muslim property is key in the production of sectarian violence in real time. For the report itself though, it sets the terms on how these practices would be interpreted by Najjadeh youth. First, to refer to the energy plant as "national" is to frame the Kata'ib as an enemy of the nation with narrow, sectarian interests. The Najjadeh's new Arab nationalism, in alignment with other leftist popular organization, is not mentioned, but it is implicitly the panacea to this enemy of the Lebanese people. Alongside populist and nationalist justifications is the claim that these youth had a "Kata'ib darkness." Throughout the report, one gets an image of maddened, sinister, and spiteful perpetrators. This imagery did not form in a vacuum, but built off earlier usage of the words punks and lads, language that turned *futuwwa* on its head. But they were not just deviant youths; they were almost animalistic. Using nonhuman imagery as a way to perform violence is echoed in the first

---

[102] *Sawt al-'Uruba*, September 24, 26, 28, and October 1, 1958.
[103] Ibid., September 24, 1958. British sources actually reported that the energy plant was quite small. FO 371/134134, Scott, no. 1381, September 23, 1958.
[104] FO 371/134134, Scott, no. 1381, September 23, 1958.
[105] *Sawt al-'Uruba*, September 24, 1958.

phase of the Lebanese Civil War in 1975–1976. The Progressive Socialist Party and its writer(s) in *al-Anba'* argue that the "isolationist" Kata'ib is no longer a legitimate political actor. Instead, the Kata'ib young men had "transformed to machines or wild animals."[106] In 1958, perhaps the language was not as blunt. But like 1975, this account also provided the dehumanization necessary to fight another citizen, Kata'ib member or otherwise, and kill them in battle, on the grounds that they were defending the people and defeating the sectarian enemy.

A later *Sawt al-'Uruba* article, published on October 4, goes beyond vandalism to describe Kata'ib acts of torture. While the article does not mention religious branding, it does point to the sinister nature of Kata'ib "attack[ing] the defenseless and innocent." Four young men, presumably affiliated with the Najjadeh, were moving furniture from the Geitawi neighborhood in east Beirut by way of a truck when Kata'ib youth stopped them. Although the Kata'ib branch president of the nearby Rmeil district intervened and allowed the truck to leave Geitawi, Kata'ib members then pursued the vehicle, smashed out the glass, and dragged the four youth back to their office. There they made them wear blindfolds as they repeatedly whipped them.[107] After the "Kata'ib punks" had their fun, they left the four men near dead in Dabas Square in the nearby Ashrafiyya neighborhood. The injured and tortured were eventually picked up by a military detachment and local police, who could not press charges or investigate Kata'ib offices in east Beirut because the assailants were unknown.[108] These acts of sect-based violence were brutal and indefensible, according both to the Najjadeh and British diplomats. The latter reported several days later on how "scores of innocent Moslems [*sic*] were picked up at random" by the Kata'ib, and in some cases, found mutilated.[109] Perhaps most importantly, the Najjadeh paper emphasizes that the Kata'ib youth were not acting directly under the orders of Kata'ib leaders. While the leadership let the men pass, the youth punks, uncontrollable, were the causers of sect violence.

Kata'ib youth also faced violence if caught in Najjadeh neighborhoods of support. A particular instance before the battle of Beirut, but one that is similar to practices of violence during the battle, is narrated in Desmond Stewart's published journal from the summer of 1958, *Turmoil in Beirut*. Stewart was a British journalist and teacher who worked for the Makassed Society, which gave him access to Sunni elements, such as Salam. One of Stewart's acquaintances, a young man associated with the Popular

---

[106] *Al-Anba'*, May 1 and December 12, 1975.   [107] *Sawt al-'Uruba*, October 4, 1958.
[108] Ibid.
[109] FO 371/134134, Scott, no. 136, 1001, 251 58, September 23, 1958. Page 7 and FO 371/134134, no. 1471 Crosthwaite, October 9, 1958.

Resistance named Adnan, spoke of a recent "captured Kataeb [*sic*] spy" he had seen. Found "wandering round the Basta streets," this spy was caught by Popular Resistance fighters wearing a Kata'ib badge under his shirt and carrying a map of Basta. The Kata'ib youth was then "shackled," had "his face bashed in," and was "being kept till nightfall, when he would be shot."[110]

The description of the youth punks, and their sect-based practices, including capturing and torturing a Muslim youth in a Christian neighborhood or vice versa, then, generated something that scholars of 1958 would later call sectarian violence. Yet, in the midst of the conflict, combatants did not often use that exact terminology, at least in an active sense. An October 9 article from *Bayrut al-Masa'* states that the paper's owner, Salam, will never let the struggle turn into a "sectarian civil war," like President Chamoun and his allies want.[111] In Salam's estimation, then, the sectarian treachery of the other will not occur because of the dedication of "the people" to defend Lebanon. Discourse like this defies the sentiments of scholars, who, like Khalaf, argue that "confessional enmity [was] aroused by the conflict."[112] Instead, when the pejorative "punk" or populist "people" were evoked, either with or without mentioning sect, these groups, alongside scholarly and popular depictions of them, were actively producing the terms of sectarian distinction making and sectarian violence.

Conclusion: Rethinking Sectarian Violence as a Discourse and Practice in the 1958 War

The evidence presented in this chapter has found that the historical construction of a distinct type of sectarian discourse and action, sectarian violence, was produced in the summer of 1958 at the hands of popular organizations. However, this conclusion is not self-evident or intuitive. First, if sectarianism is a way of explaining things, it is hard to consider 1958 the birth point of sectarian violence. More often than not, popular organizations did not refer to their opponents as sectarian. Compounding this is the rhetoric that was used in the lead-up to the war. From 1957 to 1958, both oppositional and pro-government groups mobilized constitutionalism and populism to describe their enemy, whether it be Chamoun, Nasser, the former's Western backers, or the latter's Lebanese supporters. Yet, by reading into the cultural production of popular organizations and their allies during the war, we see how coded language was used to

---

[110] Stewart, *Turmoil in Beirut*, 40.   [111] *Bayrut al-Masa'*, October 9, 1958.
[112] Khalaf, *Civil and Uncivil Violence in Lebanon*, 138.

discredit the enemy and urge the young rank and file to support and fight against it. Terms like "gangs," "lads," and "deviants" were meant to reduce the project of popular organizations to a backward plight. In a few occasions, sectarian was deployed in distinction to the other group's true popular support. Regardless, what these groups had worked long to instill, a cosmopolitan youth culture for and by the Lebanese people, however defined, was now being used against them.

Therefore, although popular organizations existed within a sect-based political culture and society, they are the agents that described the conflict in these terms. Diplomats, pundits, and scholars also contributed to this trend as well, referring to the violence as sectarian. In some cases, especially during the final battle for Beirut, they even characterized the actors at the center of this war as young men who were unable to control their sectarian inners. This linkage, however misplaced, turned youth empowerment on its head and painted young people as susceptible to sectarian violence. This is why I argue that even if not at all times, or equally, 1958 marks the production of sectarian violence, with young people at the center of its explanations.

Second, if sectarianism is a way of doing things, our task in locating sectarian violence is equally difficult. This is because in the midst of the war, whether in the Chouf or Beirut, practices, rituals, routines, and ideologies linked to youth culture, those that cannot be reduced to sect alone, were mobilized to fight this war. From waving flags to holding guns, from lecturing to drilling, from pledging to join a group to oathing to join a war, from visualizing the struggle as a call to protest to using cartoons as a call for the death of others, I find that this transition was rather seamless for young members. This is because these rituals of organizational youth culture made sense to these youth. Winning Lebanon at one time meant building the organization, but in a context like 1958, it meant defending it at all costs.

By the same token, that youth practices became central to the culture of war marks a new trend in Lebanon, different than any episode before it. 1958 was a moment of national warfare, fought primarily by young people, in which both sides began to explain their enemy as either deranged youth, or sometimes, the sectarian other. Coupled with a new discourse of sectarian violence in 1958, this performativity breathed to life the phenomenon of sectarian violence that appears so rigid, fixed, reflective, and permanent in hindsight. Therefore, to rethink sectarian violence is to chart this historical transformation, both in words and action, and I argue that popular organizations were active agents in this transformation.

The way 1958 was explained and the way it was lived echo well beyond this five-month conflict. Most immediate in comparison is the Lebanese Civil War of 1975–1990. It also raged across the country, as leaders and scholars alike explained combatants as either dying for the just cause or representative of the worst of *futuwwa*. Regarding the latter, the words of the rebel leader of the 1958 War, Jumblatt, are instructive. In a later war, days after the Kata'ib shooting of twenty-eight Palestinians on April 13, 1975, Jumblatt distinguished in *al-Anba'* between good and evil. There was the "Arab vanguard," flanked by the Progressive Socialist Party, which "forms a powerful force and leads nations and peoples of the Third World." Then there was the "conspiracy" of the Kata'ib, a "sectarian organization" with punks who have "hatred [that] has deepened in their hearts."[113] In a later set of 1976–1977 interviews, however, Jumblatt broadened his critique. He commented on the youth's "tendency to unbridled self-indulgence and looting." He continued:

It still amazes me how disappointingly immature and callow the young people turned out to be in this respect, for all their heroism, their commitment and their honesty. The young people treated the battle as a game, they threw themselves into it wholeheartedly, as if it were a sport. But as far as public and private property was concerned, they often behaved like migrating nomads or Bohemians ... [.] It was utterly disgusting; we felt they were dragging us all into the mire with them. We should have reacted more vehemently. We did try, but we also needed these strange kids aching to do battle.[114]

Nationalized, populist, and (pejoratively) youthful are adjectives that typify Jumblatt's comments. They are also adjectives that were created and linked to popular organizations in 1958. Finally, these terms can be, and are, also employed to explain other cases of sectarian violence in the latter half of the twentieth century and twenty-first century across the globe. They range from past wars in Northern Ireland to current ones in Syria.[115]

Exploring these comparisons, teasing out the relationship between discourse and practice in each, is for another study. To conclude here though, the presence of these connections does not mean the sectarian violence of 1958 in Lebanon was a blueprint or exportable. Unlike the decolonization struggles of the 1950s–1960s or the 1979 Iranian Revolution, who would want to promote or make modular sectarian

---

[113] *Al-Anba'*, May 1, 1975.

[114] Kamal Jumblatt, *I Speak for Lebanon*, trans. Michael Pallis (London: Zed Press, 1982), 111.

[115] For more information on how sectarian violence is explained and practiced elsewhere, see Allen Feldman, *Formations of Violence. The Narrative of the Body and Political Terror in Northern Ireland* (Chicago, IL: University of Chicago Press, 1991); and Nikolaos Van Dam, *Destroying a Nation: The Civil War in Syria* (London: I.B. Tauris, 2017).

violence? While one could make the claim that actors do promote sectarianism to destroy a place or divide a people, these two chapters on the 1958 War argue that the production of a new type of violent social interaction is more contextual. Indeed, trends that dominate the Global South and colonized world in the twentieth century, such as rural-urban migration, the construction of youth politics, mass political socialization, and a postcolonial context ripe for populist discourse, became wrapped up in the violence that would unfold from Belfast to Beirut.

Epilogue
Centering Youth, Remembering and Globalizing 1958

Meanwhile, Beirut was again embroiled in fire. Barricades and unrest. Lebanon was sliding in a war, pitching district against district. 1958 was already forgotten.[1]

Mona Aoueiss Zaccak, a young woman from the Chouf, got engaged in October 1957 and married in May 1958. She and her husband spent the summer of 1958 in Italy on their honeymoon. In what must have felt jarring, they experienced little of the unrest explained in the latter part of this book. The fire that Zaccak spoke of in the documentary *Honeymoon 1958* was the Lebanese Civil War of 1975–1990. By the start of that war, Zaccak was correct. What is now referred to by scholars as the "mini civil war" of 1958 had sunk into distant memory.[2]

This is in part due to the disparate size and scale of the two wars. While the fighting of 1958 resulted in no more than 4,000 deaths, over 170,000 people were killed in the war of 1975–1990.[3] This made it the most devastating conflict the region had experienced since the 1948 Arab-Israeli War. In terms of forced migration, in 1958, tens of thousands of Syrians, Palestinians, and Egyptians were deported from Lebanon by the government on grounds of subversion with the United Arab Republic.[4] This number is surpassed by some two-thirds of the entire population of Lebanon that was displaced throughout 1975–1990.[5] Whereas the 1958 War cost the country thousands of Lebanese lira in revenue, the UN reported that each year of the later civil war until 1982 tallied 2 billion USD in damages.[6] Lastly, by 1983, Syria, Israel, and the US-led

---

[1] Hady Zaccak, *Honeymoon 1958*, DVD (Rome: Istituto Luce Cinecittà, 2013).
[2] Georges Corm, *Lubnan al-Mu'asir: Tarikh wa-Mujtama'a* [Modern Lebanon: History and Society], trans. Hassan Qubaysi (Beirut: al-Maktaba al-Sharqiyya, 2004), 107.
[3] Michael Hudson, *The Precarious Republic* (1968), 108; and Khalaf, *Civil and Uncivil Violence in Lebanon* (2002), 232.
[4] FO 371/134127, Middleton, no. 962, July 10, 1958.
[5] Khalaf, *Civil and Uncivil Violence in Lebanon*, 232.
[6] Central Directorate of Statistics, *al-Nashra al-Ihsa'iyya Rub' al-Sanawiyya, 1960–1961* [Quarterly Statistical Bulletin, 1960–1961] (Beirut: Ministry of Planning, 1961), 49; and Khalaf, *Civil and Uncivil Violence in Lebanon*, 232.

multinational forces occupied Lebanon, and some of their forces did not leave until recently.[7] By comparison, in the 1958 War, the government and its supporters, including the Kata'ib, could not prove large-scale interference nor provoke global intervention until change elsewhere in the region brought US forces to the shores of Beirut.

This difference in scope and scale is one reason *Winning Lebanon* ends in 1958. That is, the events that led up to that war mark more of a rupture than a continuity. More specifically, I find 1958 to be the end of an era of youth, popular, and disruptive politics. What started during the French colonial period as a project of youth empowerment, grounded in populism, ended with young people at the center of a war. However, much of the history of popular organizations before 1958 has little to do with sustained, physical violence. Youth-centric movements were some of the first to crystalize anti-colonial, political, social, and economic platforms that carried into the early independence era. They met, sang, played – shaping new youth cultures – and discussed issues of communal, national, and global importance. Lastly, these groups placed young people, in all their shapes and forms, from Beirut to Brazil, as the makers of these politics. Hence, if this book has done anything, it is to serve as a call to center youth and their politics, not only in the history of modern Lebanon, but global politics in the twentieth and twenty-first centuries. While the former should be of interest to the historian, the latter is significant to those considering contemporary trends. They include Occupy Wall Street, the Arab Spring, and what I read as youth-centric protests of 2019, ranging from the Hong Kong protest movement to an unfolding "revolution" in Lebanon, as protesters are referring to it, a *thawra*.

Another reason this book culminates with 1958 is to work alongside others who are attempting to showcase this as a truly "revolutionary year."[8] Additionally, *Winning Lebanon* hopes to serve as a call for globalizing 1958. To do such is first to put the scholarship on 1958 in Lebanon, Iraq, Jordan, and the Arab Middle East in conversation with other works focusing on 1958 in the Global South.[9] In Africa, young intellectuals, ranging from Franz Fanon to James Baldwin, formed the backbone of the growing Tricontinental movement. They did this as they

---

[7] For more information on these interventions, see Traboulsi, *A History of Modern Lebanon* (2007), 214–227.

[8] For more information on 1958 in the region, see Wm. Roger Louis and Roger Owen, eds., *A Revolutionary Year: The Middle East in 1958* (London: I.B. Tauris, 2002); and Jeffrey G. Karam, ed., *The Middle East in 1958: Reimagining A Revolutionary Year* (London: I.B. Tauris, 2020).

[9] This sentiment comes out of conversations for a panel I organized at the American Historical Association annual meeting in January 2019 (Chicago, US), titled, "A Revolutionary Year: Centering and Globalizing 1958."

talked about, and experienced firsthand, French colonial policy in Algeria.[10] Thousands of miles away, from the Mediterranean to the Caribbean, Cuban peasants called for radical land reform in 1958 – that of which Fidel Castro would popularize years later.[11] The young Lebanese people described in this book were aware of these crises, and their significance, whether they agreed or disagreed with their premises. To globalize 1958, then, also means placing young people at the heart of this story – ten years before they become acknowledged as the center – and narrate this story from the ground-up.

Therefore, even if the Lebanese, like Zaccak following her honeymoon, forgot 1958, it has, and should continue to hold, an important place in historical scholarship. 1958 can also play a crucial role in understanding exactly what the Lebanese have forgotten: the connections between the Lebanese Civil War and the 1958 War. While one could focus on unresolved sociopolitical issues, the type of urban warfare, or the place of regional powers, I want to stress here a simple point as it relates to *futuwwa* or "youthfulness." Many of the rank-and-file men and women of different fighting forces to the Lebanese Civil War were young in 1958. Whether those as (in)famous as Bashir and Amin Gemayel (the sons of Pierre), Walid Jumblatt (the son of Kamal) and George Hawi (Lebanese Communist Party), or "ordinary" young people, the 1958 War served as their "initiation into militancy."[12] At twenty years or younger, they participated alongside their fathers, brothers, and sisters in these rituals of violence – their blood baptism so to speak. Furthermore, the type of language they practiced to make sense of the conflict (i.e., our just struggle vs. the punks and their abomination), how they performed violence (rituals of youth culture), and where they engaged in conflict (across the country) is observable in future moments of "sectarian violence" in Lebanon and beyond during the twentieth and twenty-first centuries. In the end, *Winning Lebanon* has attempted to highlight that popular organizations, and the young leaders and members within them, engineered these trends.

Lastly, 1958 can live on through popular culture, and not just that which exclusively surrounds popular organizations. While *Winning Lebanon* has highlighted the significance of this source focus in new

---

[10] For more information, see Jeffrey James Byrne, *Mecca of Revolution: Algeria, Decolonization, and the Third World Order* (New York: Oxford University Press, 2016); and Tyler Stovall, "The Fire This Time: Black American Expatriates and the Algerian War," *Yale French Studies* 98 (2000): 182–200.

[11] See Sara Kozameh, "Guerrillas, Peasants and Communists: Agrarian Reform in Cuba's 1958 Liberated Territories," *The Americas* 76, no. 4 (2019): 641–673.

[12] Khalaf, *Civil and Uncivil Violence in Lebanon*, 146.

interpretations of the past, popular culture beyond the group level is a critical element not addressed in this book. Accordingly, I call others to examine radio – both those stations operated by popular organizations and those that were not – television, and art during wartime in 1958. One set of notable artifacts that I would like to conclude with here are the paintings of Khalil Zgheib (1911–1975). Hailing from Mount Lebanon, Zgheib made several paintings depicting life around the 1958 War, one of which is on the cover of this book, titled *Le Début des Événements de 1958*, or "The Beginning of the Events of 1958." According to the owner of this painting, Zgheib likely created it on May 9, just one day after the murder of anti-Chamoun journalist Nasib al-Matni in Beirut.[13] Consequently, it serves as an immediate reaction to the war.

Many of Zgheib's admirers consider him a simpleton, part of the *Naïf* art movement. As a result, in conversations they remind me not to over-interpret his work. Even if arguable, and Zgheib was not actively considering 1958 as a metaphor or symbol, there are two noticeable aspects of this painting of downtown Beirut that relate to the themes of *Winning Lebanon*. First, is that while some individuals in the painting are shown bloodied, victims to the war, others are not. Whether it is the young woman walking her dog down the street or the Muslims praying at al-Omari Mosque, they just act as if, according to one art critic, they "don't give a damn."[14] Here Zgheib juxtaposes chaos and calm. Perhaps, then, he is speaking to the transformation in motion of everyday nonviolent rituals to practices of violence. While popular organizations may mobilize the youth culture that made sense to them – oathing, saluting, marching, telling, and visualizing stories of struggle – bystanders may go on with their quotidian existence as if nothing had happened. Whereas the latter was an act of coping, the former was an act of justifying, performing, and producing violence in 1958.

Second of importance to *Winning Lebanon* is how youth are depicted in Zgheib's work. The forty-seven-year-old painter drew three typical male *shabab*, in the back right of the painting. They appear to be protesting – one has his right hand up in the air – blocking traffic, and occupying space. These depictions reflect multiple conceptions of youth described throughout this book. Scholars, pundits, leaders, and now artists, conceived of young people before, in, or after 1958 as either activists, street nuisances, or maddened examples of the worst of *futuwwa*. Perhaps most importantly, *Winning Lebanon* has added nuance to these absolute

---

[13] Conversations with Ambassador Samir Moubarak, Aintoura Kisrawan, Lebanon, June 4, 2018.

[14] Conversations with Saleh Barakat, Beirut, Lebanon, May 25, 2018.

characterizations of young people. As I have tried to highlight, popular organizations, and the young individuals at their core, were active and do matter. Through their practices they effected change, nonviolent and violent. Whether one considers it positive or negative change is not exactly the point. *Winning Lebanon* has meant to uncover the reality that young people are not only the products of history, but its producers as well.

Bibliography

Archives and Special Collections

Foreign Relations of the United States Series
1958–1960: Lebanon and Jordan. Volume XI
Kamel Mroueh Foundation Collection. Beirut, Lebanon
Kata'ib Party Museum Collection. Haret Sakher, Lebanon
Linda Sadaqah Collection. American University of Beirut, Lebanon
1951–1952 Political Crisis Files
1958 Crisis Files
Lebanese Kata'ib Party Files
Najjadeh Party Files
Syrian Social Nationalist Party Files
Progressive Socialist Party Collection. Dar al-Taqaddumiyya, Moukhtara, Lebanon
Records at the British National Archives, London, United Kingdom
FO 371 (General Correspondence)
FO 1018 (Embassy and Consular Archives)
Records at the Lebanese National Archives, Beirut
Government Decrees and Information on Associations, Gatherings and Sports Clubs
Records at the United Nations Archives and Records Management, New York
AG-020 United Nations Office for Special Affairs (1955–1991)
AG-056 United Nations Observation Group in Lebanon (UNOGIL) (1958)
Records at the United States National Archives, College Park, MD
Record Group 59: Lebanon Crisis Files, 1958
Tala'i' Organization Collections. 'Amiliyya Islamic Benevolent Society Records.
      Beirut, Lebanon.

Organizational and Affiliated Newspapers

al-Akhbar (Lebanese Communist Party)
al-'Amal (Kata'ib Party)
al-Anba' (Progressive Socialist Party)
Ansar al-Sada (Najjadeh Party)
al-Aswaq (Syrian Social Nationalist Party)
al-Bashir (Kata'ib Party-affiliated)

Bayrut (Najjadeh Party-affiliated)
al-Bina' (Syrian Social Nationalist Party)
al-Insaniyya (Lebanese People's Party)
al-Iyman (Najjadeh Party)
al-Jarida (Syrian Social Nationalist Party-affiliated)
al-Majalla (Syrian Social Nationalist Party-affiliated)
al-Nahda (Syrian Social Nationalist Party)
al-Nashra al-Rasmiyya (Syrian Social Nationalist Party)
al-Nida' (Lebanese Communist Party)
al-Rai (Arab Nationalist Youth)
Sada al-Shamal (Syrian Social Nationalist Party)
al-Safa' (Syrian Social Nationalist Party)
al-Sahafi al-Ta'ih (Lebanese People's Party-affiliated)
Sawt al-Sha'b (Lebanese Communist Party)
Sawt al-'Uruba (Najjadeh Party)
al-Tha'ir (Arab Nationalist Youth)
al-'Urwa (Arab Nationalist Youth-affiliated)
al-Waqt (Lebanese Communist Party)
al-Zauba'a (Syrian Social Nationalist Party – Argentina)

National Newspapers and Journals

Bayrut al-Masa'
Le Commerce du Levant
al-Diyar
al-Hayat
al-Nahar
al-Siyasa
al-'Urfan

Primary Sources in Arabic

Arab Nationalist Youth. *Rawa'i' Mukhtara min al-Sha'r al-Qawmi* [Selected Masterpieces from Nationalist Poetry]. Beirut: 1952.
Central Directorate of Statistics. *Al-Nashra al-Ihsa'iyya Rub' al-Sanawiyya, 1958* [Quarterly Statistical Bulletin, 1958]. Beirut: Ministry of Planning, 1958.
    Al-Nashra al-Ihsa'iyya Rub' al-Sanawiyya, 1960–1961 [Quarterly Statistical Bulletin, 1960–1961]. Beirut: Ministry of Planning, 1961.
Friends of Kamal Jumblatt Association. *Nadwa al-Arba'a' 'ala Khata Kamal Junblatt, 2010–2011* [Wednesday Lecture in the Footsteps of Kamal Jumblatt, 2010–2011]. Beirut: Rabata Asdiqa' Kamal Junblatt, 2011.
Jumblatt, Kamal. *Fi Maraqf al-Umam* [In the Service of the Nations]. Moukhtara, Lebanon: Dar al-Taqaddumiyya, 2007.
    Haqiqat al-Thawra al-Lubnaniyya: al-Dawaf'a al-Haqqa li-l-Intifada al-Lubnaniyya al-Akhira, 1959 [The Truth of the Lebanese Revolution: The

True Motives for the Recent Lebanese Uprising, 1959]. Beirut: Lajnat Turath al-Qa'id al-Shahid, 1978.

Nahu Sigha Jadida li-l-Dimuqratiyya al-Ijtima'iyya wa-l-Insaniyya 1945 [Toward a New Formula for Humanist and Socialist Democracy 1945]. Moukhtara, Lebanon: Dar al-Taqaddumiyya, 2004.

Rihla ila al-Hind: Liqa' al-Hakim Shri Atmananda [Trips to India: Meeting with the Doctor Sri Atmananda]. Moukhtara, Lebanon: Dar al-Taqaddumiyya, 2011.

Lebanese Communist Party. *Nidal al-Hizb al-Shiyu'i al-Lubnani min khilal Watha'iqahu* [The Struggle of the Lebanese Communist Party through Its Documents], vol. 1. Beirut: Manshurat al-Hizb al-Shiyu'i al-Lubnani, 1971.

Sawt al-Sha'b Aqwa: Safhat min al-Sahafa al-Shiyu'iyya al-'Amaliyya wa-l-Dimuqratiyya 'ala Khamsin 'Ama [The Voice of the People Is the Strongest: Pages from the Communist, Working, and Democratic Press at Fifty Years]. Beirut: Dar al-Farabi, 1974.

Lebanese Kata'ib Party. *Tawsiyat al-Hizb al-Kata'ib al-Dimuqratiyya al-Ijtima'iyya al-Lubnaniyya min Mu'tamir al-Awwal ila Mu'tamir al-Thamin 'Ashir* [Recommendations of the Lebanese Social Democratic Kata'ib Party from the First Conference to the Eighteenth Conference]. Beirut: Manshurat Dar al-'Amal li-l-Taba'a wa-l-Nashr, 1993.

al-Makdisi, Toufiq. *Al-Ahzab al-Siyasiyya fi Lubnan 'Am 1959* [Political Parties in Lebanon in 1959]. Beirut: Manshurat al-Jarida wa-l-Orienan, 1959.

Min Qalb Bayrut: Muhyi al-Din al-Nasuli, 1897–1961 [From the Heart of Beirut: Muhyi al-Din al-Nasuli, 1897–1961]. Beirut: Dar al-Nahar li-l-Nashr, 1992.

Mroueh, Kamel. *Nihna fi Afriqiyya: al-Hijra al-Lubnaniyya al-Suriyya ila Afriqiyya al-Gharbiyya Madiha, Hadirha, Mustaqbala* [Us in Africa: The Lebanese Syrian Migration in West Africa, Past, Present, and Future]. Beirut: al-Makshufa, 1938.

Naqqash, Shafiq, and 'Ali Khalifa. *Al-Haraka al-Kashshafiyya fi al-Aqtar al-'Arabiyya* [The Scout Movement in the Arab Countries]. Beirut: Dar al-Kashshaf, 1936.

Progressive Socialist Party. *Anashid al-Hizb al-Taqaddumi al-Ishtiraki* [Anthems for the Progressive Socialist Party]. Beirut: Progressive Socialist Party, n.d.

Mithaq al-Hizb al-Taqaddumi al-Ishtiraki [The Charter of the Progressive Socialist Party]. Beirut: Dar al-Ahad, 195[?].

Al-Nizam al-Dakhili [The Internal Structure]. Beirut: Progressive Socialist Party, 1972.

Saadeh, Antoun. *Mabadi' al-Hizb al-Suri al-Qawmi al-Ijtima'i wa-Ghayatuh* [The Principles of the Syrian Social Nationalist Party and It Goals]. Beirut[?]: Syrian Social Nationalist Party[?], 1947.

Nushu' al-Umam: Kitab al-Awwal [The Birth of Nations: The First Book]. Beirut: 1938.

Syrian Social Nationalist Party. *Al-Hizb al-Qawmi Yarad 'ala al-Hizb al-Shiyu'i* [The Nationalist Party Responds to the Communist Party]. Beirut: Syrian Social Nationalist Party, 1945.

Al-Nizam al-Dakhili [The Internal Structure]. Beirut: Syrian Social Nationalist Party, 1955.

Zurayk, Constantine. *Ma'na al-Nakba* [The Meaning of the Disaster]. Beirut: Dar al-'Alim li-l-Malayin, 1948.

Primary Sources in English and French

Abouchdid, Eugenie Elie. *Thirty Years of Lebanon & Syria*. Beirut: The Sader-Rihani Printing Company, 1948.

Baden-Powell, Robert. *Scouting for Boys: A Handbook for Instruction in Good Citizenship* (1908). Edited by Elleke Boehmer. Oxford: Oxford University Press, 2004.

Disraeli, Benjamin. *Sybil or the Two Nations*. Oxford: Oxford University Press, 1925.

"French Mandate for Syria and the Lebanon." *The American Journal of International Law* 17, no. 3, Supplemental Official Documents (July 1923): 177–182.

Jumblatt, Kamal. *I Speak for Lebanon*. Translated by Michael Pallis. London: Zed Press, 1982.

Lebanese Kata'ib Party. *Connaissance des Kataeb: Leur doctrine et leur poltique nationales* [Knowing the Kata'ib: Their Doctrine and National Politics]. Beirut: 1948.

Office of United States Chief of Counsel for Prosecution of Axis Criminality. *Nazi Conspiracy and Aggression*, vol. 1. Washington, DC: United States Government Printing Office, 1946.

Saadeh, Antoun. *The Genesis of Nations*. Translated by the Department of Culture of the Syrian Social Nationalist Party. Beirut: Syrian Social Nationalist Party, 2004.

Schram, Stuart R., ed. *Quotations from Chairman Mao Tse-Tung*. New York: Bantam Books, 1967.

Stewart, Desmond. *Turmoil in Beirut: A Personal Account*. London: Allan Wingate, 1958.

Syrian Social Nationalist Party. *A Note Concerning the Work and Achievement of the Women's Branch in the Syrian Social Nationalist Party: For the Political and Social Emancipation and Progress of the Syrian Woman*. Beirut: 1949.

Zurayk, Constantine. *The Meaning of the Disaster*. Translated by R. Bayly Winder. Beirut: Khayat's College Book Cooperative, 1956.

Films

Assaf, Farid. *Ahzab Lubnan* [Lebanese Political Parties]. DVD series. Seattle, WA: Arab Film Distribution, 2003.

Zaccak, Hady. *Honeymoon 1958*. DVD. Rome: Istituto Luce Cinecittà, 2013.

Kamal Jumblatt: al-Shahid wa-l-Shuhada [Kamal Jumblatt: Witness and Martyr]. DVD. Beirut: Friends of Kamal Joumblatt Association, 2015.

Arabic Secondary Sources

Abu Khalil, Joseph. *Biyar al-Gemayel: Qisa Rajul wa-Watan* [Pierre Gemayel: Story of a Man and His Nation]. Beirut: Haquq al-Taba'a Mafuza li-l-Mu'lif, 2002.

Abu Salah, 'Abbas. *Al-'Azma al-Lubaniyya 'Am 1958: Fi Dawa' Watha'iq Yukshaf 'anha al-Awwal Marra* [The Lebanese Crisis of 1958: In Light of Documents Revealed for the First Time]. Beirut: al-Kursa al-Mashur, 1998.

al-Ahmad, Ahmad Salim. *Hizb al-Suri al-Qawmi al-Ijtima'i, 1932–1962: Dirasa Tarikhiyya* [The Syrian Social Nationalist Party, 1932–1962: A Historical Study]. Beirut: Dar wa-Maktabat al-Turath wa-l-Adab, 2014.

Aoun, Jean, and Joseph Abu Khalil. *Al-Sheikh Pierre: Tarikh fi Sur* [Sheikh Pierre: History in Pictures]. Translated by Joyce Badran and Darine Karkafy. Beirut: Mehanna Group, 2007.

Arab Cultural Club. *Masira al-Khamsin 'Am: al-Nadi al-Thaqafi al-'Arabi, 1944–1994* [A Fifty-Year Journey: The Arab Cultural Club, 1944–1994]. Beirut: 1994.

Al-Nadi al-Thaqafi al-'Arabi khilal 35 'Am, 1944–1979 [The Arab Cultural Club at Thirty-Five Years, 1944–1979]. Beirut: 1980.

al-'Azmah, 'Aziz. *Qustantin Zurayq: 'Arabiyyun li-l-Qarn al-'Ishriyyin* [Constantine Zurayk: Arabs for the Twentieth Century]. Beirut: Mu'assasat al-Darasat al-Filistiniyya, 2003.

Barut, Muhammad. *Harakat al-Qawmiyyin al-'Arab: al-Nash'a, al-Tatawwur, al-Musa'ir* [The Arab Nationalist Movement: Origins, Development, Fate]. Damascus: al-Markaz al-'Arabi li-l-Darasat al-Istratijiyya, 1997.

Charaf, Jean. *Tarikh Hizb al-Kata'ib al-Lubnaniyya* [The History of the Lebanese Kata'ib Party], vol. 1, 1936–1940. Beirut: Dar al-'Amal li-l-Nashr, 1979.

Tarikh Hizb al-Kata'ib al-Lubnaniyya [The History of the Lebanese Kata'ib Party], vol. 3, 1946–1952. Beirut: Dar al-'Amal li-l-Nashr, 2009.

Tarikh Hizb al-Kata'ib al-Lubnaniyya [The History of the Lebanese Kata'ib Party], vol. 4, 1953–1967. Beirut: Dar al-'Amal li-l-Nashr, 2009.

Corm, Georges. *Lubnan al-Mu'asir: Tarikh wa-Mujtama'a* [Modern Lebanon: History and Society]. Translated by Hassan Qubaysi. Beirut: al-Maktaba al-Sharqiyya, 2004.

Ghanma, Amjad Dhib. *Jam'iyyat al-'Urwa al-Wuthqa: Nash'atuha wa-Nashatatuha* [The Invisible Bond Society: Its Origins and Activities]. Beirut: Riad El-Rayyes Books, 2002.

Hardan, Nuwaf. *Sa'adeh fi al-Mahjar* [Saadeh in Exile], vol. 1, 1921–1930, Brazil. Beirut: Dar Fikr li-l-Ibhath wa-l-Nashr, 1989.

Sa'adeh fi al-Mahjar [Saadeh in Exile], vol. 2, 1938–1940. Beirut: Bisan li-l-Nashr wa-li-l-Tuzi'a, 1996.

al-Hindi, Hani, and 'Abd Ilila al-Nasurawi. *Harakat al-Qawmiyyin al-'Arab: Nashataha wa-Tatwarha 'abr Watha'iqha, 1951–1967* [The Arab Nationalist Movement: Its Activities and Developments according to Its Documents, 1951–1967], vol. 1. Beirut: Jam'iyyat al-Haquq Mahfutha al-Abhath al-'Arabi, 2001.

Harakat al-Qawmiyyin al-'Arab: Nashataha wa-Tatwarha 'abr Watha'iqha, 1951–1967 [The Arab Nationalist Movement: Its Activities and

Developments according to Its Documents, 1951–1967], vol. 4. Beirut: Jam'iyyat al-Haquq Mahfutha al-Abhath al-'Arabi, 2004.

'Issa, Ghassan Ahmed. *Munazzamat al-Tala'i' fi Lubnan min khilal Watha'iquha al-Asliyya, 1944–1947* [The Vanguard Organization of Lebanon through Its Founding Documents]. PhD diss., Lebanese University, 1992.

al-Jabburi, Fathi 'Abass Khalaf Mahanna. *Nasha'a al-Hizb al-Taqaddumi al-Ishtiraki wa-Muwaqafahu al-Dakhiliyya wa-l-Kharajiyya, 1949–1975: Darasa Tarikhiyya* [The Origins of the Progressive Socialist Party and Its Internal and External Positions, 1949–1975: A Historical Study]. Moukhtara, Lebanon: Dar al-Taqaddumiyya, 2009.

Jamhuri, Antoun Jarji. *Thikrayat: Thikrayat al-Mafud fi al-Quwwa al-Nithamiyya al-Kata'ibiyya, Ahdath 1958* [Memoirs: Memoirs of Commissionership in the Kata'ib Organizational Force, Events of 1958]. Beirut: Manshurat Dar al-'Amal, 201?.

Jazmati, Nadhir. *Musahama fi Naqd al-Harakat al-Siyasiyya fi Suriya wa-Lubnan: al-Hizb al-Shuyu'i al-Suri, 1924–1958* [Contribution to Understanding Political Movements in Syria and Lebanon: The Syrian Communist Party, 1924–1958]. Damascus: Mutaba'a Ibn Hiyan, 1990.

Jazmati, Naziy. *Al-Hizb al-Shiyu'i al-Lubnani* [The Lebanese Communist Party]. In *al-Ahzab wa-l-Harakat al-Shiyu'iyya wa-l-Markisiyya al-'Arabiyya* [The Arab Communist and Marxist Parties and Movements], vol. 1, 263–304. Damascus: Arab Centre for Strategic Studies, 2000.

Jiraj, Jibran. *Min al-Ja'aba: Marawiyat, Mustanadat, wa-Adabiyyat 'an al-Hizb al-Suri al-Qawmi al-Ijtma'i* [From the Bag: Stories, Documents, and Literature on the Syrian Social Nationalist Party], vol. 1, November 16, 1932 – November 16, 1935. Lebanon: 1985.

Min al-Ja'aba: Marawiyat, Mustanadat, wa-Adabiyyat 'an al-Hizb al-Suri al-Qawmi al-Ijtma'i [From the Bag: Stories, Documents, and Literature on the Syrian Social Nationalist Party], vol. 2, November 16, 1935 – November 16, 1936. Lebanon: 1986.

Juha, Shifaq. *Al-Haraka al-'Arabiyya al-Sirriyya: Jama'at al-Kitab al-Ahmar, 1935–1945* [The Secret Arab Movement: The Society of the Red Book]. Beirut: al-Furat, 2004.

Ma'rakat Masir Lubnan fi 'Ahd al-Intidab al-Faransi, 1918–1946 [Battle for the Fate of Lebanon in the French Mandate Period], vol. 2. Beirut: Maktabat Ra's Bayrut, 1995.

Karami, Nadiya, and Nawwaf Karami. *Waqi'at al-Thawra al-Lubnaniyya 1958* [The Reality of the 1958 Lebanese Revolution], 2nd ed. Moukhtara, Lebanon: Dar al-Taqaddumiyya, 2010.

Khir, Milya Malik. *Muhyi al-Din al-Nasuli, 1896–1961* [introduction to Nasuli's *Bayrut* newspaper microfilm]. Beirut: American University of Beirut, Jafet Library Audiovisual Materials, 1971.

al-Kubaisi, Basil. *Harakat al-Qawmiyyin al-'Arab* [The Arab Nationalist Movement]. Beirut: al-Ittihad al-'Am li-l-Kitab wa-l-Sahafahiyyin al-Filastiniyyin, 1974.

ul Luhum, Suyyid. *Musua'a Hizb al-Kata'ib al Lubnaniyya min Biyar al-Mu'sus ila Biyar al-Shahid* [Encyclopedia of the Lebanese Kata'ib Party: From Pierre the Founder to Pierre the Martyr], vol. 1, *Bidayat al-Ta'sis wa-l-Intilaq, 1936–1942* [Beginning of the Founding, 1936–1942]. Beirut: Dar al-Ittihad al-Thaqafa al-'Arabi, 2007.

Lebanese Kata'ib Party. *Al-'Amal Monthly Magazine*, vol. 14. Beirut: Dar al-'Amal, 1979.

Al-Kata'ib al-Lubnaniyya: Hizb Dimuqrati Ijtima'i [The Lebanese Kata'ib: A Social Democratic Party]. Beirut: Maslahat al-Da'ayya fi al-Kata'ib al-Lubnaniyya, 1958.

Majid, Khalil Majid. *Al-Intikhabat al-Lubnaniyya, 1861–1992: al-Quwaniyyin-al-Nita'ij* [Lebanese Elections, 1861–1992: Laws to Results]. Beirut: al-Mu'assasa al-Jam'iyya al-Darasat wa-l-Nashra wa-l-Tawaza', 1992.

Maki, Hussein. *Rashid Baydun: Qawl wa-Fi'l* [Rashid Baydun: Sayings and Actions]. Beirut: Matabi' al-Masri, 1967.

Malik, 'Adel. *1958: al-Qassa, al-Asrar, al-Watha'iq* [1958: The Story, the Secret, the Documents]. Jounieh, Lebanon: Dar Sa'ir al-Mashriq, 2011.

Matar, Fuad. *Hakim al-Thawra: Sira Jurj Habash wa-Nidalahu* [The Doctor of Revolution: Biography of George Habash and His Struggle]. Beirut: Dar al-Nahar, 2008.

Progressive Socialist Party. *Rub' Qarn min al-Nidal* [A Quarter Century of the Struggle]. Beirut: Progressive Socialist Party, 1974.

Qubrasi, 'Abdullah. *'Abdullah Qubrasi Yatathakar: Ta'sis al-Hizb al-Suri al-Qawmi al-Ijtima'i wa-Bidayat al-Nidal* ['Abdullah Qubrasi Recalls: The Founding of the Syrian Social Nationalist Party and the Beginning of the Struggle], vol. 1. Beirut: Mu'assisa Fikr al-Abhath wa-l-Nashr, 1982.

Sharabi, Hisham. *Al-Jamr wa-l-Ramad: Thikrayat Muthaqqaf 'Arabi* [Embers and Ashes: Memoirs of an Arab Intellectual]. Beirut: Dar Nelson, 1998.

Syrian Social Nationalist Party. *Antun Sa'adeh, 1904–1949*. Beirut: Syrian Social Nationalist Party, 2010.

Secondary Sources in English

Abou-Hodeib, Tofoul. *A Taste for Home: The Modern Middle Class in Beirut*. Stanford, CA: Stanford University Press, 2017.

Abu-Rish, Ziad Munif. "Conflict and Institution Building in Lebanon, 1946–1955." PhD diss., University of California, Los Angeles, 2014.

Abisaab, Malek Hassan. *Militant Women of a Fragile Nation*. Syracuse, NY: Syracuse University Press, 2010.

Agwani, M. S. *Communism in the Arab East*. New York: Asia Pub. House, 1969.

The Lebanese Crisis, 1958: A Documentary Study. New Delhi: Asia Publishing House, 1965.

Anderson, Benedict. *Imagined Communities: Reflections of the Origin and Spread of Nationalism*. Revised ed. London: Verso, 2006.

Anderson, Betty. *The American University of Beirut: Arab Nationalism and Liberal Education*. Austin, TX: University of Texas Press, 2011.

Aslanidis, Paris. "Populism and Social Movements." In *The Oxford Handbook of Populism*, edited by Cristóbal Rovira Kaltwasser, Paul A. Taggart, Paulina

Ochoa Espejo, and Pierre Ostiguy, 10–26. Oxford: Oxford University Press, 2017.

Atiyyah, Aman. "Development of Shi'ite Education in Lebanon." Master's thesis, American University of Beirut, 1972.

Attié, Caroline. *Struggle in the Levant: Lebanon in the 1950s.* London: I.B. Tauris Publishers, 2004.

Ayalon, Ami. *The Press in the Arab Middle East: A History.* Oxford: Oxford University Press, 1995.

Barak, Oren. *The Lebanese Army: A National Institution in a Divided Society.* Albany, NY: State University of New York Press, 2009.

Baroudi, Sami. "Divergent Perspectives among Lebanon's Maronites during the 1958 Crisis." *Critique: Middle Eastern Studies* 8, no. 1 (Spring 2006): 5–28.

Bashkin, Orit. *The Other Iraq: Pluralism and Culture in Hashemite Iraq.* Stanford, CA: Stanford University Press, 2009.

Baun, Dylan. "The Gemmayzeh Incident of 1949: Conflict over Physical and Symbolic Space in Beirut." *Arab Studies Journal* 25, no. 1 (2017): 92–122.

"Lebanon's Youth Clubs and the 1936 Summer Olympics: Mobilizing Sports, Challenging Imperialism and Launching a National Project." *The International Journal of the History of Sport* 34, no. 13 (2017): 1347–1365.

"Populism and War-Making: Populist Alliances, Enemy Imaging and the Left during the Early Lebanese Civil War Era." In *Mapping Populism: Approaches and Methods*, edited by Amit Ron and Majia Nadesan, 146–157. Abingdon, Oxon: Routledge, 2020.

Bayat, Asef. *Life as Politics: How Ordinary People Change the Middle East.* Stanford, CA: Stanford University Press, 2010.

Beinin, Joel. "The Communist Movement and Nationalist Political Discourse in Nasirist Egypt." *Middle East Journal* 41, no. 4 (1987): 568–584.

Workers and Peasants in the Modern Middle East. Cambridge: Cambridge University Press, 2001.

Beshara, Adel. "Antun Sa'adeh: Architect of Syrian Nationalism." In *The Origins of Syrian Nationhood: Histories, Pioneers and Identity*, edited by Adel Beshara, 341–363. New York: Routledge, 2011.

Outright Assassination: The Trial and Execution of Antun Sa'adeh, 1949. Reading, UK: Ithaca Press, 2010.

Bier, Laura. *Revolutionary Womanhood: Feminisms, Modernity and the State in Egypt.* Stanford, CA: Stanford University Press, 2011.

Bishop, Elizabeth. "Steadfast and Rejectionist Front of Arab States: Iraq's 14 July 1958 Coup and the Unraveling of the Arab Union." Conference paper, American Historical Association annual meeting. Chicago, US, 2019.

Bodron, Margaret M. "Violence in the Syrian Social Nationalist Party." Master's thesis, American University of Beirut, 1970.

Bourdieu, Pierre. *Distinction: A Social Critique of the Judgment of Taste.* Translated by Richard Nice. Cambridge, MA: Harvard University Press, 1984.

The Field of Cultural Production. Essays on Art and Literature. Edited by Randal Johnson. New York: Columbia University Press, 1993.

Language and Symbolic Power. Edited by John B. Thompson. Translated by Gino Raymond and Matthew Adamson. Malden, MA: Polity Press, 1992.

Outline of a Theory of Practice. Translated by Richard Nice. Cambridge: Cambridge University Press, 1977.

Brand, Tylor. "Lives Darkened by Calamity: Enduring the Famine of WWI in Lebanon and Western Syria." PhD diss., American University of Beirut, 2014.

Buechler, Steven M. *Understanding Social Movements: Theories from the Classical Era to the Present*. Boulder, CO: Paradigm Publishers, 2011.

Byrne, Jeffrey James. *Mecca of Revolution: Algeria, Decolonization, and the Third World Order*. New York: Oxford University Press, 2016.

Chalcraft, John. *Popular Politics in the Making of the Modern Middle East*. Cambridge: Cambridge University Press, 2016.

Cole, Juan R. I. *Colonialism and Revolution in the Middle East: Social and Cultural Origins of Egypt's 'Urabi Movement*. Princeton, NJ: Princeton University Press, 1993.

Dajani, Nabil A. *Disoriented Media in a Fragmented Society: The Lebanese Experience*. Beirut: American University of Beirut, 1992.

Davis, Natalie Zemon. "The Rites of Violence: Religious Riot in Sixteenth-Century France." *Past & Present* 59 (1973): 51–91.

Deeb, Lara. *An Enchanted Modern: Gender and Public Piety in Shi'i Lebanon*. Princeton, NJ: Princeton University Press, 2006.

Degg, Martin R. "A Database of Historical Earthquake Activity in the Middle East." *Transactions of the Institute of British Geographers* 15, no. 3 (1990): 294–307.

Dueck, Jennifer. *The Claims of Culture at Empire's End: Syria and Lebanon under French Rule*. Oxford: Oxford University Press: 2010.

Early, Evelyn. "The Amiliyya Society of Beirut: A Case Study of an Emerging Urban Za'im." Master's thesis, American University of Beirut, 1971.

Entelis, John. *Pluralism and Party Transformation in Lebanon: Al-Kata'ib, 1936–1970*. Leiden: E. J. Brill, 1974.

Erlich, Haggai. *Youth and Revolution in the Changing Middle East, 1908–2014*. Boulder, CO: Lynne Reinner Publishers, Inc., 2014.

Eveland, Wilbur Crane. *Ropes of Sand: America's Failure in the Middle East*. Toronto: W.W. Norton & Company, Inc, 1980.

Fahmy, Ziad. *Ordinary Egyptians: Creating the Modern Nation through Popular Culture*. Stanford, CA: Stanford University Press, 2011.

Fahrenthold, Stacey D. *Between the Ottomans and the Entente: The First World War in the Syrian and Lebanese Diaspora, 1908–1925*. Oxford: Oxford University Press, 2019.

Farrell, Sean. *Rituals and Riots: Sectarian Violence and Political Culture in Ulster, 1784–1886*. Lexington, KY: University Press of Kentucky, 2009.

Feldman, Allen. *Formations of Violence: The Narrative of the Body and Political Terror in Northern Ireland*. Chicago, IL: University of Chicago Press: 1991.

Firro, Kais M. *Inventing Lebanon: Nationalism and the State under the Mandate*. London: I.B. Tauris, 2002.

Fisk, Robert. *Pity the Nation: The Abduction of Lebanon*. 4th ed. New York: Thunder Mouth Press/Nation Books, 2002.

Foucault, Michel. *Discipline and Punish: The Birth of the Prison*. Translated by Alan Sheridan. New York: Vintage Books Edition, 1979.

Geertz, Clifford. "Deep Play: Notes on the Balinese Cockfight." *Daedalus* 134, no. 4 (2005): 56–86.

Gelvin, James L. *Divided Loyalties: Nationalism and Mass Politics in Syria at the Close of Empire*. Berkeley, CA: University of California Press, 1998.

Gendzier, Irene L. *Notes from the Minefield: United States Intervention in Lebanon and the Middle East, 1945–1958*. New York: Columbia University Press, 1997.

Gerges, Fawaz A. "The Lebanese Crisis of 1958: The Risks of Inflated Self-Importance." *The Beirut Review* 5 (Spring 1993): 1–24.

Gershoni, Israel, and James Jankowski. *Confronting Fascism in Egypt: Dictatorship versus Democracy in the 1930s*. Stanford, CA: Stanford University Press, 2010.

Goria, Wade R. *Sovereignty and Leadership in Lebanon 1943–1976*. London: Ithaca Press, 1985.

Gorsuch, Anne E. *Youth in Revolutionary Russia: Enthusiasts, Bohemians, Delinquents*. Bloomington, IN: Indiana University Press, 2000.

Halawi, Majed. *A Lebanon Defied: Musa al-Sadr and the Shi'a Community*. Boulder, CO: Westview Press, 1992.

Hanf, Theodor. *Coexistence in Wartime Lebanon: Decline of a State and Rise of a Nation*. London: The Centre for Lebanese Studies, 1993.

Hanssen, Jens, and Max Weiss, eds. *Arabic Thought beyond the Liberal Age: Towards an Intellectual History of the Nahda*. Cambridge: Cambridge University Press, 2016.

Harris, William. *Faces of Lebanon: Sects, Wars, and Global Extensions*. Princeton, NJ: Markus Wiener Publishers, 1997.

Havemann, Axel. "Historiography in 20th-Century Lebanon: Between Confessional Identity and National Coalescence." *Bulletin of the Royal Institute for Inter-Faith Studies* 4, no. 2 (2002): 49–69.

Hazran, Yusri. "Lebanon's Revolutionary Era: Kamal Junblat, the Druze Community and the Lebanon State." *Muslim World* 100 (January 2010): 157–176.

Hitti, Philip K. *Lebanon in History: From the Earliest Times to the Present*. 3rd ed. London: Macmillan and Company Limited, 1967.

Hottinger, Arnold. "Zu'ama' and Parties in the Lebanese Crisis of 1958." *Middle East Journal* 15, no. 2 (Spring 1961): 127–140.

Hourani, Albert. *Arabic Thought in the Liberal Age, 1798–1939*. Cambridge: Cambridge University Press, 1983.

"Ottoman Reform and the Politics of Notables." In *Beginnings of Modernization in the Middle East: The Nineteenth Century*, edited by William R. Polk and Richard L. Chambers, 41–68. Chicago, IL: University of Chicago Press, 1969.

Hudson, Leila. *Transforming Damascus: Space and Modernity in an Islamic City*. New York: Tauris Academic Studies, 2008.

Hudson, Michael. *The Precarious Republic: Political Modernization in Lebanon.* New York: Random House, 1968.

Hyland, Steven. *More Argentine Than You: Arabic Speaking Immigrants in Argentina.* Albuquerque, NM: University of New Mexico Press, 2017.

Ismael, Tareq Y., and Jacqueline S. Ismael. *The Communist Movement in Syria and Lebanon.* Gainesville, FL: University Press of Florida, 1998.

Jacob, Wilson Chacko. *Working Out Egypt: Effendi Masculinity and Subject Formation in Colonial Modernity, 1870–1940.* Durham, NC: Duke University Press, 2011.

Jobs, Richard Ivan. *Backpack Ambassadors: How Youth Travel Integrated Europe.* Chicago, IL: University of Chicago Press, 2017.

Johnson, Michael. *Class and Client in Beirut: The Sunni Muslim Community and the Lebanese State, 1840–1985.* London: Ithaca Press, 1986.

Jones, Justin. *Shi'a Islam in Colonial India: Religion, Community and Sectarianism.* Cambridge: Cambridge University Press, 2012.

Jurdak, Salwa Mansur. "The Evolution of Lebanese Party Politics: 1919–1947." Master's thesis, American University of Beirut, 1948.

Kanaan, Claude Boueiz. *Lebanon 1860–1960: A Century of Myth and Politics.* London: Saqi Books, 2005.

Karam, Jeffrey G., ed. *The Middle East in 1958: Reimagining A Revolutionary Year.* London: I.B. Tauris, 2020.

Kaufman, Asher. *Reviving Phoenicia: In Search of Identity in Lebanon.* London: I.B. Tauris & Co Ltd, 2004.

Kazziha, Walid. *Revolutionary Transformation in the Arab World: Habash and His Comrades from Nationalism to Marxism.* New York: St. Martin's Press, 1975.

Kerr, Malcolm H. *The Arab Cold War: Gamal 'Abd al-Nasir and His Rivals, 1958–1970.* 3rd ed. New York: Oxford University Press, 1971.

Khalaf, Samir. *Civil and Uncivil Violence in Lebanon: A History of the Internationalization of Communal Conflict.* New York: Columbia University Press, 2002.

Heart of Beirut: Reclaiming the Bourj. London: Saqi Books, 2006.

Khater, Akram Fouad. *Inventing Home: Emigration, Gender, and the Middle Class in Lebanon, 1870–1920.* Berkeley, CA: University of California Press, 2001.

el-Khazen, Farid. *The Breakdown of the State in Lebanon 1967–1976.* New York: I.B. Tauris, 2000.

Khuri, Fuad. *From Village to Suburb: Order and Change in Greater Beirut.* Chicago, IL: University of Chicago Press, 1975.

"Kinship, Emigration, and Trade Partnership among the Lebanese of West Africa." *Africa: Journal of the International African Institute* 35, no. 4 (1965): 385–395.

Khuri-Makdisi, Ilham. *The Eastern Mediterranean and the Making of Global Radicalism, 1860–1914.* Berkeley, CA: University of California Press, 2013.

Kozameh, Sara. "Guerrillas, Peasants and Communists: Agrarian Reform in Cuba's 1958 Liberated Territories." *The Americas* 76, no. 4 (2019): 641–673.

Lacquer, Walter Z. *Communism and Nationalism in the Middle East.* London: Routledge & Kegan Paul, 1956.

Landis, Joan B. *Women and the Public Sphere in the Age of the French Revolution.* Ithaca, NY: Cornell University Press, 1988.

Lefebvre, Henri. *The Production of Space.* Translated by Donald Nicholson-Smith. Oxford: Blackwell Publishers Ltd, 1991.

Leichtman, Mara A. "From the Cross (and Crescent) to the Cedar and Back Again: Transnational Religion and Politics among Lebanese Christians in Senegal." *Anthropological Quarterly* 86, no. 1 (Winter 2013): 35–75.

Longrigg, Stephen Hemsley. *Syria and Lebanon under French Mandate.* Oxford: Oxford University Press, 1958.

Louis, Wm. Roger. *The British Empire in the Middle East, 1945–1951: Arab Nationalism, the United States, and Postwar Imperialism.* Oxford: Oxford University Press, 1986.

Louis, Wm. Roger, and Roger Owen, eds. *A Revolutionary Year: The Middle East in 1958.* London: I.B. Tauris, 2002.

Maasri, Zeina. *Off the Wall: Political Posters of the Lebanese Civil War.* London: I.B. Tauris, 2009.

Mahmood, Saba. *Religious Difference in a Secular Age: A Minority Report.* Princeton, NJ: Princeton University Press, 2016.

Makdisi, Ussama. *The Culture of Sectarianism: Community, History, and Violence in Nineteenth-Century Ottoman Lebanon.* Berkeley, CA: University of California Press, 2000.

Maksudyan, Nazan. *Orphans and Destitute Children in the Late Ottoman Empire.* Syracuse, NJ: Syracuse University Press, 2014.

Maktabi, Rania. "The Lebanese Census of 1932 Revisited. Who are the Lebanese?" *British Journal of Middle Eastern Studies* 26, no. 2 (Nov. 1999): 219–41.

Martin, Kevin W. *Syria's Democratic Years: Citizens, Experts, and Media in the 1950s.* Bloomington, IN: Indiana University Press, 2015.

Matthiesen, Toby. *The Other Saudis: Shiism, Dissent and Sectarianism.* Cambridge: Cambridge University Press, 2015.

McAdam, Doug. *Political Process and the Development of the Black Insurgency.* Chicago, IL: University of Chicago Press, 1982.

Mikdashi, Maya. "Sextarianism: Notes on Studying the Lebanese State." In *The Oxford Handbook of Contemporary Middle-Eastern and North African History,* edited by Amal Ghazal and Jens Hanssen. Oxford Handbooks Online, 2018.

Morrison, Heidi. *Childhood and Colonial Modernity in Egypt.* New York: Palgrave Macmillan, 2015.

Nir, Omri. "The Shi'ites during the 1958 Lebanese Crisis." *Middle Eastern Studies* 40, no. 6 (2004): 109–129.

Nordbruch, Gotz. *Nazism in Syria and Lebanon: The Ambivalence of the German Option, 1933–1945.* New York: Routledge, 2009.

Norton, Augustus Richard. *Amal and the Shi'a: Struggle for the Soul of Lebanon.* Austin, TX: University of Texas Press, 1987.

Panizza, Francisco. "What Do We Mean When We Talk about Populism?" In *Latin American Populism in the Twenty-First Century,* edited by Carlos de la Torre and Cynthia J. Arnson, 85–115. Baltimore, MD: Johns Hopkins University Press, 2013.

Parsons, Laila. *The Commander: Fawzi al-Qawuqji and the Fight for Arab Independence 1914–1948.* New York: Hill and Wang, 2016.

Penrose, Stephen B. L. *That They May Have Life: The Story of the American University of Beirut, 1866–1941*. Beirut: American University of Beirut, 1970.

Picard, Elizabeth. *Lebanon, A Shattered Country: Myths and Realities of the Wars in Lebanon*. Translated by Franklin Phillip. New York: Holmes & Meier, 1996.

Pitts, Graham Auman. "'Make them Hated in All the Arab Countries': France, Famine and the Making of Lebanon." In *Environmental Histories of World War I*, edited by Richard P. Tucker, Tait Keller, J. R. McNeill, and Martin Schmid, 175–190. Cambridge: Cambridge University Press, 2018.

Provence, Michael. *The Great Syrian Revolt and the Rise of Arab Nationalism*. Austin, TX: University of Texas Press, 2005.

Qubain, Fahim I. *Crisis in Lebanon*. Washington, DC: The Middle East Institute, 1961.

Rabah, Makram. *A Campus at War: Student Politics at the American University of Beirut, 1967–1975*. Beirut: Dar Nelson, 2009.

Rabinovich, Itamar. *The War for Lebanon, 1970–1985*. Revised ed. Ithaca, NY: Cornell University Press, 1985.

Richani, Nazih. *Dilemmas of Democracy and Political Parties in Sectarian Societies: The Case of the Progressive Socialist Party of Lebanon 1949–1996*. New York: St. Martin's Press, 1998.

Rugh, William A. *Arab Mass Media: Newspapers, Radio, and Television in Arab Politics*. Westport, CT: Praeger Publishers, 2004.

Russell, Mona L. *Creating the New Egyptian Woman: Consumerism, Education, and National Identity, 1863–1922*. New York: Palgrave Macmillan, 2004.

Saadeh, Sofia. "Khalil Sa'adeh and Syrian Nationalism in the Aftermath of World War I." In *The Origins of Syrian Nationhood: Histories, Pioneers and Identity*, edited by Adel Beshara, 328–340. New York: Routledge, 2011.

Said, Edward. *Orientalism*. New York: Vintage Books, 1978.

Salibi, Kamal. *A House of Many Mansions: The History of Lebanon Reconsidered*. Berkeley, CA: University of California Press, 1988.

Crossroads to Civil War: Lebanon 1958–1976. Ann Arbor, MI: Caravan Books, 1976.

The Modern History of Lebanon. New York: Frederick A. Praeger, Inc., 1965.

Sayigh, Yezid. *Armed Struggle and the Search for State: The Palestinian National Movement 1949–1993*. Washington, DC: Institute for Palestine Studies, 1997.

Sbaiti, Nadya. "If the Devil Taught French: Strategies of Language and Learning in French Mandate Beirut." In *Trajectories of Education in the Arab World: Legacies and Challenges*, edited by Osama Abi-Mershed, 59–84. New York: Routledge, 2010.

Seale, Patrick. *The Struggle for Arab Independence: Riad El-Solh and the Makers of the Modern Middle East*. Cambridge: Cambridge University Press, 2010.

Shaery-Eisenlohr, Roschanack. *Shi'ite Lebanon: Transnational Religion and the Making of National Identities*. New York: Columbia University Press, 2006.

Shanahan, Rodger. *The Shi'a of Lebanon: Clans, Parties and Clerics*. London: I.B. Tauris, 2005.

Sharabi, Hisham. *Embers and Ashes: Memoirs of an Arab Intellectual*. Translated by Issa J. Boullata. Northampton, MA: Olive Branch Press, 2008.

El-Solh, Raghid. *Lebanon and Arabism: National Identity and State Formation.* New York: I.B. Tauris Publishers, 2004.

Stovall, Tyler. "The Fire This Time: Black American Expatriates and the Algerian War." *Yale French Studies* 98 (2000): 182–200.

Suleiman, Michael W. *Political Parties in Lebanon: The Challenge of a Fragmented Political Culture.* Ithaca, NY: Cornell University Press, 1967.

Takriti, Abdel Razzaq. "Political Praxis in the Gulf: Ahmad al-Khatib and the Movement of Arab Nationalists, 1948–1969." In *Arabic Thought against the Authoritarian Age: Towards an Intellectual History of the Present,* edited by Jens Hanssen and Max Weiss, 86–112. Cambridge: Cambridge University Press, 2018.

Thompson, Elizabeth. *Colonial Citizens: Republican Rights, Paternal Privilege and Gender in French Syria and Lebanon.* New York: Columbia University Press, 2000.

Traboulsi, Fawwaz. *A History of Modern Lebanon.* London: Pluto Press, 2007.

Tutunji, Jenab. "Pierre Gemayel." In *Political Leaders of the Contemporary Middle East and North Africa: A Biographical Dictionary,* edited by Bernard Reich, 202–212. New York: Greenwood Press, 1999.

Van Dam, Nikolaos. *Destroying a Nation: The Civil War in Syria.* London: I.B. Tauris, 2017.

Van Slyck, Abigail A. *A Manufactured Wilderness: Summer Camps and the Shaping of American Youth, 1890–1960.* Minneapolis, MN: University of Minnesota Press, 2006.

Volk, Lucia. *Memorials and Martyrs in Modern Lebanon.* Bloomington, IN: Indiana University Press, 2010.

Watenpaugh, Keith David. *Being Modern in the Middle East: Revolution, Nationalism, Colonialism, and the Arab Middle Class.* Princeton, NJ: Princeton University Press, 2006.

Weiss, Max. *In the Shadow of Sectarianism: Law, Shi'ism, and the Making of Modern Lebanon.* Cambridge, MA: Harvard University Press, 2010.

Wyatt-Brown, Bertram. *Southern Honor: Ethics and Behavior in the Old South.* New York: Oxford University Press, 2007.

Yamak, Labib Zuwiyya. *The Syrian Social Nationalist Party: An Ideological Analysis.* Cambridge, MA: Center for Middle Eastern Studies, 1966.

Yaqub, Salim. *Containing Arab Nationalism: The Eisenhower Doctrine and the Middle East.* Chapel Hill, NC: University of North Carolina Press, 2004.

Yıldız, Murat. "Mapping the 'Sports *Nahda*': Towards a History of Sports in the Modern Middle East." In *Sports, Politics, and Society in the Middle East,* edited by Danyel Reiche and Tamir Sorek, 11–40. Oxford: Oxford University Press, 2019.

Zamir, Meir. *Lebanon's Quest: The Road to Statehood 1926–1939.* New York: I.B. Tauris & Co Ltd, 1997.

Ziadeh, Hanna. *Sectarianism and Intercommunal Nation-Building in Lebanon.* London: Hurst and Company, 2006.

Zisser, Eyal. *Lebanon: The Challenge of Independence.* New York: I.B. Tauris & Co Ltd, 2000.

Index

Books in the Series